Evangelicals
★★ and ★★
Presidential
Politics
★ ★ ★ ★ ★

Evangelicals
★ ★ ★ and ★ ★ ★

FROM JIMMY CARTER TO DONALD TRUMP

Presidential
Politics

★ ★ ★ ★ ★

EDITED BY

ANDREW S. MOORE

LOUISIANA STATE UNIVERSITY PRESS
BATON ROUGE

Published by Louisiana State University Press
www.lsupress.org

Designer: Laura Roubique Gleason
Typefaces: Garamond Premier Pro & Helvetica Neue, text; Mackay Bold, display

Library of Congress Cataloging-in-Publication Data

Names: Moore, Andrew S., 1968– editor.
Title: Evangelicals and presidential politics : from Jimmy Carter to Donald Trump / edited by Andrew S. Moore.
Description: Baton Rouge : Louisiana State University Press, 2021. | Includes index.
Identifiers: LCCN 2020021763 (print) | LCCN 2020021764 (ebook) | ISBN 978-0-8071-7434-0 (cloth) | ISBN 978-0-8071-7485-2 (pdf) | ISBN 978-0-8071-7486-9 (epub)
Subjects: LCSH: Evangelicalism—Political aspects—United States. | Religious right—United States. | Christian conservatism—United States | Christianity and politics—United States. | Presidents—United States—Religion. | United States—Politics and government—1977–1981. | United States—Politics and government—1981–1989. | United States—Politics and government—1989–
Classification: LCC BR1642.U5 E899 2021 (print) | LCC BR1642.U5 (ebook) | DDC 324.7/20973—dc23
LC record available at https://lccn.loc.gov/2020021763
LC ebook record available at https://lccn.loc.gov/2020021764

Contents

Acknowledgments

Most of the essays in this book originated at a 2017 conference hosted by Saint Anselm College, entitled "Jimmy Carter and the 'Year of the Evangelicals' Reconsidered." The editor would like to thank everyone who participated in that conference. In addition to the authors whose essays appear here, Elizabeth Flowers, Hilde Løvdal Stephens, Ted Ownby, Jesse Curtis, Andrew Connolly, and Geoffrey Pollick offered up an interesting and wide range of perspectives on late-twentieth-century evangelicals and politics. Moreover, Kenneth Woodward, the *Newsweek* editor who wrote the original 1976 "Year of the Evangelicals" cover story, delivered one of the conference's public lectures and was generous with his time and insights about the rise of political evangelicalism.

The conference was made possible through the financial support of the Henry Luce Foundation and the Office of the Vice President for Academic Affairs at Saint Anselm College, Brother Isaac Murphy, OSB. In addition, the Norwin S. and Elizabeth N. Bean Lecture Foundation, the New Hampshire Institute of Politics, and the Department of History and Department of Politics at Saint Anselm College provided important financial support. William Ploog was instrumental in helping secure the Luce Foundation grant, and Laura Bellavia provided planning and logistical support that made the conference run smoothly.

Finally, the editor and authors wish to express their appreciation for the constructive criticism of Louisiana State University Press's anonymous peer reviewer.

Evangelicals
★★ and ★★
Presidential
Politics

★ ★ ★ ★ ★

Introduction

JIMMY CARTER, THE "YEAR OF THE EVANGELICALS," AND THE RELIGIOUS RIGHT

ANDREW S. MOORE

In October 1976, *Newsweek* borrowed a phrase from pollster George Gallup and proclaimed that year the "Year of the Evangelicals." This was noteworthy, according to some scholars, because for much of the twentieth century, since the 1920s, conservative Protestants had removed themselves from the public arena—or at least they had been selective in the causes they championed and the battles they joined. Instead, they concentrated on building their own subculture and largely left politics to others. That changed in 1976. The most prominent example of that turn was Democratic presidential candidate Jimmy Carter. The former governor of Georgia and self-described "born-again" Christian spoke openly about his faith and claimed that it influenced both his political decisions and his actions in daily life. Indeed, appearing two weeks before the presidential contest between Carter and incumbent Republican Gerald Ford, the cover story opened with a vignette from Plains Baptist Church, where Hugh Carter—the candidate's cousin—led a men's Bible study that included Jimmy, and the pastor, Bruce Edwards, prepared to preach a sermon about being born-again. *Newsweek* credited Carter's candidacy with focusing "national attention on the most significant—and overlooked—religious phenomenon of the 1970s: the emergence of evangelical Christianity into a position of respect and power." Catholic writer Michael Novak described "a hidden religious power base in American culture" that secular journalists could not notice. Carter especially, according to Novak, had "found it." Carter was the most prominent example of this, but both presidential candidates—Ford and Carter alike—claimed to be born-again Christians, a claim made by one-third of all Americans; significant proportions of Protestants and Catholics told Gallup's pollsters that the Bible should be taken literally, a marker of conservative evangelical Christianity. As Novak remarked, this phenomenon caught journalists by surprise, and they struggled to understand this new segment of the electorate.[1]

JIMMY CARTER: A BRIEF HISTORY

Jimmy Carter was born in 1924 in Plains, Georgia (the first president born in a hospital), and he was a child when the Depression settled in, first in the South and then across the nation. His father was a large landowner, entrepreneur, and businessman, and the family survived the Depression in relatively good financial shape. Jimmy was not quite nine years old when Franklin Roosevelt became president, and he came of age at a time when the forces of economic depression combined with the political forces of the New Deal to introduce some fundamental changes to the South's economy and (eventually) its social structure. Carter's community was a biracial one, with his father the patriarch and labor lord over as many as 260 African Americans. Carter's closest playmates were black, and he claimed never to see a color line. Nevertheless, race mattered in Carter's South, and segregation remained intact well into his adult life. After graduation from the United States Naval Academy and a brief stint in the navy, Carter returned to Plains to take his father's place as family patriarch and community leader.

Politics soon beckoned. Like his father before him, Jimmy served on the Sumter County School Board. Then, in 1962, without telling his wife, Rosalynn, he woke up one day and announced he was entering the race for state senate. The political landscape had shifted that year, after the United States Supreme Court forced Georgia to abandon its county unit system and redraw electoral districts for state elections.[2] Despite flagrant voter fraud, he ultimately prevailed in that contest and then ran unopposed for reelection two years later. After a failed run for governor in 1966, in 1970 he used what many considered to be race-baiting tactics to defeat former governor Carl Sanders in a runoff. Despite playing both sides of the race issue in the campaign, he announced at his inauguration that "the era of racial discrimination is over." While he did not prioritize civil rights for African Americans, he was true to his word. He appointed blacks to statewide positions, and he made the symbolic move of hanging Martin Luther King Jr.'s portrait outside the Governor's Office.

While Carter was governor, the Democratic Party faced an identity crisis. The coalition of white southerners and urban, blue-collar ethnic voters that had overseen the rise of the New Deal liberal state and characterized the Democratic Party for much of the twentieth century splintered. George McGovern's 1972 insurgent campaign for president attempted to remake liberalism and push the party to the left. Carter participated in unsuccessful efforts to block McGovern's nomination, but he did not fit comfortably in the anti-McGovern counterinsurgency wing of the party either.[3] Following McGovern's landslide loss, other Democrats positioned themselves to be the party's standard-bearer in 1976. After meeting many of those men who wanted to be president, Carter judged himself just as capable as any of them and asked, "Why not me?"

Carter claimed that he did not set his sights on running for the presidency until his term as governor ended. But as early as 1972, Carter aide and political strategist Hamilton Jordan plotted the governor's path forward through the Democratic primary and 1976 general election. According to Jordan, Carter could be a "better qualified and more responsible alternative to George Wallace." Jordan's pragmatic conclusion hardly served as a condemnation of Wallace on racial terms. Jordan also reviewed many of the other potential candidates and rivals to Carter for the party nomination. One conclusion he reached was that "perhaps the strongest feeling in this country today is the general distrust and disallusionment [*sic*] of government and politicians at all levels." What was more, he maintained, "the desire and thirst for strong moral leadership in this nation was not satisfied with the election of Richard Nixon."[4] Carter's White House ambitions seemed far-fetched to many at the time. He was not a party insider, and he lacked national name recognition. But as Jordan's memo suggested, Carter stood out as the potential anti-Nixon. His religiosity provided an opening, and his political instincts fueled his national ambitions.

Carter was raised in the Southern Baptist Church. Distinct from other Baptist churches, the Southern Baptist Convention (SBC) comprised a loose association of local congregations that retained autonomy over all their internal affairs. The SBC was the vehicle through which individual churches pooled resources to sponsor missionary work, publish Sunday school curricula, and maintain seminaries. Formed in 1845 over the right of slave owners to serve as missionaries, the SBC's member churches remained whites-only congregations well into the late twentieth century. Plains Baptist Church anchored Carter's community, and he was baptized at the age of eleven, regularly participating in Baptist church services and events.[5] While ostensibly Baptist theology emphasizes God's grace alone—rather than works—for salvation, behavior matters, and a disciplined moralism often determines how an individual Baptist such as Carter leads his life. That moralism often stemmed from a list of activities to be avoided—with alcohol and dancing near the top of the list. Unlike other Baptists, however, the Carters drank alcohol and danced. According to Lillian, Earl "loved to dance, and he'd go dancing. He liked to have several drinks. He could dance better if he got a little high."[6] Moral restrictions aside, the church proved to be one of the institutions that supported local life in and around Plains.

Despite the long-shot odds of victory, Carter's loss in his first bid for governor in 1966 drove him into a depression. By that point, his sister Ruth Carter Stapleton had begun what would become a highly successful evangelistic ministry. She paid him a visit in Plains to help him take spiritual stock of his life—and his soul. In response to a question about what made her seem spiritually at peace, Ruth recalled that she described the difference between the two siblings in this way: "What it amounts to in religious terms is total commitment. I belong to Jesus, everything I am."[7] Ruth encouraged Carter to seek spiritual answers for himself, and he confessed to his sister that he was not sure he could place his commitment to Jesus above his political ambitions. Not long after that, Carter's Plains pastor posed this question in a sermon, "If you were on trial for being a Christian, would there be enough evidence to convict you?"[8] For Carter, the answer was no. This became the foundation for Carter's own born-again experience; more than a recommitment of his childhood faith ("rededication" is the typical Baptist parlance), this was a heartfelt conversion, a shift away from being mere churchgoer to Christ follower. As Carter told journalist Bill Moyers a decade later: "I never had really committed myself totally to God—my Christian beliefs were superficial. Based primarily on pride and—I'd never done much for other people, and I changed somewhat for the better. I formed a much more intimate relationship with Christ. And, since then, I've had just about like a new life."[9] He went from being a "church Christian"—in Ruth's words—to wholehearted Christ follower. Within the next two years, he completed SBC-sponsored domestic mission trips to Lock Haven, Pennsylvania, and Springfield, Massachusetts, and actively encouraged others to follow Jesus.

THE YEAR OF THE EVANGELICALS

Carter won the governorship in 1970. Despite a campaign that appealed to segregationists, he governed as a moderate to liberal on race. His Baptist faith hardly distinguished him in Georgia, but by the time he was ready for a national campaign, his ambitions converged with a particular cultural moment. *Newsweek's* Year of the Evangelicals aside, other observers noted both the spiritual opportunities and problems in the 1970s. In an August 23, 1976, *New York* magazine cover story, journalist Tom Wolfe labeled the 1970s the "'Me' Decade." At the same time, he located evidence of a new spiritual movement, what he called the "Third Great Awakening."[10] Moreover, former hippies turned "Jesus People" introduced communal living in both Milwaukee and Chicago, and Christian rock 'n' roll artist Larry Norman almost single-handedly created the contemporary Christian music industry.[11]

Carter was not the only evangelical prominent on the national stage in 1976. Nixon's former White House counsel Charles Colson published his memoir, *Born Again,* that year, and a brief excerpt of the book appeared in a sidebar in the *Newsweek* cover story. Loyal to Nixon to a fault, Colson had converted to Christianity while awaiting trial for crimes related to his role in the Watergate scandal. Colson's version of evangelical Christianity more closely resembled the nascent evangelical political movement than Carter's did. There were those who came to question whether Carter was even an evangelical.

Indeed, what that label even meant was open to dispute. *Newsweek* gave readers a brief history of American evangelicalism and pointed to the difficulty in arriving at an acceptable and useful definition. Evangelicals were not confined to one denomination or region of the country, and—other than bringing the "lost" to salvation in Jesus—their public goals and styles differed. *Newsweek* predicted that division would follow hard on the heels of their newfound political influence. Nevertheless, Carter's candidacy excited enough of them to turn the election his way, and his narrow margin of victory has been attributed to their support. He garnered some two million more evangelical votes than George McGovern had in 1972.

Unfortunately, Carter proved not to be what many of his evangelical supporters had hoped for. His stance on abortion was too nuanced (he personally opposed it but would support *Roe v. Wade*) and was not strong enough to appease evangelicals, and his position on the rights of homosexuals (homosexual practice was a sin, but homosexuals deserved civil rights protection) opened him to criticism from the same quarters. Moreover, his opponents managed to saddle him, falsely, with responsibility for Internal Revenue Service policies that denied tax-exempt status to private schools and colleges that continued to practice racial segregation. Framed as a religious issue, this brought even more evangelical leaders into politics in the 1970s. As a result, evangelicals soon redirected their political support. In 1979 Rev. Jerry Falwell Sr. and other Protestant evangelicals established the Moral Majority, the foundation of the political phenomenon that came to be known as the "Religious Right."

In 1980, Ronald Reagan actively sought evangelicals' support. Reagan never lived up to their expectations; nevertheless, throughout the rest of the twentieth century, white evangelicals became one of the most reliable factions within the Republican Party. In 1992, Patrick Buchanan, who had sought in vain that year's Republican nomination for president, addressed the GOP convention and declared a "cultural war . . . for the soul of America." Republicans lost the White House to Bill Clinton, but the political alliance between white evangelicals and the Republican Party continued into the twenty-first century, with largely unsatisfactory results for most evangelicals. In October 2014, following a U.S. Supreme Court decision allowing lower court rulings in favor of gay marriage to stand, *Politico* declared that the culture war was over and the GOP had "surrendered." In many ways, that culture war was a legacy of the late 1970s and the political realignment that began in 1976. What is more, in the most recent scholarly commentary on the early twenty-first century, historian Steven Miller argues that the "age of evangelicalism"—which began in the 1970s—has ended. Observers of the election of 2016 may disagree with that conclusion. Evangelicals supported Donald Trump overwhelmingly, and Trump has successfully reenergized the culture war, albeit along different lines. To be sure, some observers question the evangelical-Trump alliance. Timothy Carney, for instance, examined the 2016 primary campaign and found far less evangelical support for Trump then than in the general election.[12]

Regardless of their support for Trump, evangelicals play a considerable public role in twenty-first-century politics. Because of an expanding body of literature by historians, political scientists, sociologists, and religious studies scholars, we understand some aspects of their public role quite well. Indeed, books ranging from William Martin's 1996 *With God on Our Side* (and the PBS companion documentary) to Daniel K. Williams's *God's Own Party: The Making of the Christian Right* (2010), among many others, provide a solid foundation for the narrative outlined here, and evangelicals' place in public life is now commonly accepted. Scholars have covered individuals—including Billy Graham, Pat Robertson, Jerry Falwell Sr., Richard Viguerie, and Paul Weyrich—fairly extensively. We understand now how prominent evangelical leaders rubbed shoulders with powerful politicians and political operatives and how they encouraged their followers into the Republican Party. What is more, because of scholars such as Darren Dochuk, we know more about the relationship between those leaders and their followers and how demographic changes contributed to conservative evangelical political activism. This movement into the Republican Party was not a given in the 1970s, to be sure, but aside from biographies of Jimmy Carter and writings of the likes of journalist E. J. Dionne Jr., much less is known about what happened within the Democratic Party to encourage this realignment. A few scholars have explored the emerging political relationship between Catholics (once reliably Democratic) and white evangelicals, and David Swartz has written a well-received book on evangelical liberals in the twentieth century.[13]

Most scholarship has treated evangelicalism as primarily a political movement, but its origins and its late-twentieth-century influence reach beyond politics. Indeed, when evangelicalism emerged in the post–World

War II period as a movement to distinguish its adherents from so-called fundamentalists, evangelical theologians' concerns centered in part on fundamentalists' anti-intellectualism. Religious studies scholars and historians of the post–World War II period have documented that attempt to resurrect an evangelical intellectual tradition. Recently, scholars have argued that evangelicalism is moving back toward anti-intellectualism—or as historian Randall Stephens and physicist Karl Giberson argue, toward the creation of a "parallel culture" inhabited by self-styled "experts." In *Apostles of Reason: The Crisis of Authority in American Evangelicalism,* Molly Worthen qualifies Stephens and Giberson's description of evangelical anti-intellectualism. Instead, she argues, there has always been an inherent tension within evangelicalism that seeks to reconcile faith and reason. Worthen describes a broader, extra-political "evangelical imagination" that was active throughout the twentieth century.[14]

Most of the essays in this collection originated at a conference at Saint Anselm College marking the fortieth anniversary of *Newsweek*'s 1976 cover story. They all use issues raised in the "Year of the Evangelicals" as starting points to address larger themes about evangelicalism and politics in the twentieth and twenty-first centuries. The first of those themes is what Randall Balmer here labels the movement's "myth of origins." As the *Newsweek* story itself suggested, these evangelicals seemed to appear from out of nowhere, after hiding out in their own subculture since the end of the Scopes Trial in 1925. And when they did appear, they told themselves and others the driving force was abortion. Balmer argues the issue was really race and the Internal Revenue Service's actions against Bob Jones University over its own persistent segregation policies. Randall Stephens challenges both the timing of evangelicals' politicization and their motivations, and Allison Vander Broek and Daniel K. Williams describe the development of a movement surrounding abortion.[15]

Other themes linking these essays include evangelicals' relationship to President Carter and the period after Carter left the White House, when evangelicals secured an alliance with the Republican Party. In a development that surprised some observers, Ronald Reagan became an unlikely evangelical champion, a phenomenon that Brooks Flippen explores. Just like the election of 1976 opened a window on the emergence of evangelicalism as a political force, the election of 2016 demonstrated that, as Ted G. Jelen and Kenneth D. Wald concluded after the 2016 election, "white evangelical Protestants have become the Republican base."[16] By 2020, evangelical support for Donald Trump remained solid, even if internal divisions had become more obvious. Essays by Jeff Frederick, Ward Holder, and Hannah Dick all dive into that evangelical support for Trump and the internal divisions that have surfaced.

Since these essays began as conference presentations and were not solicited for this volume, there are gaps in the content. Two are worth mentioning here. First, most of the actors in these essays are white men. Dan Wells's essay on Eldridge Cleaver especially depicts the racialized nature of political evangelicalism. Wells uses the former Black Panther to demonstrate the extent to which "evangelicalism" was a white phenomenon. Evangelical support for Trump has largely been white, of course, and racial division has seemingly worsened in recent years. Nevertheless, there have been attempts of late to encourage evangelicalism to address its own race problem, a movement that has met with only limited success.[17] Second, if people of color are largely absent from these essays, so are prominent women activists. As a couple of the essays here indicate, the evangelical movement of the past forty or so years has become more patriarchal, with women's voices increasingly marginalized. There are exceptions, and scholars are beginning to explore those women's contributions to this movement and the irony that their leadership occurred at the same time that women assumed greater roles in pushing the nation to consider gender equality, particularly in the form of the Equal Rights Amendment. Unlike most white evangelical men at the time, Jimmy Carter supported the ERA, and First Lady Rosalynn Carter bridged the gap between white evangelical women and women's rights activists.[18] These silences notwithstanding, these essays suggest new perspectives for considering the political evangelicalism that emerged in the 1970s and has played a significant role in politics since.

NOTES

1. "Born Again," *Newsweek*, October 25, 1976, 68–78.
2. See Jimmy Carter, *Turning Point: A Candidate, a State, and a Nation Come of Age* (New York: Three Rivers Press, 1992).
3. Bruce Miroff, *The Liberals' Moment: The McGovern Insurgency and the Identity Crisis of the Democratic Party* (Lawrence: University Press of Kansas, 2009), 265.
4. Hamilton Jordan, memo on strategy, November 4, 1972, Jimmy Carter Presidential Library and Museum, Atlanta.

5. See, among others, Niels C. Nielsen Jr. *The Religion of President Carter* (Nashville: Thomas Nelson, 1977); Betty Glad, *Jimmy Carter: In Search of the Great White House* (New York: Norton, 1980), chap. 6; Wesley G. Pippert, ed., *The Spiritual Journey of Jimmy Carter: In His Own Words* (New York: Macmillan, 1978).

6. Lillian Carter, Oral History interview by David Alsobrook, September 26, 1978, Washington, DC, Jimmy Carter Presidential Library and Museum, Atlanta.

7. Quoted in Glad, *Jimmy Carter*, 108.

8. Glad, *Jimmy Carter*, 108; Peter Bourne, *Jimmy Carter: A Comprehensive Biography from Plains to Post-Presidency* (New York: Scribner, 1997), 168–69; James and Marti Hefley, *The Church That Produced a President* (New York: Wyden Books, 1977), 59–60.

9. Quoted in Pippert, *Spiritual Journey of Jimmy Carter*, 6; and Dan Arial and Cheryl Heckler-Feltz, *The Carpenter's Apprentice: The Spiritual Biography of Jimmy Carter* (Grand Rapids, MI: Zondervan Publishing House, 1996), 48.

10. Tom Wolfe, "The 'Me' Decade and the Third Great Awakening," *New York* magazine, August 23, 1976.

11. Larry Eskridge, *God's Forever Family: The Jesus People Movement in America* (New York: Oxford University Press, 2013); Gregory Alan Thornbury, *Why Should the Devil Have All the Good Music? Larry Norman and the Perils of Christian Rock* (New York: Convergent Books, 2018); Randall J. Stephens, *The Devil's Music: How Christians Inspired, Condemned, and Embraced Rock 'n' Roll* (Cambridge: Harvard University Press, 2018).

12. On evangelicals in the 2016 election, see Mark J. Rozell and Clyde Wilcox, eds., *God at the Grassroots, 2016: The Christian Right in American Politics* (Lanham, MD: Rowman & Littlefield, 2018); on the primary campaign, see Timothy P. Carney, *Alienated America: Why Some Places Thrive while Others Collapse* (HarperCollins, 2019).

13. William Martin, *With God on Their Side: The Rise of the Religious Right in America* (New York: Broadway Books, 1996); Daniel K. Williams, *God's Own Party: The Making of the Christian Right* (New York: Oxford University Press, 2010); Daniel K. Williams, *Defenders of the Unborn: The Pro-Life Movement before Roe v. Wade* (New York: Oxford University Press, 2016); Andrew S. Moore, "Jimmy Carter's 'Catholic Problem'—Not to Mention His Protestant One: The Democratic Coalition and the Struggle over Religious Liberty in the Late 1970s," *Journal of Church and State* (Spring 2011): 183–202; David R. Swartz, *Moral Minority: The Evangelical Left in an Age of Conservatism* (Philadelphia: University of Pennsylvania Press, 2012).

14. Randall J. Stephens and Karl W. Giberson, *The Anointed: Evangelical Truth in a Secular Age* (Cambridge: Belknap Press of Harvard University Press, 2011); Molly Worthen, *Apostles of Reason: The Crisis of Authority in American Evangelicalism* (New York: Oxford University Press, 2014).

15. On race and the origins of the Religious Right, see Joseph Crespino, "Civil Rights and the Religious Right," in *Rightward Bound: Making America Conservative in the 1970s*, ed. Bruce J. Schulman and Julian Zelizer (Cambridge: Harvard University Press, 2008); Randall Balmer, *Redeemer: The Life of Jimmy Carter* (New York: Basic Books, 2014).

16. Ted G. Jelen and Kenneth D. Wald, "Evangelicals and President Trump: The Not So Odd Couple," in Rozell and Wilcox, *God at the Grassroots*, 21–22.

17. See, for example, Jemar Tisby, *The Color of Compromise: The Truth about the Amer-

ican Church's Complicity in Racism (Grand Rapids, MI: Zondervan, 2019); Eric Mason, *Woke Church: An Urgent Call for Christians in America to Confront Racism and Injustice* (Chicago: Moody Publishers, 2018); Michael O. Emerson and Christian Smith, *Divided by Faith: Evangelical Religion and the Problem of Race in America* (New York: Oxford University Press, 2001).

18. See, for example, Emily Johnson, *This Is Our Message: Women's Leadership in the New Christian Right* (New York: Oxford University Press, 2019).

Seeing Red

EVANGELICAL AND FUNDAMENTALIST ANTICOMMUNISM AND POLITICAL ENGAGEMENT

RANDALL J. STEPHENS

In his religious biography of Jimmy Carter, Randall Balmer writes about the politicization of conservative American Christians in the 1970s. "For much of the twentieth century," he argues, "evangelicals harbored deep skepticism about engaging politics directly." Their sharpened millennial beliefs, otherworldliness, and skepticism about the gritty business of political engagement, so goes the argument, kept them out of the public arena. Added to this is what Balmer and others have described as a kind of benign disinterest. Televangelist and fundamentalist political broker Jerry Falwell Sr. said as much. His 1965 sermon "Ministers and Marches" proclaimed that "our only purpose on earth is to know Christ and make Him known."[1] There are other versions of this narrative of evangelical hibernation. In her 752-page sprawling narrative on the long history of a religious movement titled *The Evangelicals: The Struggle to Shape America,* Frances FitzGerald writes that "after the Scopes trial fundamentalists had been relegated to the margins of society." Certain demagogues among the devout, says Balmer, tried to gather believers together in the common cause of anticommunism. Some evangelicals responded, but, Balmer implies, most of them remained apolitical until the mid-1970s.[2]

Late in the century, anecdotes from evangelical political leaders themselves seemed to prove this narrative. John Ashcroft—a governor of Missouri and U.S. senator who would go on to serve as George W. Bush's attorney general—recalled the insularity of his Pentecostal Assemblies of God denomination. In the years after he graduated from Yale University, in 1964, and then received his juris doctor degree at the University of Chicago in 1967, he contemplated a career in politics. Yet the church he called home offered no real examples of how to do that. He recalled only one member of his denomination, J. Roswell Flower, who ran for office. Flower had merely served as a Springfield, Missouri, city councilman. Flower spent some of his time in that position trying to convince fellow Springfielders that the fluoridation of water was part of a larger Communist conspiracy to take control of the population. In 1958, a representative of the Jaycees Fluoridation Committee pushed back, claiming, "It is almost unbelievable that a man in Mr. Flower's position of responsibility . . . could be so completely misled by half truths and outright false statements made by irresponsible opponents to fluoridation." In the end, though, Flower's faction won at the polls. With fears of Communist plots and water poisoning exercising the community, Springfield's citizens voted down fluoridation by an overwhelming margin of 4,266 to 8,672, or 33 to 67 percent.[3] As odd or paranoid as the theory might have seemed, it represented persistent and real fears of Communist subversion in small-town America. Interviewed in 1988, Ashcroft thought about the strange apolitical nature of his denomination, which Flower eventually led as its general secretary. The government, Ashcroft contemplated, was "a worldly thing—in the same way that we shunned formal education for a long time."[4]

Evangelicals like Ashcroft in the 1970s were, indeed, paying more attention to national politics and becoming aware of their collective influence. In a 1977 College of William and Mary master's thesis on evangelical political thought, Darrell Kopp observed the changes taking place. "Evangelicals," claimed Kopp, "have probably given greater attention to political theory and political affairs in recent years than to any other single area of social concern." Kopp thought that as the faithful had "begun seriously to consider society's problems, so has society begun to take evangelicalism more seriously." National magazines such as *Time, Newsweek,* and *U.S. News and World Report* as well as influential newspapers like the *New York Times,* the *Washington Post,* and the *Boston Globe* took stock of the "newly" politicized evangelicals and fundamentalists. U.S. senator Mark Hatfield of Oregon, himself an evangelical, told a UPI reporter in 1976 that "many in the evangelical community were not involved in politics; they were essentially withdrawn from the world." Referring to Democratic presidential nominee Jimmy Carter, Hatfield went on to claim that "for the first time since William Jennings Bryan," the American evangelical community "has caught fire because of the fact that a candidate uses (evangelical) nomenclature publicly."[5]

Conservative Christians seemed to be thinking about their place in the larger world in other ways too. Christian pop music stars now competed for the hearts and ears of fans with their secular rivals. Evangelicals on the left end of the spectrum called for nuclear disarmament, racial justice, and greater attention to the nation's social ills. Evangelicals Letha Scanzoni and Nancy Hardesty provided a model for born-again feminism in their influential 1974 book *All We're Meant to Be*.[6] The larger trend, however, was to the right. Evangelical and fundamentalist conservatives felt that *their* country was slipping away from them at an alarming rate. They pitched traditional family values and decried what they called secular humanism, the move for gay rights, legalized abortion, and liberal school curriculum, and lamented the banning of prayer and Bible reading in public schools. Just months before Ronald Reagan won his landslide victory over incumbent Jimmy Carter, the *New York Times's* Dudley Clendinen maintained that this "new political activism of conservative Christians arises in large part from the growth of television evangelism, whose audiences have become the political wells from which the coalition seeks to draw."[7]

But that was only part of the story, Clendinen admitted. Political power brokers and strategists such as Paul M. Weyrich, Richard Viguerie, and a host of others brought together a large grassroots movement. Such changes were stunning to anyone paying attention to local and national politics. Some leaders of the Republican fold bristled at the new coalition of the self-righteous and denounced Falwell and company. There were those who might have wished that fundamentalist activists would have just stayed in their pulpits. In 1981, Barry Goldwater upbraided the Lynchburg, Virginia, TV preacher. "I think that every good Christian ought to kick Falwell right in the ass," said the Arizona senator and one-time presidential hopeful.[8] Falwell's call for moral purity and righteous politics, especially in his opposition to the appointment of Sandra Day O'Connor to the Supreme Court, was too much for Goldwater to endure. With a sense of irony, the journalist Mike Royko noted in 1984 how much the religious-political revolution had changed the landscape. "There's little doubt," he quipped, "the Rev. Jerry Falwell and the rest of the right wing, TV Bible-thumpers have done their job. They've managed to convince a large segment of the population that God is a conservative Republican."[9]

More than ten years before journalists and national politicians noticed the trend of conservative Christian politicization, Donald A. Kruse was thinking about evangelicals and their relationship to politics. A career Foreign Service Officer, Kruse wrote in *Christianity Today* in 1964 about a kind of dilemma. "Evangelicals have problems with government," he noted bluntly. They struggled with "what it is and what it should do, what involvement they should have with it, and how it relates to the work of the Gospel." Some in the fold thought of government as a kind of "necessary evil." Not all of the faithful had neglected their civic responsibilities or had remained aloof from politics. But, Kruse lamented, "we need once more to invoke the names of Wilberforce, Beecher, Bryan, and scores of others."[10] Kruse might have just as easily mentioned the names of committed anti-liberal and anti-communist Christian crusaders, though the work of such contemporaries might have struck him as less noble than that of the cast of luminaries he mentioned.

Yet ministers like Falwell, laypeople, and denominational officials had long strayed from the narrow confines of their churches and had engaged in political work and activism, even though such activity had not been such a trial for Goldwater and other critics. Their unified opposition to Soviet aggression and the threat of homegrown communism made them alive to the political debates of the day. American evangelical and fundamentalist anticommunism was more than a passing fad or the hobbyhorse of a handful of cranky ministers. Indeed, even as Falwell counseled his Lynchburg parishioners to stay clear of politics in the 1950s and 1960s, he was also attacking the civil rights movement and painting its leaders Red. Anticommunism was one of the most striking ways that believers entered the political realm, especially in the postwar years. When evangelicals rallied against the godless Red menace, participated in anti-communist denominational campaigns, or read the countless Red Scare articles, books, and pamphlets that rolled off their church presses, they were laying claim to a particular vision of the country. Conservative traditions and organizations, in this view, were endangered by Bolsheviks, the Soviet Union, and a host of internal subversives. Believers willingly lent their support to politicians and public figures who most adamantly opposed the spread of communism around the globe and in the United States. Politicians, military leaders, and government officials such as J. Edgar Hoover, Generals MacArthur and Patton, Richard Nixon, and Barry Goldwater won the allegiance of the devout. In a 1964 piece in the fundamentalist magazine *Sword of the Lord,* John R. Rice answered the question "Why We Will Vote for Goldwater." In part, he said, it had to do with Lyndon Johnson's vice presidential pick, Hubert Humphrey. Humphrey "was one of the founders of the left-wing Americans for Democratic Action," Rice informed his 100,000 readers. "That group was so radically left wing, socialist and pink," Rice vented, "that even President Kennedy, in the last election, shunned its support, [and] would not speak at its convention."[11]

This brand of conservative anti-liberalism had been developing for decades, especially after American Protestants began to divide in the late nineteenth and early twentieth centuries over ideas about personal and social salvation, theology, and the appropriate relationship to the dominant culture. By the 1920s and 1930s, the Manichaean outlook of anticommunism well suited a conservative view of the world. It is not surprising, then, that numerous squabbles broke out between hard right fundamentalists and more moderate evangelicals concerning devotion to the anti-communist cause. Historian Axel Schäfer remarks that the "combination of projecting anti-communist resolve while rejecting fundamentalist extremism was crucial in cementing the political credentials of post-war evangelicalism."[12]

For all the disagreements fundamentalists and evangelicals had over race, ideology, and culture, the core issue of anticommunism indelibly marked both traditions. In the 1930s and 1940s, few political issues divided evangelicals and fundamentalists from their liberal mainline Protestant cousins more than communism, support of state welfare programs, and New Deal liberalism. Since the late nineteenth and early twentieth centuries, believers had made labor activists, socialists, and Communists chief targets in their sermons, editorials, and tracts. The most celebrated preacher of the 1910s and 1920s, Billy Sunday, called on Christians to reject "godless communism." Sunday, a former professional baseball player for the Chicago White Stockings, had a distinct knack for the dramatic. He illustrated his sermons with homespun wisdom about right living and the benefits of muscular Christianity. Sunday took particular aim at modernism, liberal Protestantism, and anything that seemed un-American to him. Little was as damnable, in his estimation, as communism. With a typical flare for folksy hyperbole and manly posturing, Sunday claimed, "If I had my way, I'd fill the jails so full of them [Bolsheviks] that their feet would stick out the windows." He continued, with violent rhetoric that seemed to draw on the book of Revelation: "Let them rule? We'll swim our horses in blood up to the bridles first." As World War I raged on, the barbarous "Huns" of Germany were the focus of Sunday's rage. After the Russian Revolution and the Red Scare of 1919, the Bolshevik threat became a favorite subject of scorn for the heartland evangelist. Sunday told his crowds that he would rather be in hell than be in Russia. Darwinian evolution and atheism were hallmarks of that condemned nation, he warned.[13]

Many Protestants might have been opposed to the Soviet Union or found fault in Communist ideology. But there were notable outliers. In March 1930, the editor of Boston's *Congregationalist* witnessed a Communist rally taking place near the statehouse. William E. Gilroy had pity on the sad, misguided band of malcontents, some of whom were "ill-dressed, undernourished and pathetically incompetent-looking." The police, thought the Congregationalist leader, were excessive and un-Christian in their reaction. "Had Christian society no better answer to a futile group of bitter communists and unemployed people than to confirm them in their bitterness, and hustle them off with the consciousness that the only answer to them was the answer of brute force?"[14] A few years later, the Congregationalists' General Council passed a resolution that called on members to help abolish capitalism and the "legal forms which sustain it, and the moral ideals which justify it." In the same era, an Episcopal magazine deemed the American economic order "rotten to the core." The National Council of Methodist Youth called on its members to "renounce the Capitalistic system based on economic individualism and the profit motive."[15]

Such bold statements were equally matched on the fundamentalist right by caustic denunciations of communism and the New Deal. Historian Matthew Sutton has noted that "Roosevelt's efforts to expand the power of the federal government and his internationalist inclinations seemed to parallel fundamentalists' end-times fears about the rise of totalitarian states and world rule by a Satan-inspired dictator."[16] Most would not go as far as end-times promoters such as Arno C. Gaebelein, William Bell Riley, or Gerald Winrod, who believed in the validity of the *Protocols of the Elders of Zion.* But some among them would champion Hitler as a fitting, God-ordained opponent to Stalin. In the pages of his New York City–based magazine *Our Hope,* Gaebelein rhapsodized about the Nazis in early 1934. He quoted with approval a piece that appeared in the *Presbyterian* journal:

> The Nazi[s] are militant anti-communists. They are somewhat like the Vigilantes of the old West, or the Ku Klux Klan, if you please. If the average conservative American Christian were to take a check list of avowed Nazi tenets, he would probably favor eighty per cent of the items. They are for the home. They are for marriage. They are for children. They are against these sex-saturated moving pictures. They are for nationalism as against communism. They are for the peasant, and for putting back millions of people on to privately-owned farms, the re-establishment of a stout yeomanry. They are for an industrious, God-fearing body politic. They are for Christianity, through a vigorous ecclesiastical organization. These are the sound old German virtues which we ordinarily associate with Luther and the German Bible. That is their credo on paper.[17]

In other issues of Gaebelein's journal, he lambasted Communist infiltration of America. The anti-God movement, he thundered in 1934, "started through the Satanic agencies with the second Russian Revolution. It grows the world over and is one of the most sinister signs of our time."[18] Here Gaebelein warned of a Red takeover of the the American government, the American military, colleges and universities, and the modernistic Methodist Church.

Few, however, could match the thunder of Gerald L. K. Smith, a Wisconsin native and preacher. He pastored the Seventh Christian Church in Indianapolis before heading south in 1928 to take the pulpit of the King's Highway Church in Shreveport, Louisiana. Restless and filled with pent-up rage, he soon channeled his energies into political causes. He variously backed "Kingfish" Huey Long and then William "Liberty Bill" Lemke in their campaigns against President Roosevelt. Smith hit the trail for Long, promoting his "Every Man a King" program and setting up "Share-Our-Wealth" clubs in Louisiana. The preacher took a hard right turn when he joined William Dudley Pelley's fascist Silver Shirts of America. The former minister now urged on the Silver Shirts to take back control of their nation. "We're going to drive that cripple [Roosevelt] out of the White House," he guaranteed a crowd of Pelley's supporters. Smith publicly dubbed the president "Franklin D. Jewsevelt," joining his voice with thousands of others, both Christians and non-Christians, who blamed Jews for the political and economic problems of the interwar years. His weekly Detroit radio addresses won him an ultra-right following of white nationalists. Bolsheviks and labor organizations, along with Jews, Catholics, and African Americans, were dooming the country, he proclaimed with fury. Smith drew together these threats, announcing that "Marx was a Jew, an atheist and an enemy of Christ and Christianity."[19]

With the outbreak of World War II, Smith put his efforts into isolationist causes and even ran for president with the America First Party in 1944. The U.S. Justice Department took notice of his activities. It listed his publication, the *Cross and the Flag,* as seditionist propaganda. (His magazine began with only 7,000 subscribers, but by 1951, it had climbed to 13,500. The Anti-Defamation League later estimated that it had reached a circulation of 25,000.)[20]

After the war, Smith attacked the United Nations and the U.S. Supreme Court and formed the Christian Nationalist Crusade in 1947. In 1952, he spent considerable time and effort trying to prove that Dwight Eisenhower was a Swedish Jew and therefore unfit for the presidency. America's gadfly journalist H. L. Mencken called Smith "the greatest rabble rouser seen on earth since Apostolic times." Mencken sat in the WINS studio in June 1937 to witness one of Smith's "radio harangues." He lumped the minister together with other "breast beaters," William Jennings Bryan and Billy Sunday. Smith's chief concern, according to

Mencken, seemed to be "that Communism and its associated heresies" were a "serious menace to the old flag and the old religion."[21]

Of course, most mainstream evangelicals distanced themselves from the rantings and conspiracy theories of blatant racists and hard-core xenophobes. Ministers and leaders of the fold such as Carl F. H. Henry and Harold Ockenga tried to steer a more neutral or moderate path. Far right firebrands and sectarian fundamentalists, they claimed, were not good models for believers. These and other, more centrists figures worried that race prejudice, indifference to social justice, and a disengagement from the world of ideas had persisted for far too long.[22] Yet far right figures had a readership and a following. And though they may have worked on the edges of a larger movement, their influence should not be dismissed outright. According to Leo Ribuffo, the careers of Pelley, Smith, and Winrod "show that the 'extremism' of the far right often converged with the cultural and political mainstream. These three agitators attracted intermittent support from prominent officials and businessmen, and their political techniques overlapped with those used by 'pragmatic' centrists. Most important, their favorite countersubversive, racist, and anti-Semitic motifs had long circulated through American society."[23] Nonetheless, more mainstream and acceptable anti-communist religious crusaders would rally to the cause in later years.

In the postwar era, the Australian immigrant Fred Schwarz would become one of the most influential anti-communist activists in the United States. Schwarz, a Baptist layman and medical doctor, garnered the support of laypeople as well as high-profile ministers. Prominent revivalist Billy Graham urged Schwarz on to found his Christian Anti-Communism Crusade in 1953. That organization won the support of thousands of evangelicals and fundamentalists alike. His anti-communist training schools also proved enormously popular. In the winter of 1956, Schwarz led a citywide campaign in Spokane, Washington. The event kicked off with a Rotary Club luncheon and was highlighted by a large-scale Sunday meeting at the city's Coliseum. The Australian doctor lectured his enthusiastic crowds on how the showing in Russia of the immoral, decadent musical *Porgy and Bess* played into Soviet propagandists' hands. He also cautioned that "since the communists are planning the extermination of one-third of the American people, not as an act of punishment, but as a necessary scientific step in their concept of human regeneration, every parent, citizen, and Christian must be interested."[24]

And interested they were. Schwarz's 1960 book, *You Can Trust the Communists (to Be Communist)*, sold over one million copies. Schwarz won widespread media attention as well as high-profile endorsements in the early 1960s. In these years, Ronald Reagan, Phyllis Schlafly, and William F. Buckley all signed up for his courses, which along with warnings of Red threats to Christianity and freedom, called for direct action and political involvement. Celebrities such as John Wayne, Roy Rogers, and Pat Boone pitched the school to potential students. In 1961, fifteen thousand pupils took part in Schwarz's educational programs in Southern California alone. Schwarz's organization raised over one million dollars from his 1961 drive.[25] The doctor's outlook appeared almost moderate compared to that of other contemporary crusaders.

With a much more strident tone, Oklahoma pastor Billy James Hargis also joined in the fight. In 1947, while pastor of First Christian Church in Sapulpa, Oklahoma, he founded a precursor of his Christian Crusade organization. He gave up his pastorate in 1950 to become a kind of full-time anti-communist entrepreneur. He reached out to working- and middle-class white constituents in the Midwest, West, and South. Hargis, who set up and led his Christian Crusade out of Tulsa, was at the peak of his powers in the early and mid-1960s, when Bob Jones University awarded him an honorary doctorate. Fellow Sooners described Hargis as a "bawl-and-jump" evangelist. His morally urgent message, ceaseless anti-communist campaigning, and hyper-patriotism made him appear almost like a character from Stanley Kubrick's iconic 1964 send-up *Dr. Strangelove*. Hargis's Christian Crusade, like Schwarz's Christian Anti-Communism Crusade, was one of the most well-funded, far right organizations in the nation. A tax-exempt, nonprofit, it took in an astonishing $1 million in contributions in 1963.[26] In some ways, it was a kind of religious analogue of the John Birch Society, which had similar regional strength. In his *Communist America—Must It Be?* Hargis won over Americans who felt that the Soviet Union had a clear upper hand. America, under the influence of hapless politicians and effete liberal Protestants, was weak and lacked much needed moral courage. In 1960, the first edition of Hargis's *Communist America* sold fifteen thousand copies. Then a second printing sold ten thousand. Between 1958 and 1963, the Christian Crusade's print, radio, and film income amounted to $3.5 million. That was actually far greater than what the John Birch Society raised in the same period.[27]

The Oklahoma leader, much like the Birchers, called on his readers and television viewers to fight the United Nations and oppose an activist Supreme Court, corrupt public officials, and the secular forces that were destroying the nation's public schools. Christian citizens, he urged, had to take back their country. "Our founding fathers did not intend to establish a government that did not recognize God and Jesus Christ," he wrote. The country's roots were firmly fixed in Christian soil. But now that was in danger. "Are we ashamed of our nation?" Hargis asked rhetorically. "Are we ashamed of our flag? Are we ashamed of our God? Are we ashamed of the faith of our fathers?"[28]

Hargis had a strong media presence in these years as well. His syndicated radio show aired on 500 stations. His television efforts were similarly successful, winning spots on 250 stations. The Oklahoma rabble-rouser focused on a host of foes that he was convinced were part of a broader Communist agenda. He took aim at Martin Luther King Jr. and the civil rights movement. In the mid-1960s he raised the alarm about folk music and rock 'n' roll. Civil rights agitation and Protestant Left activism, along with student protests in California, were regular targets of his campaigns. American parents, Hargis warned, were losing their children to Communist influences.[29] Hargis's young protégé David A. Noebel embarked on a speaking tour and writing campaign to warn parents, pastors, and teachers about the Beatles. The four young stars from Liverpool, according to Noebel, were using hypnotism and secret messages in their songs to ready the nation's youth for a Communist invasion.[30] Skeptics might doubt the claims made by Hargis and Noebel, but the two and their followers expected such criticism and, in some cases, even welcomed it.

Besides, they reasoned, all the public scrutiny and negative attention gave their organization much needed press coverage. Noebel's books sold well, and his speaking tours were covered in major newspapers and in *Newsweek*. Fundamentalists such as Carl McIntire, John R. Rice, Tim LaHaye, and Bob Jones III joined in the crusade against communism and rock music, following Noebel's lead. Such far right stalwarts also leveled criticisms at more mainline evangelicals for theological lapses and, like

Hargis, targeted liberalism and ecumenism in the churches. Indeed, because of the separatism and extreme rhetoric of such partisans, their influence and reach had some real limits. Yet in the broader, much larger world of evangelicalism, anticommunism remained a powerful motivating force.

Throughout the postwar years, evangelical sermons, radio programs, and public outreach campaigns featured the anti-Red message. Popular magazines such as *Christianity Today,* the *Christian Herald, Moody Monthly,* and the *King's Business* regularly reported on and diagnosed the sources of godless communism. Clergyman L. Nelson Bell, who joined his son-in-law Billy Graham in the launching of *Christianity Today,* remained a steadfast backer of the House Un-American Activities Committee well into the 1960s.[31] In stark terms, *Christianity Today* editor Carl F. H. Henry reminded readers in 1965 about the grave threats communism posed. "More than any other modern ideology," he counseled, "atheistic Communism is responsible for an all-out assault on the Christian faith." Red intellectual fads were especially gaining ground among impressionable, naive young people.[32] Christian parents and ministers needed to pay greater attention to what was going on in the lecture halls of college and university campuses.

Surely, such fears influenced evangelicals and fundamentalists in these years following the Cuban missile crisis, the fall of Eastern European nations to oppressive Communist regimes, and the escalation of American involvement in South Vietnam. In some ways, evangelicals and fundamentalists were much like other Americans in the consensus era. A Gallup poll in the early 1960s, for instance, found that 81 percent of Americans surveyed would rather fight a nuclear war than live under communism. The organization found that only 21 percent of British people surveyed thought the same.[33]

Across the United States, evangelical women joined in the work to purify the nation and to prepare for war with the Soviets. Conservative Christian women were much like their non-evangelical co-laborers in the cause. Mary C. Brennan's general observation about women anticommunists applies: "Some women acted in ways that defied conventional limits regarding female behavior. Others took a more traditional route. They joined clubs; they wrote letters, newsletters, books, and articles; they gave speeches and organized demonstrations. They even ran for public office."[34] Evangelical and fundamentalist women who joined the ideological war against Reds found common cause with other Protestants, Catholics, members of the John Birch Society, and parents of schoolchildren. *Life* magazine summed up their suspicions in a February 1962 feature: "The beliefs of the anti-Communist right begin to slide off into the murk. Some members of the right are convinced that the peril of Communism lies not so much in Khrushchev's rockets and 50-megaton bombs as it does in some secret, insidious influence in their own backyards."[35]

While such internal subversion seemed dubious to many other Americans, it was deadly serious to committed anti-communists. Some husbands and wives worked closely together toward the same urgent goal. Mel and Norma Gabler of Hawkins, Texas, a small town in the northeastern part of the state, began their long-running campaign against what they viewed as liberal, godless, or even communistic public school textbooks in the early 1960s. As with other women in the movement, Norma Gabler linked her fight with the home and child-rearing. Such conservative campaigning, even within a patriarchal system, allowed prominent women leaders to take on national roles of protest and advocacy. This principle also served in the careers of women evangelists such as Aimee Semple McPherson and later Kathryn Kuhlman. The urgency of the cause prompted action.[36] Similarly, Catholics such as Phyllis Schlafly and the John Birch Society stalwart Laurene Conner took on new roles as highly visible, engaged leaders.[37]

Historians such as Darren Dochuk, Michelle Nickerson, and Lisa McGirr have shown that middle-class women were more committed than many others, joining efforts to shape anti-communist curriculum, to monitor and protest school administrators, and to set up and take part in counter-organizations. In Southern California in the early 1950s, for instance, housewives Louise Hawkes Padelford and Frances Bartlett took on Pasadena school superintendent Willard E. Goslin. "Meeting in their living rooms," observes Dochuk, the women "amassed complaints about watered down curricula and communist insurrection and connected them to a wider protest against state infringement on the private sphere." Under pressure from these efforts, Goslin was eventually ousted in 1950.[38]

For conservative men and women—activists like the Gablers or Phyllis Schlafly—communism took on a significance and power in ways that it did in larger religious circles. The nation's largest Protestant denomination, the Southern Baptist Convention, claiming 10.2 million members and 33,000 churches in the early 1960s, addressed the Soviet threat directly. A 1957 editorial cartoon in the Jackson, Mississippi, *Baptist Record*, titled "A Humanity Curtain Greater than the Iron Curtain," expressed the hopes of many. Only the light of the Gospel could save the world from Communist aggression. The illustration, by Jack Hamm, shows a bald, hunched-over thug with a hammer and sickle on his sleeve and *Red Atheism* written on his arm. He menacingly holds a cat of nine tales in his hand as he faces off with a line of Christians, who hold hands in resistance. A large Holy Bible stands behind them, along with a passage from 1 Peter 4:14: "If ye be reproached for the name of Christ, happy are ye."[39]

Southern Baptists responded in more official ways as well. "A great wave of concern about communism has recently been evident throughout the [denomination]," church leaders noted in a 1961 press release.[40] Southern Baptists turned to a former diplomat, Paul Geren, for counsel. "Communists reject God for themselves and either hate or pity believers," he intoned. Worse yet, the Reds themselves were idolatrous. They worshipped, said Geren, the false gods of "Party, Science, Power" and the gruesome, embalmed corpses of Lenin and Stalin.[41] That theme of communism as a twisted and satanic religion occurred repeatedly in evangelical and fundamentalist circles. This was just one of the many reasons why the divide between liberal/mainline Protestants and evangelicals/fundamentalists would grow even wider during the Vietnam War era.

Taking part in this larger campaign was best-selling author and self-help apostle Norman Vincent Peale, who fused together patriotism and anticommunism. Director of the FBI J. Edgar Hoover joined such luminaries in the battle and, like Peale, was eager to speak to evangelicals and fundamentalists. Hoover tithed to the Capitol Hill Methodist Church as well as the National Presbyterian Church. He also told an interviewer in 1967 that he was particularly fond of Peale's "radio religion."[42]

Additionally, America's most famous, well-respected evangelical, revivalist Billy Graham, based much of his early and mid-career on the principles and fiery rhetoric of Red baiting. The Charlotte, North Carolina, native first attended the fundamentalist Bob Jones College in 1936, before moving on to the more mainstream evangelical Wheaton College outside of Chicago. A couple of years after graduating from there, in 1943, he began working for the Youth for Christ organization. He launched his evangelistic career in 1949 with a celebrated crusade in Los Angeles, with the crucial assistance of newspaper baron William Randolph Hearst. From what the press dubbed his "canvas cathedral," the southern preacher employed his powerful rhetorical skills and charms to win over crowds. He called them to renewed devotion and asked them to give their hearts to Jesus. He also warned of the hazards of the era, the threats to stable Christian families, and the trouble with liberalism, and he predicted the demise of the nation if it broke its covenant with God.[43]

In sermons, in print, and in radio addresses, Graham spent much of his career warning of Soviet belligerence. The stakes seemed higher than ever in the late 1950s and especially in the weeks after the USSR launched the world's first satellite, Sputnik. In late October 1957, Graham told crowds gathered at the Polo Grounds for his New York crusade that the Soviets were hatching plans to attack the country. "I was told last week on good authority," said Graham, making expert use of the passive voice, "that there is a strong element within the Kremlin that believes Russia should attack the United States within the next two years." It would be a shame, he reasoned, if President Eisenhower were not completely forthright with the American people. The president needed to tell citizens precisely about the dangers posed by the Communists. "The American people are not children," he admonished. "They want the facts straight from the shoulder." Those facts, in Graham's estimation, clearly showed that the country was engaged in a battle with dark, evil forces, both at home and abroad.[44]

The North Carolina evangelist thought that few saw the facts and dangers of the age better than J. Edgar Hoover did. In turn, Hoover was a strong supporter of Graham.[45] Whether speaking about juvenile delinquency, crime, world affairs, or spiritual lethargy, Graham was fond of quoting Hoover as an especially powerful expert. Publications such as *King's Business, Christianity Today,* and *Youth for Christ* regularly featured editorials by the FBI director on the Communist menace, juvenile delinquency, and societal decline.[46] In 1964, Hoover informed readers of *Christianity Today* about a particularly troublesome problem. Hitting on a typical theme, he wrote: "Communism has been able to make inroads into our country not so much because of its inherent strength but because of our weaknesses; not because of its superiority but because of our failure to understand its chicanery and deceit. The penalty for such a failure can be nothing but national suicide, all the more tragic since it is a camouflaged suicide."[47] Americans neglected their spiritual heritage at great cost, Hoover declared, in terms quite similar to those laid out in Graham's sermons. He concluded with solemn advice for the magazine's evangelical readers, its pastors, denominational officials, and laypeople: "Let us place our hope in the only faith that can move men to most noble purposes in life, the faith of our fathers." It was a rhetorical flourish that believers were well familiar with, and it was something that they had long been telling themselves.[48]

Graham, the leading voice of evangelicalism, found in Hoover's warnings a clear and precise moral critique of communism. And while never as strident as Hargis or McIntire, Graham had made anti-communist crusading central to his larger evangelistic work.[49] His popular religious campaigns—first aired on radio and later broadcast to national and international audiences on TV—drew millions. He called on Americans to turn from the sins of the flesh, to stop gambling, to stop using alcohol, and to quit watching destructive Hollywood films. Graham frequently told the press and his own audiences that he did not want to take part in political debates and bitter theological feuds. He was neutral, he declared. Yet in fact, he was far from neutral. And as the Cold War got hotter, the real threat of communism was a frequent topic of discussion and of his sermons.[50]

One of Graham's 1947 sermons, two years before he stepped onto the national stage with his large-scale crusades, made clear his point of view. After a series of revivals in Europe, he was thinking more and more about the future status of his country in the new global order. Could the nation fall as quickly as it rose? Might it be another Babylon or Rome? "The wages of a nation's sin, the wages of an organization's sin, the wages of individual sin," he remarked, "is death." The country was founded on the Bible. The founding fathers had staked much on Christian virtue. Yet, Graham argued, at present Christian America was encircled by the forces of hell—higher criticism, climbing divorce rates, and atheism. "America as we know it today," the revivalist speculated, "cannot possibly reach 1975."[51]

The pastor who would become the most visible evangelical perhaps in the world seemed to be especially conscious that he not appear to be too political. He often castigated the extremes of the Left and the Right, as did Carl Henry and Harold Ockenga, offering mild critiques of fundamentalists such as Carl McIntire, Bob Jones II, and others on the hard right. But in the 1950s, Graham remained an ardent Cold Warrior. He hoped that Congress would go after "Fifth Columnists," found ways to commend the work of Senator Joseph McCarthy, and castigated those who erred in giving too much to the Soviets at the 1945 Yalta Conference.[52] Behind the scenes, Graham supported candidates like Richard Nixon who would be tough on Communists and would project American strength around the globe. In 1960, Graham and Peale, along with other leading voices of evangelicalism, considered how best they could oppose the Catholic presidential candidate, John F. Kennedy.[53]

In October 1964, as another presidential campaign was coming to a close, Graham spoke to a near-capacity crowd as part of his Boston Crusade. He took aim at big government, communism, and welfare handouts. The nation was on the path to a major showdown with the Reds. As if catching himself in an uncharacteristic public statement, he told the crowd: "I'm not political. Not even my wife knows who I'm going to vote for, and I won't tell her after I do." Bertram G. Waters, reporting on the meeting in the *Boston Globe,* remained unconvinced of the minister's self-proclaimed neutrality. "Billy Graham started to sound like Barry Goldwater," he commented.[54] Graham, like so many evangelicals in these years, regularly told reporters and the audiences that gathered to hear him speak that he shunned politics. But it was only a certain kind of politics that he shunned. Asked in 1963 about the March for Jobs and Freedom that Martin Luther King Jr. had led in Washington, DC, Graham said, "Only when Christ comes again will little white children of Alabama walk hand in hand with little black children." Other believers who looked to the swift return of Jesus had deep suspicions about government spending, an activist state, and liberal Protestants' social justice work.[55]

Sylvester Johnson notes that by the early 1960s, "anti-communism increasingly functioned as an ideological weapon against civil rights." But within black churches, there were strains of anticommunism, an unsurprising development considering how the reactionary movement shaped so many aspects of American life. Martin Luther King Jr. even delivered a staunchly anti-communist sermon in September 1962 titled "Can a Christian Be a Communist?" King concluded that "no Christian can be a communist because communism leaves out God. It regards religion psychologically as wishful thinking, regards religion intellectually as the product of fear and ignorance." He further noted that another reason "we can't accept communism is that its methods are opposed to Christianity. Since for the communist there is no divine government or no absolute moral order, there are no fixed, immutable principles." Still, King's words rang hollow to numerous white and black evangelical critics, who were convinced that King himself, and the civil rights movement as a whole, was either part of a secret Communist plot or had been duped into carrying out the Kremlin's agenda.[56]

The influential black holiness preacher, songwriter, and radio broadcaster Elder Lightfoot Solomon Michaux made anticommunism one of his special causes. In 1952, for example, he held his Washington, DC, mass rally "Crusade against Communism," drawing thousands of participants. Michaux's later rivalry with and intense opposition to King had much to do with Michaux's anti-communist political orientation.[57] Similarly, the African American Baptist minister and a founder of the Montgomery Improvement Association, Uriah J. Fields, would also take a hardline anti-communist position. As a result, Fields would break with his former co-laborer King. Like Michaux, Fields painted his former colleague Red in published works and speeches delivered around the country.[58] Such examples were clearly in the minority, yet they speak to the power and widespread appeal of anticommunism.

The stridency and scope of white evangelical and fundamentalist anticommunism was unmistakable. This form of political activity had helped define the movement for decades before Jimmy Carter won the presidency in 1976. It was perhaps the way that millions of believers were drawn into the conservative camp and later the GOP, in particular. Anticommunism informed the faithfuls' views about the family, nationalism, and capitalism. The historian Jonathan P. Herzog addresses the matter in *The Spiritual-Industrial Complex:* "Evangelical anti-Communism, if measured by its depth, surpassed its predecessors. The anti-Communist Christians of the late 1950s and 1960s did more than watch Fulton Sheen on television, attend church, and say a prayer for the nation each night before bed. They also traveled to attend lectures, subscribed to a variety of shoe-string-budget newsletters, discussed their beliefs with neighbors, and campaigned for the removal of anti-Christian, anti-American literature from library shelves."[59] This became a kind of holy war, notes Herzog, that especially energized the devout. The National Association of Evangelicals, one of the largest religious groups in the United States, made fighting the Red menace one of its central concerns.[60]

Indeed, for all the talk about being more concerned with heavenly matters than earthly ones, evangelicals were political in ways that even they might not have immediately recognized as such.[61] The devout supported Cold Warriors in calling for government officials to clamp down on internal subversives and attempting to stop Red curricula in their schools, just as they hoped that missionaries might counter godless communism around the globe.

NOTES

1. Randall Balmer, *Redeemer: The Life of Jimmy Carter* (New York: Basic Books, 2014), xvi. Falwell's "Ministers and Marches" sermon, quoted in Macel Falwell, with Melanie Hemry, *Jerry Falwell: His Life and Legacy* (New York: Simon & Schuster, 2008), 96.

2. Frances FitzGerald, *The Evangelicals: The Struggle to Shape America* (New York: Simon & Schuster, 2017), 144. For more on evangelicals as apolitical or disengaged before the 1976 election, see Mark J. Rozell, "The Religious Right in American Politics," in *Routledge Handbook of Political Management,* ed. Dennis W. Johnson (New York: Routledge, 2009), 241.

3. "In Statements Made against Fluoridation Flower 'Misled,' Jaycees Charge," *Springfield (MO) Leader and Press,* August 27, 1958, 17. See also "Fluoridation Vote Sept. 9: Council Sets Date after Public Debate," *Springfield Leader and Press,* August 12, 1958, 9; Ann Fair Dodson, "Fluoridation and Pensions Up for Decision of Voters," *Springfield Leader and Press,* September 7, 1958, 37; and "Fluoridation Loses by Lopsided Margin," *Springfield Leader and Press,* September 10, 1958, 17; and Flower's letter to the local paper: "Flower Opposed to Fluoridation," *Springfield Leader and Press,* August 26, 1958, 9.

4. Ashcroft, quoted in Dan Betzer, *Destiny: The Story of John Ashcroft* (Springfield, MO: Revivaltime Media Ministries, 1988), 15. See also John Wicklein, "Extremists Try to Curb Clergy: Moves to Ban Social Issues Causing Protestant Rift," *New York Times,* March 28, 1960, 1, 25.

5. Hatfield, quoted in David E. Anderson, "Sen. Mark Hatfield Challenges Label of Religious Conservative," *Tampa Bay Times,* August 28, 1976, 56.

6. "Religion: Return to Conservatism," *U.S. News and World Report,* January 5, 1976, 52; cover: "Born Again! The Evangelicals," *Newsweek,* October 26, 1976; Clint Confehr, "Jerry Falwell's Marching Orders: Washington Is Taking Note of Jerry Falwell and His

Army of Followers—Whose Political Clout Is Growing," *Saturday Evening Post,* December 1980, 58–59, 99; Maria Karagianis, "The Rise of the Right," *Boston Globe,* September 14, 1980, H12; Susan Friend Harding, *The Book of Jerry Falwell: Fundamentalist Language and Politics* (Princeton, NJ: Princeton University Press, 2000), 10, 17, 77, 126, 165, 219; Pete Daniel, *Standing at the Crossroads: Southern Life in the Twentieth Century* (Baltimore: Johns Hopkins University Press, 1996), 224–25; Mark A. Noll, Nathan O. Hatch, and George M. Marsden, *The Search for Christian America* (Westchester, IL: Crossway Books, 1983), 14; Seth Dowland, *Family Values and the Rise of the Christian Right* (Philadelphia: University of Pennsylvania Press, 2015), 129–30, 136–37; David R. Swartz, *Moral Minority: The Evangelical Left in an Age of Conservatism* (Philadelphia: University of Pennsylvania Press, 2012).

7. Dudley Clendinen, "'Christian New Right's' Rush to Power," *New York Times,* August 18, 1980, B7.

8. Goldwater, quoted in Jon Margolis, "The 2 Faces of American Conservatives," *Chicago Tribune,* July 12, 1981, 4.

9. Mike Royko, "Say Yer Prayers, Ron, or Shut Up," *Chicago Tribune,* August 31, 1984, 3.

10. Donald A. Kruse, "Evangelicals in Government," *Christianity Today,* August 28, 1964, 13, 16.

11. John R. Rice, "Why We Will Vote for Goldwater," *Sword of the Lord,* October 16, 1964, 1. See also "The GOP Ticket: The Religious Factors," *Christianity Today,* July 31, 1964, 39; Jerry L. Faught, "Independent Baptists," in *The Baptist River: Essays on the Many Tributaries of a Diverse Tradition,* ed. W. Glenn Jonas Jr. (Macon, GA: Mercer University Press, 2008), 117; Warren L. Vinz, "The Sword of the Lord, 1934–," in *The Conservative Press in Twentieth-Century America,* ed. Ronald Lora and William Henry Longton (Westport, CT: Greenwood Press, 1999), 132; Thomas Aiello, "Constructing 'Godless Communism': Religion, Politics, and Popular Culture, 1954–1960," *Americana: The Journal of American Popular Culture* 4, no. 1 (Spring 2005), www.americanpopularculture.com/journal/articles/spring_2005/aiello.htm.

12. Axel R. Schäfer, "What Marx, Lenin, and Stalin Needed Was . . . to Be Born Again: Evangelicals and the Special Relationship between Church and State in U.S. Cold War Foreign Policy," in *America's "Special Relationships": Foreign and Domestic Aspects of the Politics of Alliance,* ed. John Dumbrell and Axel R. Schäfer (London: Routledge, 2009), 229 n. 237.

13. Billy Sunday, quoted in George Sirgiovanni, *An Undercurrent of Suspicion: Anti-Communism in America during World War II* (New Brunswick, NJ: Transaction, 1990), 27. See also Robert Moats Miller, *American Protestantism and Social Issues, 1919–1939* (Westport, CT: Greenwood Press, 1977), 186, 194–95; Robert Wenger, "Social Thought in American Fundamentalism, 1918–33" (PhD diss., University of Nebraska, 1973).

14. William E. Gilroy, "The Editor Sees a Riot," *Congregationalist,* March 20, 1930, 373, 374.

15. Resolutions quoted in Margaret Bendroth, *The Last Puritans: Mainline Protestants and the Power of the Past* (Chapel Hill: University of North Carolina Press, 2015), 140, 141–42.

16. Matthew Avery Sutton, "Was FDR the Antichrist? The Birth of Fundamentalist Antiliberalism in a Global Age," *Journal of American History* 98, no. 4 (March 2012): 1052; Richard V. Pierard, "Evangelical Christianity and the Radical Right," in *The Cross and*

the Flag, ed. Robert G. Clouse, Robert D. Linder, and Richard V. Pierard (1972; reprint, Eugene, OR: Wipf & Stock, 2005), 99–118.

17. "An Unbiased Report on the Conditions in Germany," *Our Hope* (January 1934): 413.

18. "The Increasing Anti-God Movement," *Our Hope* (November 1934): 295.

19. "Gerald L. K. Smith Dead; Anti-Communist Crusader," *New York Times,* April 16, 1976, 27. Leonard Dinnerstein, *Antisemitism in America* (New York: Oxford University Press, 1994), 134. Smith, quoted in Glen Jeansonne, "The Cross and the Flag, 1942–1977," in *The Conservative Press in Twentieth-Century America,* ed. Ronald Lora and William Henry Longton (Westport, CT: Greenwood Press, 1999), 392. "Rev. Gerald L. K. Smith's Federation Is Suspended," *Chicago Daily Tribune,* December 9, 1939, 23.

20. Peter R. D'Agostino, "The Cross and the Flag," in *Antisemitism: A Historical Encyclopedia of Prejudice and Persecution,* vol. 1: *A–K,* ed. Richard S. Levy (Santa Barbara, CA: ABC-Clio, 2005), 152. George Sokolsky, "These Days . . . Hate, Incorporated," *Washington Post,* December 8, 1954, 17.

21. H. L. Mencken, quoted in Glen Jeansonne, in *Gerald L. K. Smith: Minister of Hate* (Baton Rouge: Louisiana State University Press, 1997), 39. "New York, June 19, 1937," in *The Diary of H. L. Mencken,* ed. Charles A. Fecher (New York: Vintage Books, 1991), 99–100.

22. Garth M. Rosell, *The Surprising Work of God: Harold John Ockenga, Billy Graham, and the Rebirth of Evangelicalism* (Grand Rapids, MI: Baker Academic, 2008), 14–16, 143–47. Carl F. H. Henry, *The Uneasy Conscience of Modern Fundamentalism* (Grand Rapids, MI: Eerdmans, 1947).

23. Leo P. Ribuffo, *The Old Christian Right: The Protestant Far Right from the Great Depression to the Cold War* (Philadelphia: Temple University Press, 1983), xii. See also "Long Ally Now Heads a Drive against Reds: Aide Says Smith Has Pledges of $1,500,000 Chest from Financial Leaders," *New York Times,* October 18, 1936.

24. Schwarz, quoted in "Porgy, Bess Showing in Russia Is Termed Red Propaganda Aid," *Spokane Daily Chronicle,* February 2, 1956, 5. For parallel conversations, see also "Atheism in Communism: How Stable?" *Christianity Today,* January 17, 1964, 46; J. C. Pollock, "Christian Youth in Soviet Schools," *Christianity Today,* August 28, 1964, 5.

25. David Farber, *The Rise and Fall of Modern American Conservatism: A Short History* (Princeton: Princeton University Press, 2010), 107. Daniel K. Williams, *God's Own Party: The Making of the Christian Right* (New York: Oxford University Press, 2010), 61.

26. Harold H. Martin, "Doomsday Merchants of the Far Right," *Saturday Evening Post,* April 28, 1962; Travis Hughs, "Hargis Loves a Revival," *Palm Beach Daily News,* December 22, 1964, 4.

27. Heather Hendershot, *What's Fair on the Air? Cold Wear Right-Wing Broadcasting and the Public Interest* (Chicago: University of Chicago Press), 11. For related reactionary developments among evangelicals, see Henry A. Buchanan and Bob W. Brown, "The Ecumenical Movement Threatens Protestantism," *Christianity Today,* November 20, 1964, 21–23; "None So Blind," *Christianity Today,* March 12, 1965, 32; and Carl F. H. Henry, "The World Council and Socialism: Geneva Conclave of Ecumenical Churchmen Will Reflect WCC Attitudes on Political Involvement," *Christianity Today,* July 8, 1966, 3–7.

28. Billy James Hargis, *Communist America—Must It Be?* (Tulsa, OK: Christian Crusade, 1960), quotations on 31 and 37.

29. Billy James Hargis, "Please Act Immediately," fundraising letter, April 15, 1967, Wilcox Collection, Spencer Library, University of Kansas. Robert D. McFadden, "Billy James Hargis, 79, Pastor and Anticommunist Crusader, Dies," *New York Times,* November 29, 2004, www.nytimes.com/2004/11/29/obituaries/billy-james-hargis-79-pastor-and-anticommunist-crusader-dies.html?_r=0. See also "Christian Responsibility and the Law," *Christianity Today,* July 17, 1964, 20–21.

30. David A. Noebel, *Communism, Hypnotism, and the Beatles: An Analysis of the Communist Use of Music, the Communist Master Music Plan* (Tulsa, OK: Christian Crusade Publications, 1965), 1. See also David Hitchcock, "Stop the Communist Use of Music," *Christian Crusade,* October 1966, 26.

31. Philip Jenkins, *The Cold War at Home: The Red Scare in Pennsylvania, 1945–1960* (Chapel Hill: University of North Carolina Press, 1999), 178, 179.

32. Carl F. H. Henry, "Communist Assault on Christian Faith," *Christianity Today,* August 27, 1965, 3.

33. "The Long and Bitter Worldwide Struggle to Contain the Reds," *Life,* November 10, 1961, 98.

34. Mary C. Brennan, *Women Arise: The Red Threat on the Domestic Scene* (Boulder: University Press of Colorado, 2008), 85. Allison Hepler, *McCarthyism in the Suburbs: Quakers, Communists, and the Children's Librarian* (Lanham, MD: Lexington Books, 2018), 39, 86, 88.

35. Keith Wheeler, "Who's Who in the Tumult of the Far Right," *Life,* February 9, 1962, 117.

36. Lee Jones, "Witnesses Argue Textbook Content," *Shreveport (LA) Times,* August 17, 1976, 11.

37. Donald T. Critchlow, *Phyllis Schlafly and Grassroots Conservatism: A Woman's Crusade* (Princeton, NJ: Princeton University Press, 2008). Claire Conner, *Wrapped in the Flag: A Personal History of America's Radical Right* (Boston: Beacon Press, 2013).

38. Darren Dochuk, *From Bible Belt to Sunbelt: Plain-Folk Religion, Grassroots Politics, and the Rise of Evangelical Conservatism* (New York: Norton, 2010), 201. Lisa McGirr, *Suburban Warriors: The Origins of the New American Right* (Princeton, NJ: Princeton University Press, 2003), 56, 71, 86. Michelle M. Nickerson, *Mothers of Conservatism: Women and the Postwar Right* (Princeton, NJ: Princeton University Press, 2012), 23, 136. Chester G. Hanson, "Pasadena Schools Row Flares Anew," *Los Angeles Times,* September 27, 1952, 15.

39. Jack Hamm, "A Humanity Curtain Greater than the Iron Curtain," *Baptist Record* (Jackson, MS), August 1957, 4.

40. Benson Y. Landis, ed., *Yearbook of American Churches* (New York: Office of Publication and Distribution, National Council of Churches of Christ in the USA, 1964), 23.

41. "Baptist Features, Produced by Baptist Press News Service of the Southern Baptist Convention," June 12, 1961, 1, 2, Southern Baptist Historical Library and Archives, Nashville, TN.

42. Jeremiah O'Leary, "J. Edgar Hoover's Life: Routine and Temperance," *Boston Globe,* December 31, 1967, 12. Republication of interview with Hoover from Billy Graham's *Decision* magazine: "Hoover Tells How Christianity Shaped His Life," *Washington Post,* July 3, 1971, A21.

43. Grant Wacker, *America's Pastor: Billy Graham and the Shaping of a Nation* (Cambridge: Belknap Press of Harvard University Press, 2014), 157–58, 199, 231–33.

44. Graham, quoted in "Graham Says He Hears Some Reds Want U.S. War within 2 Years," *New York Times,* October 28, 1957, A10.

45. Michael J. McVicar, "Apostles of Deceit: Ecumenism, Fundamentalism, Surveillance, and the Contested Loyalties of the Protestant Clergy during the Cold War," in *The FBI and Religion: Faith and National Security before and after 9/11,* ed. Sylvester A. Johnson and Steven Weitzman (Berkeley: University of California Press, 2017), 90–91, 97; K. A. Cuordileone, *Manhood and American Political Culture in the Cold War* (New York: Routledge, 2005), 82.

46. Steven P. Miller, *Billy Graham and the Rise of the Republican South* (Philadelphia: University of Pennsylvania Press, 2009), 23, 94. J. Edgar Hoover, "The Danger of Civil Disobedience," *King's Business* (February 1966): 14; Hoover, "Trade Softness for Firmness," *Youth for Christ* (Wheaton, IL) (August 1957): 12; Hoover, "Spiritual Priorities: Guidelines for a Civilization in Peril," *Christianity Today,* June 22, 1962, 3–4. On Hoover's writing in *Christianity Today,* see David E. Settje, *Faith and War: How Christians Debated the Cold and Vietnam Wars* (New York: New York University Press, 2011), 31.

47. J. Edgar Hoover, "The Faith of Our Fathers," *Christianity Today,* September 11, 1964, 6.

48. Ibid., 7.

49. See *Christianity Today*'s coverage of Hargis and his troubles with the IRS, in "Battle on the Right," *Christianity Today,* December 4, 1964, 47.

50. William C. Martin, *With God on Our Side: The Rise of the Religious Right in America* (New York: Broadway Books, 2005), 33–34. Anticommunism and Christian patriotism sparked the imaginations of Bob Jones University administrators, students, and faculty. The school became a bastion of Christian Americanism in the stormy 1960s. Mark Taylor Dalhouse, *An Island in a Lake of Fire: Bob Jones University, Fundamentalism, and the Separatist Movement* (Athens: University of Georgia Press, 1996), 105–6.

51. Billy Graham, "America's Hope," in *The Early Billy Graham: Sermon and Revival Accounts,* ed. Joel Carpenter (New York: Garland, 1988), 12, 13–15, 17, 19. The author is indebted to John G. Turner for pointing him to this source.

52. Leo P. Ribuffo, *The Old Christian Right: The Protestant Far Right from the Great Depression to the Cold War* (Philadelphia: Temple University Press, 1983), 260. Marshall Frady, *Billy Graham: A Parable of American Righteousness* (New York: Simon & Schuster, 2006), 238. See also Graham's 1949 sermon in Los Angeles on "Why God Allows Communism to Flourish and Why God Allows Christians to Suffer," October 23, 1949, Billy Graham and the 1949 Christ for Greater Los Angeles Campaign, www2.wheaton.edu/bgc/archives/exhibits/LA49/05sermons01.html.

53. Randall Balmer, *God in the White House: A History: How Faith Shaped the Presidency from John F. Kennedy to George W. Bush* (New York: HarperOne, 2009), 26–31.

54. Graham, quoted in Bertram G. Waters, "Graham's Talk Leans to Politics," *Boston Globe,* October 11, 1964, 5.

55. Graham, quoted in William Martin, *A Prophet with Honor: The Billy Graham Story*

(New York: Morrow, 1991), 286. Jerry Falwell, *Strength for the Journey: An Autobiography* (New York: Simon & Schuster, 1987), 276.

56. Sylvester A. Johnson, *African American Religions, 1500–2000* (Cambridge: Cambridge University Press, 2015), 340. Martin Luther King Jr., "'Can a Christian Be a Communist?' Sermon Delivered at Ebenezer Baptist Church," Atlanta, September 30, 1962, https://kinginstitute.stanford.edu/king-papers/documents/can-christian-be-communist-sermon-delivered-ebenezer-baptist-church.

57. Sherry S. DuPree, *African-American Holiness Pentecostal Movement: An Annotated Bibliography* (New York: Routledge, 2013), 416.

58. Jack Morton, "Negro Speaker Says: Communists Stir Both Negro and White in Racial Unrest," *Binghamton (NY) Press and Sun-Bulletin,* September 21, 1963, 3. For an account that locates black anticommunism within a long tradition, see Eric Arnesen, "The Traditions of African-American Anti-Communism," *Twentieth Century Communism* 6, no. 6 (March 2014): 124–48.

59. Jonathan P. Herzog, *The Spiritual-Industrial Complex: America's Religious Battle against Communism in the Early Cold War* (New York: Oxford University Press, 2011), 207.

60. "Evangelical Parley Will Open Monday," *Chicago Daily Tribune,* April 24, 1960, 26.

61. An editorial in a 1964 issue of *Christianity Today* is revealing. Ralph Bonacker, director of the Episcopal Mission Society in the Diocese of New York, doubted the effectiveness of the "War on Poverty" and other large-scale social welfare efforts. A "ministry to the souls of men," he wrote, echoing Billy Graham, "is ultimately the only solution to our vast problems of poverty, racial turmoil, crime and delinquency, alcohol and narcotics addiction, and divorce and family breakdown." Ralph Bonacker, "The Church and Social Welfare," *Christianity Today,* September 11, 1964, 11, 13.

Full Circle

THE RELIGIOUS RIGHT FROM BOB JONES TO DONALD TRUMP

RANDALL BALMER

At a remove of more than four decades, it is easy to lose sight of the improbability of Jimmy Carter's ascent to the presidency in the mid-1970s. In November 1974, just before Carter announced his candidacy for the Democratic nomination, Gallup conducted a survey to gauge support for thirty-two potential candidates for president of the United States; Carter's name was not among them. The following month, however, the governor of Georgia announced his candidacy and headed for the precincts of New Hampshire and the prairies of Iowa. "Jimmy Who?" worked harder than anyone else. "I can will myself to sleep until ten-thirty and get my ass beat," he told a relative, "or I can will myself to get up at six o'clock and become President of the United States." His rivals took notice. "Seems like everywhere I've been lately, they tell me Jimmy Carter was just through there a week or so ago," Morris Udall, one of Carter's rivals for the Democratic nomination, complained. "The sonofabitch is as ubiquitous as the sunshine."[1]

On January 19, 1976, Carter finished first in the Iowa precinct caucuses, and he won the New Hampshire primary on February 24. Soon his campaign began to resemble a juggernaut. In Florida, Carter scored his most important, but underappreciated, victory when he dispatched a fellow southern governor. Carter's win on March 9 effectively ended the political career of one of the nation's most notorious segregationists, George C. Wallace of Alabama.

Having secured the Democratic nomination in July, Carter cruised into the general election with what was shaping up as a landslide victory over Gerald Ford. Carter's carefully calibrated campaign, however, very nearly imploded over a miscalculation by the candidate. On September 20, just weeks before the election, *Playboy* magazine hit the newsstands. Carter had intended that his interview would dispel any notion of smug self-righteousness on his part, but the media picked up on his statement about lusting after women other than his wife. For evangelicals, that statement was utterly unremarkable—let us remember Jesus's words at the Sermon on the Mount—although a fellow Southern Baptist, picking up on another quote from the interview, allowed that "well, 'screw' is just not a good Baptist word." The media had a field day. One editorial cartoon depicted the Democratic nominee staring at the Statue of Liberty in a state of undress, and Carter dropped fifteen percentage points in the polls.[2]

Another magazine arguably rode to Carter's rescue. On the basis of Carter's insurgent candidacy and the popularity of Charles Colson's autobiography, *Born Again,* the October 25 issue *Newsweek* proclaimed 1976 the "Year of the Evangelical." Days later, Americans went to the polls and narrowly elected a born-again Southern Baptist Sunday school teacher president of the United States. Carter, by most accounts, did not win a majority of evangelical voters, but he came close, faring far better than previous Democratic nominees. Many evangelicals relished the opportunity to cast their votes for one of their own.

I have often argued that Kenneth Woodward and *Newsweek* were four years premature in anointing 1976 the Year of the Evangelical. In 1980, we had not one, not two, but three candidates for president who claimed to be evangelicals: Carter, the incumbent; John B. Anderson, Republican member of Congress from Illinois (a member of the Evangelical Free Church and my former boss as head of the House Republican Conference); and Ronald Reagan, episodic churchgoer and former governor of California.

This time around, evangelicals, prompted by leaders of the Religious Right, lavished their votes on Reagan, the Republican nominee who arguably had the most tenuous hold on the label *evangelical.* Therein lies a tale.

The Religious Right's most cherished and durable myth is its myth of origins. According to this well-rehearsed narrative, articulated by Jerry

Falwell Sr., Pat Robertson, and countless others, evangelical leaders were shaken out of their political complacency by the United States Supreme Court's *Roe v. Wade* decision of January 22, 1973. Falwell even recounted, albeit fourteen years later, his horror at reading the news in the January 23, 1973, edition of the *Lynchburg (VA) News.* "The Supreme Court had just made a decision by a seven-to-two margin that would legalize the killing of millions of unborn children," Falwell wrote. "I sat there staring at the *Roe v. Wade* story growing more and more fearful of the consequences of the Supreme Court's act and wondering why so few voices had been raised against it." This myth of origins has Falwell and other evangelical leaders emerging like a mollusk out of their apolitical stupor to fight the moral outrage of legalized abortion. Some even went so far as to invoke the moniker "new abolitionists" in an apparent effort to ally themselves with their antebellum evangelical predecessors who sought to eradicate the scourge of slavery.[3]

The abortion myth, however, collapses in the face of historical scrutiny. In 1968, twenty-six evangelical theologians gathered under the aegis of the Christian Medical Society and the flagship evangelical magazine *Christianity Today* to discuss the ethics surrounding abortion. The participants came up with several justifications for abortion, including "individual health, family welfare, and social responsibility," but they could not reach a consensus that abortion was sinful. Two successive editors of *Christianity Today,* Carl F. H. Henry and Harold Lindsell, also equivocated on abortion. Henry affirmed that "a woman's body is not the domain and property of others"; Lindsell declared that "if there are compelling psychiatric reasons from a Christian point of view, mercy and prudence may favor a therapeutic abortion."[4]

In 1970, the United Methodist Church General Conference called on state legislatures to repeal laws restricting abortion, and in 1972, the Methodists acknowledged "the sanctity of unborn human life" but also declared that "we are equally bound to respect the sacredness of the life and well-being of the mother, for whom devastating damage may result from unacceptable pregnancy." Meeting in St. Louis, Missouri, during the summer of 1971, the messengers (delegates) to the Southern Baptist Convention passed a resolution that stated, "We call upon Southern Baptists to work for legislation that will allow the possibility of abortion under such conditions as rape, incest, clear evidence of severe fetal deformity, and carefully ascertained evidence of the likelihood of damage to the emotional, mental, and physical health of the mother." The Southern Baptist Convention, hardly a redoubt of liberalism, reaffirmed that position in 1974, the year after the *Roe* decision, and again in 1976.[5]

When the *Roe* decision was handed down, W. A. Criswell, former president of the Southern Baptist Convention and pastor of First Baptist Church in Dallas, Texas, expressed his satisfaction with the ruling. "I have always felt that it was only after a child was born and had a life separate from its mother that it became an individual person," one of the most famous fundamentalists of the twentieth century declared, "and it has always, therefore, seemed to me that what is best for the mother and for the future should be allowed."[6]

Baptists especially applauded the decision as an appropriate articulation of the line of division between church and state, between personal morality and state regulation of individual behavior. "Religious liberty, human equality and justice are advanced by the Supreme Court abortion decision," W. Barry Garrett of *Baptist Press* wrote. Floyd Robertson of the National Association of Evangelicals disagreed with the *Roe* decision, but he believed that legal redress should not be a priority for evangelicals. "The church and state must be separate," Robertson said. "The actions and conduct of Christians transcend the secular community for which the state is responsible."[7]

The real origins of the Religious Right are rather more prosaic and less high-minded. In May 1969, a group of African American parents in Holmes County, Mississippi, filed suit to prevent three new whites-only academies from securing tax exemption from the Internal Revenue Service; each of the schools had been founded to evade desegregation of the public schools. In Holmes County, the number of white students enrolled in the public schools had dropped from 771 to 28 during the first year of desegregation; the following year, that number fell to zero. The court case, known as *Green v. Kennedy,* won a temporary injunction against the "segregation academies" in January 1970, and later that year, Richard Nixon ordered the IRS to enact a new policy that would deny tax exemptions to segregated schools. In July 1970, the Internal Revenue Service announced that in accordance with the provisions of the Civil Rights Act of 1964, which forbade racial segregation and discrimination, it would no longer grant tax-exempt status to private schools with racially discriminatory policies. Such institutions were not—by definition—charitable organizations, and therefore they had no claims to tax-exempt status; similarly, donations to such organizations would no longer qualify as tax-deductible contributions. On November 30, 1970, the IRS sent letters of inquiry to schools in question in an effort to ascertain whether or not they discriminated on the basis of race. Bob Jones University, a fundamentalist school in Greenville, South Carolina, responded that it did not admit African Americans.[8]

Meanwhile, the *Green v. Kennedy* suit was joined with a similar suit to become *Green v. Connally*. On June 30, 1971, the United States District Court for the District of Columbia issued its ruling in the *Green v. Connally* case: "Under the Internal Revenue Code, properly construed, racially discriminatory private schools are not entitled to the Federal tax exemption provided for charitable, educational institutions, and persons making gifts to such schools are not entitled to the deductions provided in case of gifts to charitable, educational institutions."[9]

Paul Weyrich, who became the architect of the Religious Right, saw his opening. Ever since Barry Goldwater's campaign for the presidency in 1964, Weyrich had been trying to organize evangelicals politically. Their numbers alone, he reasoned, would constitute a formidable voting bloc, and he aspired to marshal them behind conservative causes. "The new political philosophy must be defined by us in moral terms, packaged in non-religious language, and propagated throughout the country by our new coalition," Weyrich wrote in spelling out his vision. "When political power is achieved, the moral majority will have the opportunity to re-create this great nation." Weyrich believed that the political possibilities of such a coalition were unlimited. "The leadership, moral philosophy, and workable vehicle are at hand just waiting to be blended and activated," he wrote. "If the moral majority acts, results could well exceed our wildest dreams."[10]

But Weyrich's dreams, still a hypothetical coalition that he already referred to as the "moral majority" (lowercase letters), needed a catalyst—not simply an event or issue that would ignite all the indignation that had been accumulating but also a standard around which to rally. For nearly two decades, Weyrich, by his own account, had tried various issues to pique evangelical interest in his scheme, including pornography, school prayer, the proposed Equal Rights Amendment to the Constitution, and abortion. "I was trying to get these people interested in those issues and I utterly failed," Weyrich recalled in 1990. "What changed their mind was Jimmy Carter's intervention against the Christian schools, trying to deny them tax-exempt status on the basis of so-called de facto segregation."[11]

Because the *Green v. Connally* ruling was "applicable to all private schools in the United States at all levels of education," Bob Jones University stood directly in the IRS crosshairs. Founded in Florida by arch-fundamentalist Bob Jones in 1926, the school had been located for a time in Cleveland, Tennessee, before moving to South Carolina in 1947. In response to *Green v. Connally,* Bob Jones University admitted a married black man, a worker in the school's radio station, as a part-time student. He dropped out a month later. Out of fears of racial mixing, the school maintained its restrictions against admitting unmarried African Americans until 1975. Even then, however, the school stipulated that interracial dating would be grounds for expulsion, and the school also promised that any students who "espouse, promote, or encourage others to violate the University's dating rules and regulations will be expelled."[12]

The Internal Revenue Service pursued its case against Bob Jones University and on April 16, 1975, notified the school of the proposed revocation of its tax-exempt status. On January 19, 1976, the IRS officially revoked Bob Jones University's tax exemption, effective retroactively to 1971, when the school had first been formally notified of the IRS policy. As Bob Jones University sued to retain its tax exemption, Weyrich pressed his case. Evangelical leaders, especially those whose schools were affected by the ruling, were angry, electing to construe the decision as government intrusion in religious matters. Weyrich used the *Green v. Connally* case to rally evangelicals against the government. When "the Internal Revenue Service tried to deny tax exemption to private schools," Weyrich said in an interview with *Conservative Digest,* that "more than any single act brought the fundamentalists and evangelicals into the political process." The IRS action "kicked a sleeping dog," Richard Viguerie, one of the founders of the New Right, said. "It was the episode that ignited the religious right's involvement in real politics." When *Conservative Digest* cataloged evangelical discontent with Carter in August 1979, the Internal Revenue Service regulations headed the list. Abortion, on the other hand, was not mentioned.[13]

In ramping up for political activism, evangelicals portrayed themselves as defending what they considered the sanctity of the evangelical subculture from outside interference. Weyrich astutely picked up on those fears. "What caused the movement to surface was the federal government's moves against Christian schools," Weyrich reiterated in 1990. "This absolutely shattered the Christian community's notions that Christians could isolate themselves inside their own institutions and teach what they pleased." For agitated evangelicals, Weyrich's conservative gospel of less government suddenly struck a responsive chord. "It wasn't the abortion issue; that wasn't sufficient," Weyrich recalled. "It was the recognition that isolation simply would no longer work in this society."[14]

Although leaders of the Religious Right in later years would seek to portray their politicization as a direct response to the *Roe v. Wade* ruling of 1973, Weyrich and other organizers of the Religious Right have been emphatic in dismissing this abortion myth. *Green v. Connally* served as the catalyst, not *Roe v. Wade*. Although many evangelicals certainly felt troubled by abortion and viewed it as part of the broader problem of promiscuity in American society, most of them regarded it as a "Catholic issue" in the realm of politics until the late 1970s. (Falwell acknowledged as much when he preached against abortion for the first time on February 26, 1978, from his pulpit at Thomas Road Baptist Church.) Evangelical leaders, prodded by Weyrich, chose to interpret the IRS ruling against segregationist schools as an assault on the integrity and the sanctity of the evangelical subculture, ignoring the fact that exemption from taxes is itself a form of public subsidy. And that is what prompted them to action and to organize into a political movement. "What caused the movement to surface," Weyrich reiterated, "was the federal government's moves against Christian schools," which, he added, "enraged the Christian community."[15]

Ed Dobson, formerly Falwell's assistant at Moral Majority, has corroborated Weyrich's account. "The Religious New Right did not start because of a concern about abortion," he said in 1990. "I sat in the non-smoke-filled back room with the Moral Majority, and I frankly do not remember abortion being mentioned as a reason why we ought to do something." More recently, still another conservative activist, Grover Norquist, has confirmed that the *Roe v. Wade* decision did not factor into the rise of the Religious Right. "The religious right did not get started in 1962 with prayer in school," Norquist told Dan Gilgoff, of *U.S. News & World Report,* in June 2009. "And it didn't get started in '73 with *Roe v. Wade.* It started in '77 or '78 with the Carter administration's attack on Christian schools and radio stations. That's where all of the organization flowed out of. It was complete self-defense."[16]

The actions of the Internal Revenue Service especially affected Bob Jones University, goading those associated with the school into political activism. Elmer L. Rumminger, longtime administrator at the university who became politically active in 1980, remembered that the IRS case "alerted the Christian school community about what could happen with government interference" in the affairs of evangelical institutions. "That was really the major issue that got us all involved to begin with—at least it was for me." What about abortion? "No, no, that wasn't the issue," he said emphatically. "I'm sure some people pointed to *Roe v. Wade,* but that's not what got us going. For me it was government intrusion into private education."[17]

The IRS pursuit of Bob Jones University and other schools may have captured the attention of evangelical leaders, but Weyrich was clever enough to realize that the political mobilization of evangelical and fundamentalist leaders represented only half of the equation. Unless these leaders could enlist rank-and-file evangelicals, Weyrich's dream of a politically conservative coalition of evangelicals would remain unfulfilled. And here is where abortion finally figures into the narrative. During the 1978 midterm elections, the Democratic Party suffered a net loss of three seats in the Senate and fifteen seats in the House of Representatives. Though not unexpected for the party in power—Republicans suffered far greater losses in the previous by-election year of 1974, the year of Nixon's resignation—those reading the election returns could see that abortion had the potential to emerge as a political issue for evangelicals, especially in light of the Senate contests in New Hampshire, Iowa, and Minnesota.

Weyrich could barely contain his delight with the 1978 election returns, especially the Senate elections in Iowa and in New Hampshire, where Roger Jepsen defeated Dick Clark and Gordon Humphrey ousted Thomas J. McIntyre, respectively. "The election of Roger Jepsen and Gordon Humphrey to the U.S. Senate is true cause for celebration, especially in view of the fact that two of the most liberal senators went down to defeat," Weyrich wrote. Even more notable, however, was how it happened: with the support of politically conservative evangelicals. Weyrich immediately set about fortifying the nascent coalition. On December 5, just a month after the election, Weyrich brought Humphrey, the senator-elect from New Hampshire, and his wife to a gathering of evangelical activists. The following day, Robert Billings penned an exultant letter to Weyrich, praising him for his "wise remarks" and congratulating him on the "smashing success" of an evening. "Paul, we did something that no-one has done in years—we brought together the three main factions of the fundamentalist community," Billings wrote. "I believe something was started last night that will pull together many of our 'fringe' Christian friends." Billings concluded his handwritten letter: "Thank you for your important part. God bless you![18]

In persuading evangelicals that abortion was a moral issue that demanded their political activism, Weyrich received help from an unlikely source, a goateed, knicker-wearing philosopher and Presbyterian minister, Francis A. Schaeffer, who, together with his wife, ran a community and study center in Switzerland. Schaeffer, considered by many the intellectual godfather of the Religious Right, began to weigh in about the pervasiveness of what he called "secular humanism" in American society. He lamented the loss of "basically a Christian consensus" and said that "we now live in a secularized society."[19]

By the late 1970s, Schaeffer was beginning to cite abortion as one consequence of a troubling cultural shift away from the mores of evangelical Christianity and toward the reviled secular humanism. Schaeffer viewed abortion as the inevitable prelude to infanticide and euthanasia, and he wanted to sound the alarm. He did so through his writings and lectures, but he also teamed with C. Everett Koop, a pediatric surgeon, to produce a series of five films, collectively titled *Whatever Happened to the Human Race?* Although Francis Schaeffer died in 1983 and his son, Frank Schaeffer, now claims that his father was appalled at the machinations of Religious Right leaders, the films, together with a companion book by the same title, served to introduce abortion to evangelicals as a moral concern. "By the end of the *Whatever Happened to the Human Race?* tour," Frank Schaeffer recalled, "we were calling for civil disobedience, the takeover of the Republican Party, and even hinting at overthrowing our 'unjust pro-abortion government.'" Years later, Robert Maddox, Jimmy Carter's liaison for religious affairs, recounted his only encounter with Schaeffer, who was visiting the office of Alonzo McDonald, an evangelical who served as Carter's deputy chief of staff. "I think you've caused a great damage here with this abortion stuff," Maddox said. Schaeffer's quiet response, according to Maddox: "Could be."[20]

Weyrich's prescience about expanding abortion from a preponderantly "Catholic issue" into an evangelical preoccupation was nothing short of brilliant. His success in blaming Carter for the IRS action against Christian schools may also have been brilliant, but it was also mendacious because Carter bore no responsibility for that. After years of warnings, the Internal Revenue Service finally rescinded the tax exemption of Bob Jones University on January 19, 1976, because of its persistent racist policies. That date was a notable one for Jimmy Carter—but not because he was in any way responsible for the action against Bob Jones University. Carter won the Iowa precinct caucuses on January 19, 1976, his first major step toward capturing the Democratic presidential nomination. He took office as president a year and a day later. Weyrich and the Religious Right, however, persuaded many evangelicals that Carter, not Gerald Ford, who was then president, was somehow responsible for this unconscionable "assault" on Christian schools. In Weyrich's words, "Jimmy Carter's intervention against the Christian schools, trying to deny them tax-exempt status on the basis of so-called de facto segregation," prompted preachers like Jerry Falwell Sr. to mobilize against him.[21]

For politically conservative evangelicals in the late 1970s, Jimmy Carter's refusal to seek a constitutional amendment banning abortion came to be seen as an unpardonable sin, despite his long-standing opposition to abortion and the efforts of his administration to limit the incidence of abortion. Carter, in fact, had a longer and more consistent record of opposing abortion than Ronald Reagan.

Still, the Reagan-Bush campaign remained uneasy about abortion as a political issue. In his address to fifteen thousand evangelicals crowded into Reunion Arena in Dallas on August 22, 1980, Reagan talked about creationism and affirmed that if he were stranded on a desert island, the one book he wanted was the Bible. He decried the IRS actions against segregated schools—and said nothing whatsoever about abortion.

A consideration of the origins of the Religious Right makes it easier to understand why evangelicals voted so overwhelmingly for Donald Trump in 2016. Aversion to the Democratic nominee, stoked by decades of vitriol, was undeniably a factor, but evangelical political activism from the late 1970s—only secondarily concerned with the defense of biblical or family values—played a key role. The Religious Right is rooted in the defense of racial segregation, and no amount of bluster or historical revisionism can alter that fact. In casting their lot with Weyrich and the far right fringes of the Republican Party, evangelicals not only abandoned one of their own, Jimmy Carter, in the 1980 election; they also forfeited the prophetic voice that had been characteristic of evangelical political activism dating back to the nineteenth century and reiterated in the Chicago Declaration of Evangelical Social Concern, an activism that advocated for peace, adopted a critical posture toward unbridled capitalism, and more often than not took the part of those on the margins of society, especially women and people of color.

The Faustian bargain that Falwell and others struck with the Republican Party gave them access to power in the 1980s and beyond—or at least the illusion of access. In exchange, however, the prophetic voice of evangelicalism was struck dumb, and evangelicals themselves began to secularize. The evangelicalism of my childhood was both a subculture and a counterculture; we understood ourselves as standing against the depredations of the larger society. Beginning with the 1980 presidential campaign, however, evangelicalism remained a subculture, with its own institutions, jargon, and celebrities. But it ceased to be a counterculture. Leaders of the Religious Right offered nary a whimper of protest when the

Reagan administration enacted tax cuts that overwhelmingly favored the affluent at the expense of those less prosperous. They stood by in silence when the Reagan administration flouted environmental protections and exploited natural resources. Prosperity theology, a variant of trickle-down economics, rose to new heights of popularity during the "greed is good" era of the 1980s. Similarly, evangelicals offered no protest when George W. Bush initiated military engagements that would not meet even the barest criteria for a just war. Time and again, the loyalties of the Religious Right have centered on the Republican Party and Republican politicians rather than the New Testament or the noble traditions of evangelical social activism in the nineteenth and early twentieth centuries. Opposition to abortion and support for "family values," at least in the hands of cynical evangelical leaders, became effective, albeit transitory, bludgeons against anyone they regarded as a political adversary.

And in 2016, when their preferred party nominated someone with a history of shifting positions on their supposed signature issue, an irreligious casino owner and confessed sexual predator with a patchy marital past, leaders of the Religious Right simply abandoned the rhetoric of family values and retreated to the redoubt of racism that undergirded the formation of their political movement. The so-called defense of "religious freedom" was little more than an attempt to deny constitutional liberties to others. Trump's race-baiting and his excoriation of immigrants, together with his party brand, were sufficient to retain the loyalty of Religious Right leaders; 81 percent of white evangelical voters followed their lead.

The reluctance of historians—most recently Frances FitzGerald—to acknowledge the principal catalyst for the Religious Right ultimately hobbles their attempts to interpret the 2016 election. Rather than draw on definitive historical research (as well as the testimony of Paul Weyrich, Ed Dobson, Grover Norquist, Richard Viguerie, and others) that locates the origins of the Religious Right in the defense of tax exemptions for segregated schools, many still opt for the catalog approach—school prayer, *Roe v. Wade,* gay rights, opposition to the Equal Rights Amendment— explanations that have been explicitly disavowed by the aforementioned founders of the Religious Right. The 2016 election allowed evangelicals finally to dispense with the fiction that their political behavior was motivated by moral concerns or family values and concede that the movement had become a wholly owned subsidiary of the Republican Party. Evangelical support for Trump represented a definitive break from the noble tradition of Charles Grandison Finney and nineteenth-century evangelicalism; tolerance for Trump's racist rhetoric signaled a return to the founding principles of the Religious Right, a movement born out of racism. The path from Bob Jones to Donald Trump may not have been narrow—it bulged at times with ancillary issues—but it was straight. To shift the geometrical metaphor, the election of 2016 saw evangelicals return full circle to the charter principles of the Religious Right.

NOTES

1. Quoted in Marshall Frady, *Southerners: A Journalistic Odyssey* (New York: New American Library, 1980), 354, 344.

2. Quoted in Daniel K. Williams, *God's Own Party: The Making of the Christian Right* (New York: Oxford University Press, 2012), 126.

3. Jerry Falwell, *Strength for the Journey* (New York: Simon & Schuster, 1987), 334–35.

4. Walter O. Spitzer and Carlyle L. Saylor, eds., *Birth Control and the Christian: A Protestant Symposium on the Control of Human Reproduction* (Wheaton, IL: Tyndale House, 1969), 141, xxv–xxvi, xxviii; Carl F. H. Henry, "Abortion: An Evangelical View," in *Jerry Falwell and the Rise of the Religious Right: A Brief History with Documents,* ed. Matthew Avery Sutton (Boston: Bedford / St. Martin's, 2013), 95; Harold Lindsell, *The World, the Flesh, and the Devil* (Minneapolis: World Wide Publications, 1973), 100, 101.

5. Quoted in Mark Tooley, *Methodism and Politics in the Twentieth Century* (Anderson, IN: Bristol House, 2012), 222, 224–25; *Annual of the Southern Baptist Convention, 1972* (Nashville: Executive Committee, Southern Baptist Convention, 1972), 72. On the reaffirmations of the 1971 resolution, see *Annual of the Southern Baptist Convention, 1974* (Nashville: Executive Committee, Southern Baptist Convention, 1974), 76. The 1976 resolution was more measured, calling on "Southern Baptists and all citizens of the nation to work to change those attitudes and conditions which encourage many people to turn to abortion as a means of birth control"; but it also affirmed "our conviction about the limited role of government in dealing with matters relating to abortion, and support the right of expectant mothers to the full range of medical services and personal counseling for the preservation of life and health." *Annual of the Southern Baptist Convention, 1976* (Nashville: Executive Committee, Southern Baptist Convention, 1976), 58.

6. Quoted in "What Price Abortion?" *Christianity Today,* March 2, 1973, 39 [565].

7. "Abortion and the Court," *Christianity Today,* February 16, 1973, 32 [502]; quoted in "What Price Abortion?" *Christianity Today,* March 2, 1973, 39 [565]; Floyd Robertson, *United Evangelical Action* (Summer 1973): 8–11, quotations from 11.

8. For a superb review of the circumstances surrounding the *Green v. Kennedy* case, see Joseph Crespino, "Civil Rights and the Religious Right," in *Rightward Bound: Making*

America Conservative in the 1970s, ed. Bruce J. Schulman and Julian E. Zelizer (Cambridge: Harvard University Press, 2008), 90–105. Crespino correctly identifies this case, together with *Green v. Connally*, as the catalyst for the Religious Right.

9. *Green v. Connally, 330 F. Supp. 1150 (D. D.C.) aff'd sub nom. Coit v. Green, 404 U.S. 997 (1971)*.

10. "The Moral Majority," MS, n.d., box 19, Paul M. Weyrich Papers, American Heritage Center, University of Wyoming (hereafter cited as Weyrich Papers).

11. Quoted in William Martin, *With God on Our Side: The Rise of the Religious Right in America* (New York: Broadway Books, 1996), 173. As early as February 1979, several months before the formation of an organization by that name, Howard Phillips was using the term *moral majority*. See letter, Howard Phillips to Jerry Falwell, February 27, 1979, Evangelist Activism, box 15, Weyrich Papers. According to historian Robert Freedman: "The Supreme Court's banning of public school prayer (1962) and legalization of abortion (1973) outraged many evangelicals and fundamentalists. However, few decided to participate actively in politics as a result." He adds, "Weyrich believes that the Carter administration's policy toward Christian Schools was the turning point." Robert Freedman, "The Religious Right and the Carter Administration," *Historical Journal* 48 (March 2005): 236. Michael Lienesch writes, "The Christian conservative lobbyists were originally concerned with protecting the Christian schools from Internal Revenue Service investigations over the issue of racial imbalance." Michael Leinesch, "Right-Wing Religion: Christian Conservatism as a Political Movement," *Political Science Quarterly* 97 (Fall 1982): 409. On the importance of schools to the nascent Religious Right, see also J. Charles Park, "Preachers, Politics, and Public Education: A Review of Right-Wing Pressures against Public Schooling in America," *Phi Delta Kappan* 61 (May 1980): 608–12.

12. "'Most Unusual': No Time for a Change," *Christianity Today*, December 17, 1971, 34. Bob Jones III insisted that "there was no connection between the enrollment of this one black student and the major threats facing the university."

13. Paul Weyrich, "The Pro-Family Movement," *Conservative Digest* 6 (May–June 1980): 14; Freedman, "Religious Right and the Carter Administration," *Historical Journal* 48 (March 2005): 238, 240; Wilfred F. Drake, "Tax Status of Private Segregated Schools: The New Revenue Procedure," *William and Mary Law Review* 20 (1979): 463–512; "Jimmy Carter's Betrayal of the Christian Voter," *Conservative Digest*, August 1979, 15; Michael Sean Winters, *God's Right Hand: How Jerry Falwell Made God a Republican and Baptized the American Right* (San Francisco: HarperOne, 2012), 110; Crespino, "Civil Rights and the Religious Right," 99–100.

14. Quoted in *No Longer Exiles: The Religious New Right in American Politics*, ed. Michael Cromartie (Washington, DC: Ethics and Public Policy Center, 1993), 26.

15. Quoted ibid., 26; quoted in Martin, *With God on Our Side*, 173. Falwell declared in his sermon: "The Roman Catholic church is to be commended for their diligent and persistent battle against abortion. They have done far more to my knowledge than any other one segment of our society, to try to stop abortion." Jerry Falwell sermon (transcript), "Abortion-on-Demand: Is It Murder?" Genesis 1:26, 27, February 26, 1978, SE-126, Liberty University Archives.

16. Quoted in Cromartie, *No Longer Exiles*, 52; Dan Gilgoff, "Exclusive: Grover

Norquist Gives Religious Conservatives Tough Love," God & Country: On Faith, Politics, and Culture (blog), *U.S. News & World Report,* June 11, 2009, www.usnews.com/blogs/god-and-country.

17. Elmer L. Rumminger, telephone interview with the author, July 17, 2010.

18. Letter, Paul Weyrich to Daniel B. Hales, December 31, 1978, box 3, Weyrich Papers; letter, Robert "Bob" Billings, Christian School Action, Inc., to Paul Weyrich, December 6, 1978, box 3, Weyrich Papers.

19. Philip Yancey, "Schaeffer on Schaeffer, Part II," *Christianity Today,* April 6, 1979, 25.

20. Frank Schaeffer, *Crazy for God: How I Grew Up as One of the Elect, Helped Found the Religious Right, and Lived to Take All (or Almost All) of It Back* (New York: Carroll & Graf, 2007), 283, 259, 293; Maddox, interview with the author, Bethesda, MD, December 6, 2012. According to his son, Francis Schaeffer had initially balked at bringing up abortion because he didn't "want to be identified with some Catholic issue." Schaeffer, *Crazy for God,* 266. The companion volume for the film series is Francis A. Schaeffer and C. Everett Koop, *Whatever Happened to the Human Race? Exposing Our Rapid yet Subtle Loss of Human Rights* (Old Tappan, NJ: Revell, 1979). In his paean to Schaeffer, Cal Thomas declared, "No man contributed as much to the conservative side of the ideological battle than did Dr. Francis Schaeffer, who died of cancer last month at the age of 72." Cal Thomas, transcript, *Moral Majority Report,* June 28, 1984, Liberty University Archives.

21. Quoted in Martin, *With God on Our Side,* 173.

An Evangelical Black Panther

THE POLITICS OF RACE AND THE CONVERSION
OF ELDRIDGE CLEAVER

DAN WELLS

On November 18, 1975, Eldridge Cleaver surrendered to American authorities in Paris, France, after living for seven years in fugitive exile under charges of assault with intent to kill, stemming from a 1968 shootout with the Oakland, California, Police Department. While in exile in Cuba, Algeria, China, Russia, North Korea, North Vietnam, and France, Cleaver served as the director of the international branch of the Black Panther Party and planned for a violent overthrow of the United States government. While living in the South of France in 1975, Cleaver claimed to have a vision while standing on his apartment balcony. One night while gazing into a "star-spangled sky," he saw his own face in the full moon, accompanied by Fidel Castro, Karl Marx, Friedrich Engels, Mao Zedong, and Jesus Christ.[1] On the balcony, Cleaver collapsed in a moment of both "desperation" and "ecstasy," weeping uncontrollably while reciting the Lord's Prayer and the Twenty-Third Psalm.[2] He felt that God had called him to surrender to Jesus Christ and the American justice system.[3] The "old Eldridge Cleaver was no more."[4] This essay will recount the transformation of Eldridge Cleaver from radical Black Panther to born-again evangelical. This essay will illustrate how Cleaver was remade in the image of white evangelicalism. As a result, Cleaver enacted and participated in a campaign that sought to maintain and extend the unifying commitments of twentieth-century American evangelicalism. Cleaver's story of transformation demonstrates the pervasive power of evangelicalism and how American evangelicalism created distinct categories of race and white respectability that were written upon the mind, body, religious belief, and practice of Eldridge Cleaver.

Eldridge Cleaver rose to prominence in the late 1960s as a leading black intellectual and political revolutionary. While incarcerated in California's Folsom State Prison for sexual assault, Cleaver penned his 1968 *New York Times* best-selling memoir, *Soul on Ice*. In this book, Cleaver vividly articulated his thoughts on race and African American sexuality, rejection of U.S. capitalism, and the sins of U.S. imperialism. Upon release, Cleaver joined the Black Panther Party, quickly earning the attention of FBI director J. Edgar Hoover, who branded him "the nation's greatest threat."[5] As the minister of information for the Black Panthers, Cleaver became a symbol of rebellion and resistance for those seeking change in the midst of that tumultuous age. Following a shootout with an Oakland Police "Red Squad" in April 1968 that left seventeen-year-old Bobby Hutton dead in the street, he fled the country and established the international branch of the Black Panther Party. Cleaver's time abroad was marked by constant surveillance and harassment conducted by the American intelligence community. This action was not completely unfounded, as Cleaver admitted that he was actively pursuing options for violent Marxist revolution in the United States.[6] By 1975, it is likely that no one would have ever associated Cleaver with the predominantly white, middle-class American evangelicalism. In fact, Cleaver often spoke out against the evangelicals of the day. However, this all changed when, in the final year of Cleaver's seven-year exile, Jesus Christ called him home to America.

Upon arrival to the United States in November 1975, Cleaver was detained and jailed to await trial for his charges from 1968. In the Alameda County Jail, Cleaver met "a troop of three people who called themselves the 'God Squad.'" The God Squad was an evangelical prison ministry that led weekly Christian worship services and Bible studies inside the county jail. The God Squad, like other evangelical prison ministries, believed that inmates could be fully rehabilitated through a "personal relationship with Jesus Christ." These prison ministries enacted a "colorblind Christianity" that sought to remake inmates of color in the image of white evangelicalism. In many ways, these ministries were the natural product of twentieth-century conservatism and a crusade against communism. The prison ministries were the expression of evangelical conservatism in the prison system, a place in which many evangelicals saw Christianity and capitalism directly threatened by the growth of Black Nationalist groups, many of which Cleaver supported.

In the mid-twentieth century, Black Nationalist groups proliferated in American prison systems. Evangelicals saw this development as a direct assault on Christianity inside the prison and a "ticking time bomb" waiting to explode as inmates were reintroduced into society. In order to combat the growth of these "anti-Christian, militant, communist, liberal, atheistic Black Nationalist groups," crusading prison ministries sought to fight back the encroachment of "the work of Satan" in America's prisons. If the Nation of Islam, Black Israelites, the Black Guerilla Family, or even the Black Panthers were making inroads with the prison system, evangelicals believed that a significant Christian response was necessary. In the process, evangelical prison ministries sought to transform the souls of prisoners and strip them of their "blackness" through the rhetorical milieu of "colorblindness." Under the guise of colorblindness, evangelicals positioned their religious movement as reputable and racially moderate. In doing so, they helped do the same for the cause of punishment—bolstering the justice system's claims to neutrality and its insistence that punishment could be colorblind, even as it increasingly incarcerated people of color. Cleaver saw this dynamic at work, commenting that these ministries only existed to police the conduct of incarcerated black men. Outside of prison, Cleaver later experienced a similar program of surveillance under the watchful eye of white evangelicals.

As Cleaver observed the God Squad in the Alameda County Jail, he kept his distance. They "would join hands, close their eyes and say a little prayer." "I couldn't get all hung up on that," Cleaver said, "I wasn't particularly fond of closing my eyes around the people who were in the tank."[7] Cleaver could not trust a white man looking to save his soul while imprisoning his mind and body. Speaking later to an audience in Milwaukee, he told them that something kept bothering him about the group. Regardless of his numerous attempts to convince the God Squad that their Bible studies and prayer circles were merely an extension of American empire, they refused to abandon the project of converting the Black Panther Party minister of information. "Finally, I went and sat down," Cleaver said.[8]

Through the leadership of the God Squad, Cleaver told students at Iona College, a Roman Catholic institution in New York, he realized "there was a vacuum within me, a gulf, that had to be filled . . . that could only be filled by God through his Son Jesus Christ."[9] Cleaver was freed from his former life of black nationalism, Marxism, and radicalism and delivered to Jesus Christ.

In 1976, the insurance mogul and evangelical financier Arthur S. DeMoss paid Cleaver a visit at the Alameda County Jail, discovering that Cleaver was now a born-again Christian. After that visit, Cleaver's "legal maze" unraveled, and on August 13, 1976, he was released free of charges.[10] Cleaver was overwhelmed with media attention. The *New York Times, Newsweek, Rolling Stone,* the NBC television network, and a host of other media outlets each sought opportunities to interview him.[11] This newfound national interest was a result not of Cleaver's "controversial" stances on race, incarceration, or capitalism in America but, rather, of his new religious life. President and chairman of the life insurance company National Liberty Corporation, DeMoss pioneered a number of mass-marketing policies via direct mail and television advertisements. After his death, the DeMoss fortune was used to fund antiabortion, anti–marriage equality, and abstinence campaigns, Jerry Falwell's Liberty University, Pat Robertson's American Center for Law and Justice, and Newt Gingrich's political action group, GOPAC.[12]

Two months after Cleaver's release, Donn Downing of *People* magazine asked Cleaver about his conversion experience. "Would you describe yourself now as a born-again Christian?" Downing asked. Cleaver responded: "The label doesn't bother me. I just wish I could be born again every day." He continued in the interview to discuss his denouncement of the Black Panther Party, disillusionment with Marxism, and his subsequent embrace of American conservatism. The former Black Panther, author of the best-selling memoir that sent shivers down the moral spines of Christian conservatives, who had once spoken of rape as the ultimate form of protest against the white man and Christianity but a tool of the capitalist elite, was now a born-again Christian.[13] To conclude the interview, Downing asked Cleaver about his future. Downing inquired, "Are you going to undertake some sort of Christian activist crusade?" "I have no plans like that," Cleaver said.[14]

Following the publication of the *People* interview, Cleaver was immediately sought out by the most recognizable figures who occupied "The Year of the Evangelical." His plans for a nationwide crusade ministry quickly changed. Evangelical personalities such as Billy and Ruth Graham, Charles Colson, Pat Robertson, Robert Schuller, and Jerry Falwell Sr. each met or opened personal correspondence with Cleaver. Cleaver's own recollection of these meetings and the surviving letters show that these white evangelicals all encouraged him to undertake a nationwide evangelical crusade ministry.[15] Writing in his post-conversion memoir, *Soul on Fire,* Cleaver recalled that Billy Graham had offered him a piece of advice: "Eldridge, one thing you must never forget—never embarrass the Lord."[16] Although Graham believed that Cleaver could make a contribution to God's Kingdom, he wanted Cleaver to know that his conduct was being policed, surveilled, and that in order for him to survive in the world of American evangelicalism, he had to behave. By the end of 1976, the Eldridge Cleaver Crusades ministry was founded.

As long as Cleaver was on his best behavior, measuring his words, proclaiming Christ, and condemning his former life, the Billy Graham Evangelistic Association (BGEA) would fund his endeavors. Early in his crusade ministry, Cleaver received assurance from his mentor, Chuck Colson. "I am sure that the Billy Graham Association will make a substantial contribution to help get your foundation off the ground,". Colson wrote. Not only was Colson confident that the BGEA would fund Cleaver's ministry, but he received word that Graham had tapped Robert Pierce to offer Cleaver the full resources of the missionary service organization, World Vision, giving the Eldridge Cleaver Crusades a global reach. George Wilson, whom Billy Graham credited with growing the BGEA into one of the world's largest charitable organizations, worked closely with Cleaver. Wilson helped Cleaver negotiate book deals and film production and connected him to the Graham network of conservative capitalists and cultural power brokers.[17] With the funding of the Graham empire, Eldridge Cleaver Crusades was poised to speak out against the ills of Marxist communism, "conspiracies of racial reconciliation," the evils of "feminism that threatened the American family," and a host of other issues at the core of evangelicalism.[18]

Beginning his nationwide tour, white evangelicals explained that

God was offering Cleaver a unique opportunity. In the words of Chuck Colson, God called Cleaver to be transformed and separated from the "volatile black figures that preached an anti-Christian message of racial division."[19] Under the guidance of evangelical celebrities and conservative businessmen and politicians, Eldridge Cleaver was stripped of his "black-ness" in order to combat advocates of black liberation and civil rights—those Colson called "volatile black figures." Cleaver was told that in order to reach his audience, he had to demonstrate that the Lord had trans-formed him in every aspect of life. If Cleaver held on to any vestige of his old life—his iconic leather jacket, "regional euphemisms," commitment to liberation, and even his Afro hairstyle—his new life with Jesus and conservatism would be rendered useless in a crusade against the "forces of communism." The new Eldridge Cleaver could not afford to be associated with "volatile black figures that preached an anti-Christian message."[20] Surveilled by his conservative associates, the crusading Eldridge Cleaver helped evangelicals reinforce their distinct markers of religion, politics, and race—Christianity, conservatism, and white respectability.

For almost four years, the Eldridge Cleaver Crusades ministry toured the country, selling copies of *Soul on Fire* and proclaiming "God's story" of delivering the former Black Panther out of radicalism.[21] Cleaver's ministry mimicked those of his white evangelical counterparts in style, message, venue, and audience. At each speaking engagement, Cleaver spoke out against his former life, the evils of communism, racial division, and the politics of the Left, all while making an appeal to the saving power of Jesus Christ in front of a predominantly white middle-class audience.[22] *Faith at Work* announced the Eldridge Cleaver Crusades to its predominantly white middle-class Protestant readership in June 1978 in an article enti-tled "The Prodigal Returns Home." Recounting Cleaver's time in exile in Cuba, Algeria, and France, the article read, "His disillusionment with the Communist world catapulted him into a confrontation with a new kind of leader he had not yet met: Jesus Christ."[23] If readers of *Faith at Work* wanted to hear more from the born-again Black Panther, they could at-tend a meeting of the Eldridge Cleaver Crusades, subscribe to its mailing list, or purchase Cleaver's new book, *Soul on Fire,* which documented his troubled childhood, life of crime, former plans for Marxist revolu-tion, and conversion to conservative politics and evangelicalism.[24] Once a champion of Marxist communism domestically and internationally, Cleaver was thrust into evangelicalism as a new leader credentialed with the experience to speak on the dangers of communism, American race relations, and the transforming power of his newfound faith. However, this thought was not completely revolutionary for Cleaver.

Although Cleaver spoke the language of his conservative white audiences, his personal journal reflects frustration with the almost three years' worth of touring the country crusading for Christ. In one journal entry dated March 15, 1979, Cleaver wrote about a white woman named Judith who was the coordinating host for the night's crusade. "Judith: you really are the worst kind of a bitch—with no enthusiasm about life."[25] A few notebook pages later, Cleaver recounts a confrontation between Kate Millet and his spouse, Kathleen Cleaver. According to Eldridge, Kate called Kathleen "a mole communist," an allusion to the constant question of Cleaver's conversion authenticity. A page later, Cleaver scribbled down the words of an individual he spoke with after a 1979 crusade stop. "Niggers who specialize in being mean and cruel ain't got no future," Eldridge wrote without comment.[26]

At each stop on the Eldridge Cleaver Crusades tour, audiences were offered a range of Eldridge Cleaver publications and merchandise. While touring the country, Cleaver sold thousands of copies of his memoirs, including the incendiary and controversial *Soul on Ice,* to predominantly white middle-class audiences. *Soul on Ice,* in which Cleaver chronicles "protest rapes" and a life of crime, may have sat on the same evangelical nightstand with *My Utmost for His Highest* or the latest Billy Graham devotional. Also available at Cleaver crusades was a new biography that recounted Eldridge's transformation. The 1977 biography *Eldridge Cleaver: Reborn* by John A. Oliver played a vital role in presenting Cleaver's brand of the crusade aesthetic to a conservative, white middle-class audience. According to Eldridge, Oliver was a reporter who visited him regularly in the Alameda County Jail shortly after his return to the United States. Oliver was also a writer for the evangelical publishing press Logos International, funded by Arthur DeMoss. Cleaver said that Oliver would often "share the Gospel of Jesus Christ" and "do whatever he could to cheer me up."[27]

Following news that Cleaver was now a born-again Christian, Oliver approached Eldridge with a proposal to write a biography. The biography would recount Cleaver's early political activity and ideology, with an emphasis on just how radical Cleaver was. Giving readers an "inside look" into the tortured and conflicted life of Cleaver, Oliver concluded the biography by demonstrating how the power of God could even transform a man who once talked about rape as an act of protest and plotted to destroy America through Marxist revolution. Whitewashing Cleaver of the narratives he carried with him by inhabiting a black body, Oliver told readers that Cleaver's story, while on the surface different from those of the majority white readership, was no different than anyone else's. For Oliver, Eldridge was coming from the same place—the place of a sinner—but God had saved him from leftist politics, Marxist ideology, sin, death, and the type of blackness evangelicals saw in the Black Panthers.[28] On one occasion, Oliver told Cleaver, "Whenever you get out of here, we'll see if we can arrange for you to come to our church." Less than a year later, Cleaver was speaking at Oliver's Valley Christian Center in Dublin, California, and Oliver's book on Cleaver was for sale outside the church auditorium.[29]

As Cleaver toured the country, he had to continually reassure his new evangelical friends that he was not going to "embarrass the Lord." Eldridge Cleaver later told audiences that he was saved both from the pits of hell and also the blackness associated with African Americans who held political and religious beliefs different than white conservatives. Following his release from prison and negotiations with financiers and evangelical powerhouses, Cleaver was instructed in every detail on how to market himself to a "respectable" audience. The first bit of advice that Cleaver received was to "tone it down." At the request of both Billy Graham and Charles Colson, Cleaver was told that he needed to measure his speech, being careful not to speak in a manner that might remind audiences of the "old Eldridge." Long remembered as the passionate firebrand of the Black Panther Party, evangelicals desired a more subdued African American crusader. He was advised to maintain a degree of decorum, avoiding slang or "regional euphemisms." This advice was meant to extend beyond the crusade stage and into his private life, setting an example as the head of a Christian household.

In addition to a more somber oration—and some Crusades recordings are borderline sleep inducing—Cleaver was advised to change his appearance. He could not be seen in clothing that mimicked the Black Panthers or those "volatile black figures that preached an anti-Christian message of racial division." Cleaver was seen in clothing similar to his white crusading counterparts—light-colored shirts and muted suits that seemed to hang loose on his athletic frame. Cleaver traded his iconic black leather jacket and turtleneck for a leisure suit. If his clothing was not enough, Cleaver shaved his goatee down to a trim mustache and cut his revolution-inspiring Afro to a short crew cut. If Cleaver had dreams of black liberation, they were to be realized within the structures of evangelicalism, cast in the image of an African American who was not too passionate, was appropriately dressed, and was respectable.

White Christian crusaders reveled in the opportunity to welcome a person of color into their ranks, acknowledging the cultural power of a black man who had disowned a former life of Marxist communism and black nationalism. Over the course of nearly four years, Cleaver spoke to thousands across the United States and reached thousands more through his evangelical-funded writing projects. Evangelicals shared stories of Eldridge's impact in their thoroughly white contexts. Arthur DeMoss recounted one encounter Cleaver had with a Virginia police officer. After preaching at Jerry Falwell's Thomas Road Baptist Church in Lynchburg, Virginia, a "southern policeman" greeted Cleaver. After shaking hands, the policeman remarked to Eldridge, "Gosh, I doubt I'll ever want to wash that hand!" Reflecting on this story, DeMoss remarked, "When I think of what intense and total polarization existed here before these two men came to a saving knowledge of Jesus Christ, I am reminded again of the tremendous unifying power of the gospel." Ralph Wilkerson, pastor of a large evangelical church in Southern California, often told the story of arranging a police escort for the Cleaver family following a bomb threat made on the church. Wilkerson believed that the threat was made after Communists "learned that Eldridge would be giving his testimony there that evening." Forced to explain to his six-year-old son, Maceo, why the police were escorting their family away from the church, Wilkerson recalled that Eldridge told Maceo that the police were protecting them. According to Wilkerson, Maceo responded, "I thought the cops hated us!" to which Eldridge responded, "No, son, that was the *old* Eldridge

Cleaver." "Eldridge, the former militant and a man who has spent almost half of his life in prison, and who is even now awaiting trial for assault with intent to kill, is now engaged in a crusade against violence," DeMoss wrote in *Soul on Fire*.[30]

Cleaver was forced to navigate his own identity in public, under constant surveillance by the circles he once inhabited and the conservative Christian circles he was crusading for. Fighting to liberate himself from the racial stereotypes that each crusade audience placed upon him, Cleaver turned to the man who had helped create his identity as a born-again crusader. "I believe Eldridge, deep down in his own way, has always wanted to help people," Arthur DeMoss wrote. "He is extremely bright, intelligent, and articulate." Credentialing Cleaver in the boilerplate language of colorblind Christianity, DeMoss called on his Christian "brothers and sisters" to pray for the former radical. "Ever since his release from prison," DeMoss wrote, "he has been inundated with every conceivable kind of request, proposition, financial lure, and temptation." According to DeMoss, Cleaver would not be able to navigate his new world without the guiding prayers of the faithful "that he might be able to know and do God's perfect and holy and wonderful will for his life." Stripped of his blackness and agency, DeMoss believed, Cleaver was free to crusade for Christ. At the same time, the most popular figures of evangelicalism believed themselves liberated from the notion that black folk were excluded from the ranks of their religious community, pointing to Cleaver as the embodiment of what Jesus could do for even the "most wretched of sinners."[31]

After touring for almost four years, Cleaver exchanged the preaching circuit for the campaign trail. Having once run for president in 1968 on the Marxist Peace & Freedom ticket, Cleaver became a leading voice for the GOP in California. During an unsuccessful congressional campaign, Cleaver echoed the rallying cry of post–World War II Republicans: "I have taken an oath in my heart to oppose communism until the day I die."[32] He claimed his "red fighting" emerged out of a deep conviction that God had called him completely out of his old life, religiously and politically. When Eldridge Cleaver passed on May 1, 1998, he was memorialized as the unlikely "Black Panther Who Became GOP Conservative."[33]

Eldridge Cleaver's journey into American evangelicalism must have read like something out of a storybook to those who inhabited its networks. Cleaver was a well-known African American from a life of crime and radicalism transformed by the Gospel of Jesus Christ and the American way. White evangelicals could not have written a better story. Behind the scenes, however, Cleaver possessed a degree of hesitation with his white Christian counterparts. On numerous occasions, Cleaver noted that he believed he was being toured around the country like an evangelical sideshow.[34] He also recognized that enduring the years of crusade ministry was an avenue to be weathered, an avenue that would open the door to future opportunity. Some could say that Cleaver was serving the discourse of white evangelicalism in order to open the way for his own pursuit of cultural power and profit. Nevertheless, this story is more than the introduction of an African American into evangelicalism or of one man's religious experience. Eldridge Cleaver serves as a window into the manner in which evangelicalism fashioned distinct understandings of race: one needed to be remade in the image of Christian whiteness and dedicated to defending the American way of life against the forces that threatened it.

In the late 1980s, after his two failed congressional campaigns, resignation from public ministry, and a drug addiction, Cleaver was cast out of the ranks of white evangelicalism.[35] While there was never an official statement from any leading evangelical that marked this divorce, it was readily apparent throughout the 1980s. When white evangelicals were flexing their cultural muscle, Cleaver left "traditional" evangelicalism to found a new church movement he called "Christlam"—a hybrid of evangelical Christianity and his former affiliation with the Nation of Islam. Cleaver continued to sample the religious marketplace. He was a regular speaker on college campuses on behalf of Rev. Sun Myung Moon, attended Baptist and Catholic churches, and later converted to Mormonism. Alongside Cleaver's increasingly "heterodox" beliefs, his drug addiction further alienated him from conservatives and his own family. Between 1987 and 1992, he was arrested numerous times for possession of illegal substances and related crimes. In 1994, Cleaver came close to death following a drug-related assault.[36] While recovering from his injuries, he allegedly had another conversion experience, once again surrendering to Jesus Christ. This time around, however, the open arms of white evangelicals did not welcome Cleaver back. His old friends Graham, Robertson, and even his former confidant Colson were nowhere to be found. The evangelicals who were quick to capitalize on his 1975 rejection of black identity, radicalism, and embrace of conservatism had abandoned him.

When Eldridge Cleaver passed in 1998, those old evangelical friends reemerged to comment on his "magnificent contributions to the kingdom of God." Cleaver was not remembered as the religious sojourner stricken with the pain of drug addiction and forgotten by those who claimed to care about him. In news reports, there was no mention of his efforts to distance himself from "volatile black figures," his addictions, his religious experiments, or family strife. Conservatives and mainstream media outlets remembered Cleaver as the former black radical and rapist who found himself in Jesus and the GOP. Cleaver's story is more than the introduction of an African American into conservative evangelicalism or of one man's religious experience. Eldridge Cleaver acts as a window into the role of African Americans in the historiography of twentieth-century evangelicalism. Surveying the presence of African Americans in the historiography, one is hard-pressed to find a serious treatment. Often, African Americans are pushed to the periphery because of perceived differences in theology, religious practice, or aspects of cultural expression. However, the example of Eldridge Cleaver makes clear that African Americans regularly find themselves in the popular historiography only when they serve the discourse of white conservative evangelicalism. White evangelicals used Eldridge Cleaver to legitimize, police, and extend their collective power and identity.[37]

Exactly three months before his death, Cleaver offered his final public comment: "We have an excellent opportunity to fulfill the American dream, to complete the American Revolution, and to reconcile to each other and to our creator."[38] Although Cleaver had escaped a police shootout in 1968, avoided the long arm of the American intelligence community in exile for seven years, and survived the tumults of living as a black religious wayfarer in the United States, he could not escape the conservative evangelicalism that remade him.

NOTES

1. Eldridge Cleaver, *Soul on Fire* (Waco, TX: Word Books, 1978), 213.
2. John A. Oliver, *Eldridge Cleaver: Reborn* (Plainfield, NJ: Logos International, 1977), 213.

3. Cleaver, *Soul on Fire*, 217.

4. Oliver, *Eldridge Cleaver*, 217–18.

5. Jenifer Warren, "Former Black Panther Eldridge Cleaver Dies at 62," *Los Angeles Times*, May 2, 1998, http://articles.latimes.com/1998/may/02/news/mn-45607.

6. Cleaver, *Soul on Fire*, 99–100.

7. Eldridge Cleaver, "Untitled, On Return from Exile to U.S.," n.d., 18, carton 2, folder 85, Eldridge Cleaver Papers, 1964–88, Bancroft Library Special Collections, University of California, Berkeley (hereafter cited as Cleaver Papers).

8. Eldridge Cleaver, "Interfaith Ministries Milwaukee," September 1977, carton 9, folder 58, Cleaver Papers, 1964–88.

9. Cleaver Papers, 1964–88.

10. Ibid., 225. DeMoss paid Cleaver's $100,000 bail in 1976 and funded the majority of the Eldridge Cleaver Crusade ministry and Cleaver's memoir *Soul on Fire*. DeMoss died in 1979.

11. Cleaver, *Soul on Fire*, 229–32.

12. David Van Biema, "Who Are Those Guys?" *Time*, August 1, 1999, http://content.time.com/time/magazine/article/0,9171,28859-1,00.html.

13. Eldridge Cleaver, *Soul on Ice* (New York: McGraw-Hill/Ramparts, 1968), 14.

14. Donn Downing, "Ex-Panther Eldridge Cleaver: 'I Just Wish I Could Be Born Again Every Day,'" PEOPLE.com, October 25, 1976,http://www.people.com/people/archive/article/0,,20067024,00.html.

15. Correspondence, 1975–81, Cleaver Papers, BANC MSS 91/213 c.

16. Cleaver, *Soul on Fire*, 232.

17. Charles W. Colson, "Letter to Eldridge Cleaver," June 27, 1977, carton 7, folder 41, Cleaver Papers, 1964–88.

18. Charles W. Colson, "Letter to Eldridge Cleaver," May 12, 1977, 1, carton 7, folder 41, Cleaver Papers, 1964–88.

19. Colson, "Letter to Eldridge Cleaver," May 12, 1977.

20. Charles W. Colson, "Letter to Eldridge Cleaver," April 6, 1978, carton 7, folder 41, Cleaver Papers, 1964–88.

21. Cleaver, *Soul on Fire*, 231–32.

22. Ibid., 231; Oliver, *Eldridge Cleaver*, 279–80. In its first year the Eldridge Cleaver Crusades appeared on fifty-eight university campuses, in scores of churches and service clubs, on television programs, and in multiple prisons (two of which he was a former inmate).

23. Eldridge Cleaver, "The Prodigal Returns Home," *Faith at Work*, June 1978, 5, carton 2, folder 21, Cleaver Papers, 1964–88.

24. Ibid., 5.

25. It's likely that Judith would not have agreed with Cleaver's notes about purchasing "Rum & Coke" either. Eldridge Cleaver, "Personal Notebook," 1979, 53, carton 4, folder 3, Cleaver Papers, 1964–88.

26. Examining the imprint of these entries, it appears that Cleaver was writing with a greater sense of physical writing pressure than in other journal entries. Cleaver, "Personal Notebook," 53–54.

27. Eldridge Cleaver, "The Golden Shower: Testimony of Eldridge Cleaver" (1977), 2, carton 2, folder 83, Cleaver Papers, 1964–88.

28. Oliver, *Eldridge Cleaver,* 284.

29. Cleaver, "Golden Shower," 2.

30. Cleaver, *Soul on Fire,* 236–37.

31. Ibid., 237–38. See Jemar Tisby, *The Color of Compromise: The Truth about the American Church's Complicity in Racism* (Grand Rapids, MI: Zondervan, 2019).

32. Bob Cain, "'He Was a Symbol': Eldridge Cleaver Dies at 62," *CNN Interactive* (blog), May 1, 1998, http://www.cnn.com/US/9805/01/cleaver.late.obit/.

33. John Kifner, "Eldridge Cleaver, Black Panther Who Became GOP Conservative, Is Dead at 62," *New York Times,* May 2, 1998, http://www.nytimes.com/1998/05/02/us/eldridge-cleaver-black-panther-who-became-gop-conservative-is-dead-at-62.html.

34. Notebooks, 1977–81, n.d., Cleaver Papers, BANC MSS 91/213 c.

35. Cleaver for Congress, 1973–84, Cleaver Papers, BANC MSS 91/213 c.

36. General Legal Files, 1957–87, Cleaver Papers, BANC MSS 91/213 c.

37. Kifner, "Eldridge Cleaver, Black Panther."

38. Don Hewitt, *60 Minutes,* CBS, February 1, 1998.

Building Bridges and a
Broad-Based Movement

OUTREACH TO EVANGELICALS AND
RIGHT-TO-LIFE STRATEGY, 1972–1980

ALLISON VANDER BROEK

In the spring of 1973, Dr. C. Everett Koop, future pro-life leader and Reagan administration pick for surgeon general, gave a speech at the commencement ceremony at Wheaton College, a small, evangelical college just outside Chicago. He noted recent disturbing rulings from the Supreme Court—on pornography, capital punishment, and most gravely, abortion, and he lamented that the ruling in *Roe v. Wade* was "on the opposite side of the fence from the traditional teachings of Judaism and Christianity throughout the ages."[1] He advised the new graduates: "You have the obligation of knowing the issues . . . you can make your desires known to legislators . . . you can and must protest in any effective Christian manner."[2] Less than six months after the Supreme Court's ruling to legalize abortion, Koop urged these young evangelical graduates to educate themselves and to actively oppose abortion. Attempts to recruit evangelicals into right-to-life activism did not stop there.

Over the course of 1973 and into the first few months of 1974, the National Right to Life Committee (NRLC) debated the merits of a broad-based right-to-life movement and the strategies necessary to achieve it. The mix of Protestants in the group, both mainline and evangelical, as well as their Catholic counterparts expressed confidence that evangelicals and fundamentalists would be a fruitful target for the NRLC's outreach efforts. All the right-to-lifers needed to do was get organized and reach out to educate the vast untapped population of evangelicals in the nation.[3] But how would they convince evangelicals to join their cause, especially since it was devoted to an issue that some had characterized as "the Catholic Issue"?

Although presently considered to be natural allies, the right-to-life movement and evangelicals have not always had such a happy union. In fact, it took years of concerted effort on the part of many right-to-lifers to convince evangelicals to join the burgeoning movement. While many scholars have addressed the relationship between evangelicalism, the New Right and Religious Right, and the abortion issue in the 1980s, most have paid less attention to the work of the right-to-life movement to reach out to evangelicals in the years immediately before and after *Roe v. Wade*.[4] The usual narrative of evangelical involvement in abortion politics generally ignores the early efforts of right-to-lifers to reach out to evangelicals and also ignores the evangelicals who were already active in the movement prior to the 1980s, such as Bob Holbrook of Baptists for Life, Judy Fink of the NRLC, the Lutheran Church–Missouri Synod, and the Christian Action Council. Historians such as Daniel Williams, Randall Balmer, and Neil Young have recently begun to reshape this narrative and complicate the story of the rise of the New Right and its relationship to the antiabortion movement. Nevertheless, many scholars still take it for granted that in the early 1980s, conservative evangelicals and conservative Catholics suddenly found common cause in opposing abortion and overcame their theological animosity to work together on an issue both camps saw as life-or-death.[5]

Yet the influx of evangelicals into the right-to-life movement only occurred after nearly a decade of work to make the movement and its organizations a welcoming place for evangelicals and fundamentalists. Throughout the 1970s, interdenominational outreach, especially to evangelical churches, was central to right-to-life strategy. The movement spent these years working on plans to make the initial contact with evangelical denominations, to educate evangelicals on the abortion issue, and to recruit them to join the movement. The right-to-lifers cared little about political affiliation or religious practice, but they believed that they shared foundational views on morality with evangelicals, including the view that abortion was murder. Most important, right-to-lifers believed that if they could only reach evangelical churches and denominations, evangelicals would also become convinced to take action to oppose abortion. In a way, right-to-lifers believed that evangelical Protestants were already their allies—evangelicals just did not realize it yet. But with steadfast work and mobilization efforts, the right-to-life movement was confident that evangelicals would join the cause and take part in the political work the movement was already doing to elect right-to-life candidates and push for a human life amendment. Persisting in this belief, the activists got to work.

This essay will examine the attempts by the right-to-life movement and its leaders to broaden their base of support, begin their appeal to evangelicals, and find common ground on the abortion issue among the various religious traditions represented in their constituency. Right-to-lifers accomplished this task in three main ways over the course of the 1970s. First, they worked to resolve the internal tensions between Catholics and Protestants that sometimes plagued the movement. Mostly, this process involved figuring out what role the institutional Catholic Church had in abortion politics and trying to elevate more Protestants to leadership roles. Second, right-to-lifers developed a vision for a broad-based movement that welcomed Americans of all religious faiths. As they implemented this vision, right-to-lifers included evangelicals as a specific part of their agenda. Third, and most important, the right-to-life movement always acted on the belief that evangelical Christians already opposed abortion and that the only thing the movement needed to do to mobilize them into political activism was to reach out and educate evangelicals on abortion and right-to-life strategy.

RESOLVING TENSIONS BETWEEN CATHOLICS AND PROTESTANTS

In order to make the right-to-life movement a welcoming place for evangelicals and to develop and implement a vision for broad-based support, the movement first had to deal with the internal divisions that often arose between Catholics and Protestants in its leadership roles. How were right-to-lifers supposed to welcome evangelicals if Catholics and Protestants could not get along and work together in the NRLC, the movement's main organization? The activists also had to contend with what the role of the institutional Catholic Church would be in an independent right-to-life organization. Up to 1973, the institutional Catholic Church had a hand in much of the movement's organizing and funding, such as in starting the NRLC, and because of this, the movement was often portrayed as a Catholic endeavor alone. But as the movement became more prominent in national politics, its leaders wanted to clarify the roles of Protestants and other non-Catholics in their organizations and temper the involvement of the Catholic Church hierarchy both within the NRLC as well as in important public events, such as hearings before Congress. Resolving the tensions was no easy task, and tempers often flared as Protestants pushed for a greater role in right-to-life activism and Catholics tried to figure out what their new roles would be within a more broad-based movement. Though these early discussions centered on Protestants more generally, rather than evangelicals specifically, their resolutions would have major implications for evangelical involvement over the course of the decade. But in the early 1970s, it remained unclear whether the movement could be a place where evangelicals and other Protestants felt welcomed and included.

It was imperative that right-to-lifers deal with these Catholic-Protestant divisions, partly because abortion rights supporters loved to exploit the Catholic makeup of the movement and portray it as solely a Catholic endeavor. Claims of Catholic domination haunted the new right-to-life movement when it first began in the 1960s as well as throughout the 1970s. Starting the NRLC had been the Catholic Church's attempt to "shift attention away from the so-called 'exclusively Catholic opposition,'" but the abortion rights movement seized on the fact that the Catholic Church hierarchy had been responsible and saw its chance to portray the movement as completely controlled by church officials.[6] The National Abortion Rights Action League (NARAL) characterized opposition to abortion as "the influence of one church whose dogma that human life begins with conception has been, in effect, foisted upon the body politic."[7] Such allegations of a Catholic conspiracy were ubiquitous in abortion rights rhetoric throughout the 1970s and even made their way into the letters of ordinary people to their representatives and local newspapers and into the historiography of the right-to-life movement itself.[8] As early as 1972, NRLC members such as Jack Willke were expressing concern about connections to the Catholic Church that perpetuated "'Catholic' labeling of Right to Life groups by opposition."[9] The right-to-lifers recognized that if they were going to attract evangelicals and other non-Catholics to join their cause, they had to break away from the stereotype that the right-to-life movement was solely a Catholic undertaking.

Despite the church's overt role in founding and funding the NRLC in its early years and the claims that the hierarchy orchestrated the entire opposition to legalized abortion, ordinary Americans, both Catholic and non-Catholic—oftentimes laypeople—had been the main driving force behind antiabortion activity at the state and local level. The movement had never been made up of only Catholics; nevertheless, right-to-lifers feared that the abortion rights movement's tactic might be keeping more Protestants from joining. The growing push for the repeal of abortion laws culminating in *Roe v. Wade* in 1973 intensified the urgency felt by right-to-lifers about bringing more non-Catholics into right-to-life activism. Though these early right-to-lifers publicly placed great emphasis on the religious diversity of the movement, some members privately expressed concerns about the role of Protestants in the movement, the lack of Protestants and other non-Catholics in leadership positions, and the role of the Catholic Church hierarchy.

In a series of meetings in 1973 and 1974, the NRLC officially became incorporated and shed its official ties to the Catholic Church, but during the transition, the tensions between Protestants and Catholics erupted into open conflict. The Protestant leadership, including Marjory Mecklenburg, a Methodist, Judy Fink, a Baptist, and Warren Schaller, an Episcopalian, wanted to know if Protestants would only be non-Catholic fronts in the movement or if they would be given real leadership roles in the NRLC. As the reconstituted NRLC took shape, Fink complained that the NRLC's newly formed Policy Committee only consisted of Catholic men: "Since the prolife movement must be broad-based and pluralistic if it is to grow and remain healthy, I feel that it is a serious mistake for a Committee of this importance to not seat any individuals except male Roman Catholics."[10] She warned her Catholic colleagues that changes would have to take place. Mecklenburg believed the problems went beyond the makeup of the committees and feared that the Catholic hierarchy wanted to retain a large level of influence in the movement. She said that she felt "the institutional Catholic church appears to be locked into a power struggle with us for control of the organization, the position and the movement."[11] She also relayed the following account: "One of Fr. McHugh's confidants recently proposed to a Protestant on the executive committee that if the Catholic church could come up with 20 million dollars and could guarantee they could win an amendment, would the Protestants be willing to be window dressing—no rocking the boat?"[12] Mecklenburg wondered if it were even possible for the Catholic Church to work with an independent right-to-life organization and if Protestants would ever truly share equal responsibility in such an organization. If not, Protestants might be forced to form their own independent right-to-life groups.

It was unclear whether the movement would be able to resolve this tension and make the NRLC accommodating to both Catholics and Protestants. In observing the battle for control, Warren Schaller commented that he believed it was about fundamental differences between Catholics and Protestants: "It's a Protestant thing, you see, that authority rests in the people of God."[13] Catholic right-to-lifers also expressed frustrations. Randy Engel countered the Protestants' claims, writing that Mecklenburg used "her Protestantism as a battering ram to hit Catholics over the head and cow them into silence."[14] Similar to Mecklenburg, she questioned whether Protestants and Catholics could effectively work together to fight abortion. The factions ultimately reached an uneasy truce within the NRLC and attempts to include Protestants became the norm for the movement, though Robert Greene, a former executive director of the NRLC, noted that the effects of this tension still lingered several years later, and Marjory Mecklenburg and Judy Fink ultimately left the NRLC to start their own organization.[15]

Another way right-to-lifers eased the tension between Catholics and non-Catholics was by clarifying the role of the institutional Catholic Church and the extent to which church officials should be involved in right-to-life politics. This debate revolved around shaping the public voice of the movement. Again, right-to-life leaders were looking for ways to expand Protestant involvement and visibility as well as to combat stereotypes that their movement was exclusively Catholic. Their organizations already had Protestant members and leaders, but they were too often passed over when it came to public hearings or debates in favor of the more visible opponents to abortion, such as the Catholic bishops. In one memorable instance in 1974, the Senate held a hearing on pending abortion legislation, but only four Catholic cardinals were invited to represent the religious opposition to abortion. Protestant right-to-lifers immediately expressed their dismay that no Protestant clergy or laypeople were invited. The cardinals initially defended their decision to speak, arguing that they were representing all right-to-lifers and that they were simply asking the government to abide by the precepts in the nation's founding documents.[16]

In an important shift of position in this instance, church officials acknowledged the complaints of Protestant right-to-lifers, and they, too, expressed concern about the invitation of the four cardinals as a way to continue portraying the right-to-life movement as thoroughly Catholic.[17] Additionally, church officials encouraged greater visibility of Protestant right-to-lifers in future public events, such as testimony before the House Judiciary Subcommittee in March 1976.[18] And in a sign of easing tension, some Protestant right-to-lifers affirmed the church's assessment that ignoring Protestant activists was an attempt to smear the movement with the false Catholic label, rather than a concerted effort by the church to keep Protestants out of the limelight. Jean Garton, a member of the Lutheran Church–Missouri Synod, blamed the press for framing the abortion issue as a Catholic versus Protestant issue while Protestant and Jewish right-to-lifers were ignored.[19] In turn, the NRLC urged Catholics to be sensitive to Protestant involvement in the right-to-life movement, and its Intergroup Liaison Committee gave advice to its Catholic members on dealing with Protestants. "Sit down and examine your terminology," they urged Catholics. "Does it smack of Romanism? . . . Learn some of the Protestant terms. Some are so simple and yet so foreign to Catholics."[20] As they worked out the role of the Catholic Church in right-to-life activism, the NRLC continued to prioritize the recruitment of potential non-Catholic allies.

As with speaking out to make sure right-to-life committees were religiously diverse, Protestants continued to emphasize the need of having a mix of religious persons testify in opposition to abortion.[21] And in the mid-1970s, the Catholic Church began to listen and agree that Protestants needed to have a more prominent role in the right-to-life movement. Lay

Catholics agreed with Garton's assessment of the 1974 hearings, arguing that "the Protestant voice must be heard."[22] And when the House Judiciary Committee only invited the Catholic bishops to represent the right-to-life side in March 1976, William Cox urged Bishop James Rausch to delay their testimony until Protestant right-to-lifers were included, while Michael Taylor recommended the bishops testify but strongly denounce the failure to invite Protestants.[23] Ultimately, Jean Garton and Eugene Linse of the Lutheran Church–Missouri Synod provided the Protestant testimony at the hearing.[24] The NRLC as well as leaders within the Catholic Church clearly considered the Protestant-Catholic divide a vital and urgent problem to resolve and looked for ways to avoid creating tension between Catholics and Protestants in the movement.

Although none of these endeavors explicitly targeted evangelicals, their result was to reshape the right-to-life movement to be more open to non-Catholics and to add religiously diverse voices to spread the right-to-life message. They also helped Catholics and Protestant learn to work together. Ultimately, evangelical Protestants would be some of the biggest beneficiaries of the changes made by the movement in the early to mid-1970s. Evangelicals would not have to have their own separate organizations if they did not want to, and existing Protestant groups could work with the main wing of the movement. In working to resolve the lingering tensions between Catholics and Protestants in the right-to-life movement, right-to-lifers made it into something that any Protestant could be free to join, take on a leadership role, and fight against abortion.

BUILDING A BROAD-BASED MOVEMENT

Along with resolving the tensions between Protestants and Catholics, the right-to-lifers also began to articulate a vision for a broad-based movement. By *broad-based,* they meant a movement that welcomed any person who opposed legalized abortion regardless of their political or religious affiliation. As mentioned previously, the movement's leaders had long emphasized that their work was not just a Catholic project. When it came to articulating the vision for a broad-based movement, right-to-lifers argued again and again that opposition to abortion did not come solely from Catholic Church teaching. Both Catholic and non-Catholic activists insisted that their concerns were universal rather than denominational. Americans United for Life (AUL) founder and Unitarian George Huntston Williams summed up this stance in 1971: "There is nothing sectarian in the hitherto almost universal concern to safeguard embryonic life."[25] Right-to-lifers hoped that framing their cause in such terms would bring Americans of all religious backgrounds into right-to-life activism.

From the early 1970s and into the early 1980s, many right-to-lifers in a number of different organizations reiterated visions for a broad-based movement. In 1972, Dr. Joseph Stanton told members of AUL that he had "pleaded for a broad-based committee organized regardless of race, creed or color, that would seek out the broad area of general agreement among men of good will in opposing the attack on life."[26] He professed his confidence that such an organization was the only way to achieve success and overcome infighting. In 1976, American Citizens Concerned for Life (ACCL) again emphasized the need to continue to work for a "multi-denominational religious coalition."[27] Likewise, Marjory Mecklenburg observed, "The Life Movement has broad appeal and under its umbrella is the widest representation . . . a wise course for participants to follow is to continue to make room under the pro-life umbrella for all who see the inhumanity of abortion and the value of life."[28] This approach was a matter not just of reaching more people but also of developing the strongest and most effective strategy. A few years earlier, Mecklenburg had stated this position decisively: "The strongest possible kind of organization is one composed of concerned citizens rather than separate organizations of concerned Catholics or concerned Baptists . . . . Acting from a broad base an organization multiplies its appeal and its possibility to be an effective voice."[29] For most right-to-lifers, the only path forward for the movement was encouraging its religious diversity, and it soon became clear that evangelicals and their churches would be an important pillar in this plan. The right-to-life movement just needed to figure out how to apply this vision to take practical steps that would recruit more evangelicals and convince them to actively oppose abortion.

The implementation of this vision in regard to evangelicals took place in a few different ways. Right-to-lifers worked to put Protestants in visible leadership positions and to privilege their stances in the movement's own literature and in newspaper articles on their activities. They highlighted the work of people such as Bob Holbrook, Judy Fink, Dr. J.A.O. Preus of the Lutheran Church–Missouri Synod, and others. Sometimes it was about using a style that Protestants were familiar with and encouraging interfaith cooperation. For example, in 1972, Dr. Joseph Witherspoon suggested the Catholic Church build off the evangelical idea of "revival" to work for a revival on the right-to-life issue with Catholics and non-Catholics.[30] Early on, these efforts at outreach were sometimes thwarted—such as when Charles Rice tried to organize "a broadly-based, national program" only to be rejected by the Catholic bishops.[31] He castigated the bishops for what he saw as their "attempt to discredit and discourage Catholic participation in an ecumenical effort."[32] Yet in the following years, the Catholic Church became more supportive of such measures, such as when AUL made a point to diversify its board membership. Bishop Bernardin called this measure the "wisest course."[33] Following the Supreme Court's decision in 1973, Father McHugh, too, reiterated the need for more interfaith work to oppose the abortion issue.[34] As with resolving tensions between Catholics and Protestants, putting more Protestants and evangelicals in leadership positions and encouraging interfaith work within the movement became important ways to implement the vision of a more religiously diverse right-to-life movement and hopefully attract more Protestants activists.

Another prime example of the development of this vision for a broad-based movement was in the NRLC's conversations regarding its policy on birth control. The group's leaders sought to clarify the organization's official position on contraceptives in order to avoid alienating potential evangelical allies. There was a precedent for such action. As early as 1971, some groups were discussing how to accommodate Protestants in their organizations and in their policy statements. Some groups tweaked their stance on abortion, such as the Value of Life Committee, which in 1971 discussed changing its stance on abortion to oppose "abortion on demand" rather than all abortions as a way to bring in more Protestants.[35] The NRLC would ultimately adopt a neutral stance on contraceptives, but this decision only came after Judy Fink's strong statements in favor of excluding opposition to birth control in its official organizational policy positions. Fink, herself an evangelical Christian, believed that the abortion rights movement would capitalize on the NRLC's opposition to contraceptives if its members took such a stance. Most important, she had evangelicals in mind in particular when she made this recommendation. Fink worried that a statement of total opposition to birth control would "count out the participation of the 12 million Southern Baptists in the nation . . . the huge rapidly growing Independent, Fundamentalist, and Pentecostal Protestant groups . . . need I go on?"[36] The risk was too great—the NRLC had to remain neutral on birth control, largely to avoid alienating evangelical Christians from the right-to-life movement. If the movement was to be broad-based, as it claimed it wanted it to be, NRLC leaders could not take any action that risked alienating evangelicals.

Finally, right-to-lifers fostered ongoing dialogue with evangelical Christians on the involvement of non-Catholics in the right-to-life movement to show they were committed to including evangelicals. In addition to facilitating discussions through their denominational contacts, such as Bob Holbrook and Southern Baptists or Dr. Preus and the Lutheran Church–Missouri Synod, and facilitating interdenominational events such as a National Prayer Breakfast for Life, the right-to-lifers also used religious newspapers and magazines to keep an open dialogue on abortion politics from both Catholic and evangelical perspectives. In 1976, for example, several articles appeared in Catholic and evangelical publications about Catholics, evangelicals, and the abortion issue. In 1976, *Christianity Today* ran the article "Is Abortion a Catholic Issue?" while *America* featured "An Evangelical Perspective on the Abortion Issue." The first article quoted Bob Holbrook, who noted increasing opposition to abortion among evangelicals and called the charge that abortion was a Catholic issue alone a "smokescreen."[37] The latter article tried to explain the Protestant standpoint on abortion for Catholics and the primacy of using biblical arguments against abortion when discussing the issue with evangelicals.[38] Both articles served to make each group aware of the other and hopefully help Catholics and evangelicals find common ground on the abortion issue, even if they sometimes discussed the issue in different terms. If right-to-lifers were serious about creating a broad-based movement, Catholics and non-Catholics needed to start learning how to work together and needed to know that they agreed on the abortion issue.

In the 1970s, the right-to-life movement not only articulated a vision for a broad-based and religiously diverse movement, but right-to-lifers also took steps to enact that vision. They worked to reshape their leadership and highlight evangelical voices. They carefully considered their policy on issues such as birth control, keeping evangelical Christians specifically in mind. And they encouraged ongoing dialogue between evangelicals and Catholics on the abortion issue. Right-to-life activists hoped that by resolving the tensions between Protestants and Catholics, as well as by articulating and publicizing their vision for a broad-based program, evangelicals and other religious Americans would flock to join them.

REACHING THEIR EVANGELICAL ALLIES

Perhaps most important, from the early 1970s, right-to-lifers persisted in the belief that evangelical Protestants were a prime target for recruitment if they could only reach out and educate evangelicals on the abortion issue. Right-to-lifers firmly believed that evangelical Protestants were their natural allies and already opposed to abortion, even if they did not know it yet. The belief came up again and again in meetings and correspondence in the 1970s. In 1974, Fink argued: "There is a large and mostly silent prolife untapped constituency in the United States and they are ours to teach. We have only to do it."[39] In a meeting of the executive committee of the NRLC, the group again agreed that the twenty-five million Baptists in the United States would "be prolife if fully informed."[40] And former executive Robert Greene reminded the NRLC to target evangelicals as he stepped down from leadership in the organization.[41] This belief, in turn, shaped their strategy on the ground. For example, in discussing Willke's *Handbook on Abortion,* the National Right to Life Committee urged right-to-lifers: "Church groups are frequently interested.... Do not dismiss any specific church as automatically pro-abortion."[42] The NLRC indicated that evangelical denominations such as Baptists, Church of Christ, and "most biblically oriented fundamentalist churches" might be the most receptive. Even when Marjory Mecklenburg and a few other right-to-lifers split off to form American Citizens Concerned for Life, a more progressive organization, they still listed several evangelical right-to-life groups as potential groups to invite to a Congress of National Right to Life Organizations.[43] The belief that evangelicals were already opposed to abortion convinced the right-to-lifers to take decisive action in order to bring evangelicals into the right-to-life movement.

Evangelicals and other Protestants in the movement themselves spoke out, indicating that their denominations would be fruitful targets for right-to-lifers. Bob Holbrook, a Southern Baptist, noted, "The Protestant churches have 'grass-roots' support for pro-life but this support is neutralized by a failure to energize and mobilize."[44] His report urged immediate action—it had been less than a year since the *Roe v. Wade* decision, and right-to-lifers needed to work quickly to mobilize evangelical support. Another NRLC report by Judy Fink noted that "Protestant Christians can, and must, be brought into the prolife movement .... Those of us who are Protestants are keenly aware that not only do the vast majority of us reject the Supreme Court decision, we reject it on scriptural grounds."[45] Later on in the report, Fink again reiterated that evangelicals were ready and waiting—all activists needed to do was to reach out and work to educate them on the issue. These evangelicals confirmed the right-to-life leaders' contention that evangelicals were already on their side and that evangelical denominations could be a vital resource and recruiting ground for the movement.

The right-to-life movement let this belief guide its strategy in the mid-1970s. Immediately after the NRLC was officially incorporated and in the frenzy following the *Roe v. Wade* decision in 1973, the NRLC formed the Intergroup Liaison Committee. The group was supposed to focus on reaching out to other churches and organizations that might want to join the right-to-life movement now that abortion was legal nationwide, but much of the group's focus immediately turned to evangelical Protestants and their denominations, especially the Southern Baptists. They set their "first priority" as "building bridges with certain Protestant religious groups."[46] In January 1974, Fink prepared a report on the group's activities over the past year and identified a number of recommendations the group intended to pursue if it could secure adequate funding. These included running advertisements in a variety of religious periodicals, holding workshops for clergy, and sending speakers to lead workshops at seminaries and Bible colleges. By the time the report was put together, the committee had already spoken with representatives from the Lutheran Church–Missouri

Synod; helped form Baptists for Life; met with the project director of Americans Against Abortion, a newly formed evangelical antiabortion group; and sent over three thousand letters to Southern Baptist pastors.[47]

Even in this frenzy of activity, the group tried to be sensitive to the various approaches different denominations had to abortion. In making recommendations on forming right-to-life groups in various states, it warned, "It is simply not possible to ask an Independent Baptist to speak to the issue of prolife concerns from a Roman Catholic viewpoint, for example . . . working on an inter-denominational basis requires considerable education regarding proper outreach."[48] To help avert any issues, the Intergroup Liaison Committee allowed its members to make contacts within their own denominations. For instance, committee member Bob Holbrook, who was also part of the organization Baptists for Life, developed a proposal to circulate right-to-life ads in Baptist papers across the South.[49] In 1975, he helped the group work with Baptists for Life to lobby the Southern Baptist Convention in support of a right-to-life resolution.[50] The plan was very detailed, listing a series of small steps to take in the months leading up to the convention. These steps included meetings with various Baptist leaders, running advertisements in Baptist periodicals, developing an educational program to use in Baptist churches, and sending out special mailings.[51] In all of its outreach activity in the mid-1970s, the Intergroup Liaison Committee coordinated a vital segment of right-to-life strategy, allowing the NRLC to make many inroads with evangelical Christians and utilizing the skills and knowledge of evangelical right-to-lifers.

Even beyond the NRLC, state groups, such as Minnesota Citizens Concerned for Life (MCCL), also believed that evangelicals could be brought into the movement and developed plans to target southern states using contacts it had made with southern evangelicals. In 1976, MCCL launched an endeavor to support a human life amendment, which they called "Mission Possible." One of their main projects in that program was targeting the South, the Bible Belt, and giving grants to help right-to-life groups in states like Alabama and North Carolina. The group had already reached out to southern evangelicals such as Ray Dutton, a radio preacher and member of the Church of Christ from Alabama, and in 1976, MCCL even helped organize a right-to-life conference in Dutton's home state.

Dutton, like many others, believed that more people in Alabama would be actively opposed to abortion if only they heard the right-to-life message.[52] MCCL's work in the South was ambitious, and the group managed to raise a total of fourteen thousand dollars, which they planned to use in several southern states. MCCL activists hoped to spread their message and build support for a human life amendment by working with contacts they had made in the Church of Christ and with other southern evangelicals.[53] Using Mission Possible funds, MCCL also gave a grant of three thousand dollars to Baptists for Life as the organization worked to pass an antiabortion resolution at the Southern Baptist Convention.[54] For MCCL, it seemed reasonable that a state right-to-life group could make a big impact in the South and especially among southern evangelicals.

Finally, the right-to-life movement treated the 1976 presidential election as a major opportunity to reach out to evangelical Protestants. Although Jimmy Carter was an evangelical himself, the right-to-lifers thought evangelicals might reject him based on his views on abortion, and they pointed to his support of abortion rights as a way to dissuade both Catholics and Protestants from voting for him. Many right-to-lifers had strongly supported Ronald Reagan, but when Gerald Ford was chosen as the candidate, they fell in line behind him, though his views were far from what they saw as truly pro-life.[55] Carter, on the other hand, was completely unfit, even though he professed to be personally pro-life.[56] Right-to-lifers, from ordinary Americans to the Catholics bishops, pointed to his unacceptable views on abortion as the main reason to vote for Ford.

Evangelical right-to-lifers helped make abortion a campaign issue, reminding their fellow evangelicals as well as both Ford and Carter that evangelicals viewed legalized abortion as a grave problem. Eugene Linse, of the Lutheran Church–Missouri Synod, sent out a letter to all pastors in his denomination with a not-so-subtle suggestion that only one candidate was in line with "the Judeo-Christian heritage" when it came to abortion.[57] The Christian Action Council, along with other Protestant right-to-lifers, sought a meeting with President Ford to discuss the abortion issue in light of the upcoming election, reminding him of the "vast numbers of biblical Protestants . . . who are deeply distressed by the present Court-mandated, taxpayer-funded policy of mass extermination of the unborn."[58] And Marjory Mecklenburg, who had joined Ford's campaign officially, reminded the campaign that Catholics and also Southern Baptists were paying attention to the abortion issue and that the campaign should highlight the candidates' differing stances on abortion in upcoming debates.[59] Their rhetoric seemed to have some effect as the right-to-lifers kept the abortion issue in the spotlight throughout the campaign. A *Washington Post* article noted President Ford's use of the abortion issue to try to woo evangelicals, even as it reported that evangelical support for Carter was slipping.[60] Right-to-lifers did not believe that Carter's evangelical faith would automatically give him the evangelical vote. They were confident that evangelicals already recognized the seriousness of the abortion issue and would vote accordingly.

The rhetoric and actions of the right-to-life movement in the early to mid-1970s showed that right-to-lifers believed evangelicals would be a vital part of their cause. Not only did they think evangelicals would be good recruits; activists also viewed evangelicals as their natural allies who already opposed abortion and just needed to be encouraged to join the right-to-life movement. The work of the NRLC's Intergroup Liaison Committee, the MCCL, and the many activists who opposed Carter's campaign for the presidency allowed right-to-lifers to act on their belief that evangelicals already opposed abortion and just needed a clear avenue to joining the movement. Through this persistence, they would ultimately find success as the late 1970s and early 1980s saw evangelical Christians firmly commit to the right-to-life cause.

Although evangelicals did not join the right-to-life movement in droves until the late 1970s, they were a vital part of the movement throughout the decade; however, even their participation at the end of the decade was not a given. It was only possible after years of work within the right-to-life movement to develop and enact a vision for a broad-based and religiously diverse movement. In the early 1970s, right-to-lifers had to resolve tensions between Protestants and Catholics. Without resolving these lingering tensions and figuring out the role of Protestants in antiabortion politics, the movement risked alienating potential evangelical allies. Their efforts in the 1970s opened the door for further cooperation between evangelicals and Catholics. The right-to-lifers also articulated a vision for a broad-based movement that welcomed evangelicals and Americans of other faiths, emphasizing their mutual concern for the unborn and what they argued was the universal recognition that abortion was immoral. Moreover, the movement took concrete steps to implement this vision, such as remaining neutral on contraception and engaging in dialogue with evangelicals on the abortion issue.

Most important, the right-to-lifers firmly believed that evangelicals were their natural allies in the fight to oppose abortion. They sought to emphasize their common ground on abortion and to convince evangelicals that such a grave issue required political action. And this belief encouraged right-to-lifers to develop a bold strategy for reaching evangelicals across the country, from the local level all the way to Congress and the presidency. Without these efforts in the 1970s, right-to-life activists might never have formed a strong and united coalition during the Reagan years. Their efforts created a movement that encouraged cooperation with evangelicals, placed evangelicals in leadership roles, and started to take cues from evangelicals on rhetoric and strategy. The vital and foundational work of the right-to-lifers in the 1970s laid the groundwork for mass evangelical involvement in the right-to-life movement in the late 1970s and early 1980s.

NOTES

1. C. Everett Koop, "Of Law, of Life, and the Days Ahead," Commencement Address given at Wheaton College, Wheaton, IL, June 4, 1973, box 16, folder 4, George Huntston Williams Papers, Andover-Harvard Theological Library, Harvard Divinity School, Harvard University, Cambridge (hereafter cited as Williams Papers).

2. Ibid.

3. National Right to Life Executive Committee Meeting Minutes, October 26–27, 1973, box 5, folder 1, American Citizens Concerned for Life, Inc., Records, Gerald R. Ford Library, Ann Arbor, MI (hereafter cited as ACCL Records); Minutes, National Right to Life Committee Executive Committee Meeting, January 4–5, 1974, box 7, folder 10, ACCL Records; Intergroup Liaison Committee, "Midyear Report," January 1974, box 6, folder 8, ACCL Records.

4. Robert N. Karrer, "The Pivotal Year and the New Narrative: Evangelicals and Fundamentalists Join the Pro-Life Movement," *Human Life Review* 40, no. 2 (Spring 2014); Dallas Blanchard, *The Anti-Abortion Movement and the Rise of the Religious Right: From Polite to Fiery Protest* (New York: Twayne Publishers, 1994); Robert O. Self, *All in the Family: The Realignment of American Democracy since the 1960s* (New York: Hill & Wang, 2012); James Risen and Judy L. Thomas, *The Wrath of Angels: The American Abortion War* (New York: Basic Books, 1998). Neil Young and Daniel Williams have recently challenged

this consensus, offering more complex and nuanced analyses of the emergence and growth of the right-to-life movement in the 1960s and 1970s. Neil Young, *We Gather Together: The Religious Right and the Problem of Interfaith Politics* (New York: Oxford University Press, 2016); Daniel K. Williams, *Defenders of the Unborn: The Pro-Life Movement before* Roe v. Wade (New York: Oxford University Press, 2016).

5. Williams, *Defenders of the Unborn,* 144; Young, *We Gather Together,* 98.Williams notes that evangelicals started to take notice of the abortion issue and the right-to-life movement in the early 1970s as it became clear that abortion rights supporters were seeking to legalize "abortion on demand," while Young describes the difficulties encountered by Catholics, evangelicals, and Mormons in trying to develop conservative ecumenism on the abortion issue in the 1960s and early 1970s. For a good description of the role of evangelicals and the New Right in building a pro-family platform, see Self, *All in the Family.* He argues that family values issues were at the center of the shift in American politics. Because of 1960s protest that pushed for more liberal positions on issues of family, gender, and sexuality, many people felt unsettled by the rapid changes in American society, and the New Right promoted the idea that the traditional American family was in serious crisis.

6. James T. McHugh, letter, January 10, 1969, box 79, folder: Abortion, 1968–69, United States Conference of Catholic Bishops Records, Catholic University of America University Archives, Washington, DC (hereafter cited as USCCB Records).

7. Lester Breslow, MD, "Abortion: The Case for Repeal," February 15, 1969, box 1, folder 20, National Abortion Rights Action League Records, 1968–76 (MC 313), Schlesinger Library, Radcliffe Institute, Harvard University, Cambridge (hereafter cited as NARAL Records).

8. Connie Paige, *The Right to Lifers: Who They Are, How They Operate, and Where They Get Their Money* (New York: Summit Books, 1983); Faye Ginsburg, *Contested Lives: The Abortion Debate in an American Community* (Berkeley: University of California Press, 1989); Marie Saunders, "Not Decision of Church or State," *Minneapolis Tribune,* April 21, 1969, reel 3, Minnesota Citizens Concerned for Life Newspaper Clippings Microfilm Collection, Minnesota Historical Society, St. Paul (hereafter cited as MCCL Newspaper Clippings); Nan Turner to State Senator Anthony Beilenson, March 4, 1967, box 78, folder 2, Anthony C. Beilenson Papers (Collection 391), UCLA Special Library Collections, Charles E. Young Research Library, Los Angeles (hereafter cited as Beilenson Papers).

9. Untitled: meeting notes, December 9, 1972, box 4, folder 9, ACCL Records.

10. Judy Fink, "Composition of Policy Committee," memo to Professor Joseph Witherspoon, July 1, 1973, box 5, folder 7, ACCL Records. In a meeting later that week, Fink again brought up the issue, asking the NRLC Executive Committee to consider seating Protestants and Jews on the Public Policy Committee. Minutes of Conference Call Meeting of the Executive Committee of the National Right to Life Committee, July 5, 1973, box 5, folder 7, ACCL Records.

11. Marjory Mecklenburg, memo to Martin Ryan Healy, September 3, 1976, box 4, folder 15, ACCL Records.

12. Marjory Mecklenburg, memo to Martin Ryan Healy, September 3, 1976, box 4, folder 15, ACCL Records.

13. Warren Schaller, Untitled: handwritten notes, 1973, box 4, folder 6, ACCL Records.

14. Randy Engel, "NRLC—Past, Present," and Future, memo to Board of Directors, NRLC, March 30, 1974, Records, box 8, folder 4, ACCL Records.

15. Robert F. Greene, "Evaluation and Critique of Past Efforts with Recommendations," memo to NRLC Board of Directors, May 23, 1975, box 10, folder 4, ACCL Records; Young, *We Gather Together,* 133.

16. USCC, "Four American Cardinals Testify on Behalf of Pro-Life Amendment," March 7, 1974, box 62, folder: Ad Hoc Committee, January–June 1974, USCCB Records.

17. Russell Shaw, memo to Bishop Rausch, "Criticism of Cardinals' Testimony—Conference Response," March 18, 1974, box 62, folder: Ad Hoc Committee, January–June 1974, USCCB Records.

18. William Cox, memo to Bishop James Rausch, "Bishops' Testimony before House Judiciary Subcommittee on Civil and Constitutional Rights," March 4, 1976, box 63, folder: NCCB Ad Hoc Committee, March 1976, USCCB Records.

19. "Pro-Life Leader Says Senate Committee Set Up Catholic vs. Protestant 'Scenario,'" March 14, 1974, box 62, folder: Ad Hoc Committee, January–June 1974, USCCB Records.

20. Paulette Stander, "Establishing a Pro-Life Group on an Inter-Denominational Theme," January 2, 1974, box 6, folder 8, ACCL Records. In the same midyear report, Mary Ann Henry wrote an article solely devoted to Catholics learning to reach out to non-Catholics. Mary Ann Henry, "Reaching Non-Catholics: The Catholic Problem," January 2, 1974, box 6, folder 8, ACCL Records.

21. Marjory Mecklenburg, letter to Bishop James Rauch, February 24, 1976, box 63, folder: NCCB Ad Hoc Committee, February 1976, USCCB Records.

22. "Pro-Life Leader Says Senate Committee Set Up Catholic vs. Protestant 'Scenario.'"

23. Cox, memo to Bishop Rausch, "Bishops' Testimony"; Michael Taylor, memo to Bishop James Rausch, "Testimony before the House Judiciary Subcommittee on Civil and Constitutional Rights, March 24," March 5, 1976, box 63, folder: NCCB Ad Hoc Committee March 1976, USCCB Records.

24. "Lutheran Leaders Urge Legal Protection for Unborn Children," press release, March 24, 1976, box 16, folder 13, ACCL Records; Eugene Linse, "Statement of Dr. Eugene Linse Jr. before the Subcommittee on Civil and Constitutional Rights Committee on the Judiciary House of Representatives," March 24, 1976, box 63, folder: NCCB Ad Hoc Committee March 1976, USCCB Records; testimony of Jean Garton for the Lutheran Church–Missouri Synod before the Subcommittee on Civil and Constitutional Rights Committee on the Judiciary House of Representatives," March 24, 1976, box 63, folder: NCCB Ad Hoc Committee March 1976, USCCB Records

25. George Huntston Williams, "Protecting the Unborn," *Boston Herald Traveler,* February 26, 1971, box 6, folder 4, Williams Papers.

26. Joseph R. Stanton, MD, memo to Americans United for Life Board, January 28, 1972, box 6, folder 4, Williams Papers.

27. Marjory Mecklenburg, Recent Items of Interest, memo to ACCL Advisory Board, March 26, 1976, box 27, folder 10, ACCL Records.

28. Marjory Mecklenburg, "Recent Letters to the Editor Commenting on My Point of View," August 28, 1979, box 15, folder 6, ACCL Records.

29. Marjory Mecklenburg, "Don't Misinterpret," 1973, box 35, folder 4, ACCL Records.

30. Dr. Joseph Witherspoon, letter to Bishop Joseph Bernardin, February 7, 1972, box 79, folder: Abortion 1972, USCCB Records.

31. Charles E. Rice, letter to James McHugh, February 18, 1971, box 79, folder: Abortion 1971, USCCB Records.

32. Ibid.

33. Bishop Joseph Bernardin, letter to Dr. J.A.O. Preus, January 7, 1972, box 79, folder: Abortion 1972, USCCB Records.

34. Father McHugh, Constitutional Amendment on Abortion, memo to Family Life Directors, Respect Life Coordinators, and State Catholic Conference Directors, July 12, 1973, box 62, folder: NCCB Ad Hoc Committee July–August 1973, USCCB Records.

35. William A. Lynch, letter to Value of Life Committee, July 2, 1971, box 11, folder 9, Williams Papers.

36. Judy Fink, "Policy Statement of NRLC concerning 'Birth Control,'" memo to Ed Golden et al., May 15, 1973, box 4, folder 12, ACCL Records.

37. "Is Abortion a Catholic Issue?" editorial, *Christianity Today,* January 16, 1976, box 63, folder: NCCB Ad Hoc Committee, January 1976, USCCB Records.

38. Harold O. J. Brown, "An Evangelical Looks at the Abortion Phenomenon," *America,* September 25, 1976, box 46, folder 5, ACCL Records.

39. Judith Fink, *Midyear Report of the Intergroup Liaison Committee of National Right to Life Committee, Inc.,* January 1974, box 6, folder 8, ACCL Records.

40. NRLC, "Minutes: NRLC Executive Committee Meeting," January 4–5, 1974, box 7, folder 10, ACCL Records.

41. Robert F. Greene, "Evaluation and Critique of Past Efforts with Recommendations," memo to NRLC Board of Directors, May 23, 1975, box 10, folder 4, ACCL Records.

42. *Handbook on Abortion: Ideas for Its More Effective Use,* n.d. (ca. 1972–73), box 3, folder 10, ACCL Records.

43. Sandy Simmons, memo to Marjory Mecklenburg, November 19, 1974, box 15, folder 5, ACCL Records.

44. Robert Holbrook, "Proposed Plan for Pro-Life Ads in State Baptist Papers," January 2, 1974, box 6, folder 8, ACCL Records.

45. Judy Fink, Alliance from NRLC, Inc., with Protestant Judiciaries, 1973, box 4, folder 6, ACCL Records.

46. NRLC, Intergroup Liaison Committee, 1973, box 6, folder 8, ACCL Records.

47. Fink, *Midyear Report.*

48. Ibid.

49. Holbrook, "Proposed Plan for Pro-Life Ads."

50. Judy Fink, "Information concerning BFL's Plan for Passing Pro-Life Resolution at Southern Baptist Convention in June 1975," memo to National Committee for a Human Life Amendment, November 25, 1974, box 67, folder: NCHLA January–March 1975, USCCB Records.

51. Baptists for Life, "Work Plan—January 1, 1975–June 30, 1975 in re. Southern Baptists Convention," box 67, folder: NCHLA January–March 1975, USCCB Records.

52. "MCCL Helps Spread the Word to Pro-Lifers in Alabama," *MCCL Newsletter,* May 1976, box 12, folder 16, ACCL Records.

53. Peggy O'Keefe, "MCCL Mission to Make South Pro-Life Called Possible with Money, Education," *Catholic Bulletin,* March 26, 1976, box 12, folder 4, ACCL Records.

54. "Baptists Reject Easy Abortion," *MCCL Newsletter,* August–September 1976, box 12, folder 16, ACCL Records.

55. Alice Hartle, "GOP to Focus on Abortion," *National Right to Life News* 3, no. 9 (September 1976), box C25, folder 2, President Ford Committee Records, Gerald R. Ford Library, Ann Arbor, MI (hereafter cited as Ford Committee Records).

56. "Carter-Mondale Ticket: Anathema to Pro-Life Movement," *Wanderer,* July 29, 1976, box 46, folder 5, ACCL Records.

57. Eugene Linse, letter to Pastor, October 25, 1976, box 45, folder 2, ACCL Records.

58. Harold O. J. Brown, letter to James Barker, October 15, 1976, box 46, folder 5, ACCL Records.

59. Marjory Mecklenburg, memo to Stu Spencer, "Presidential Debates—Suggestions on Abortion Issue," October 21, 1976, box C25, folder 1, Ford Committee Records.

60. Myra MacPherson, "Evangelicals Seen Cooling on Carter: Many Evangelicals Having Second Thoughts about Carter," *Washington Post,* September 27, 1976, box C25, folder 1, Ford Committee Records.

Evangelicals and Abortion

THE 1976 PRESIDENTIAL ELECTION AND EVANGELICAL PRO-LIFE PARTISANSHIP

DANIEL K. WILLIAMS

In 1976, Jerry Falwell's Moral Majority was still three years away from being formed, and some of the nation's most prominent Southern Baptist ministers were endorsing Democratic candidate Jimmy Carter for president. According to much of the scholarship on evangelical politics, evangelicals in 1976 were still a "sleeping giant" who had not yet become politically mobilized on the issues that would later become the central points of focus for the Christian Right. And nowhere was that more evident, they have said, than on abortion. Randall Balmer, for instance, has argued that evangelicals did not begin to demonstrate much concern about abortion until the late 1970s.[1] There is some truth to this narrative; evangelicals did indeed demonstrate far less concern than conservative Catholics did about abortion in the 1970s, and abortion was also far less of a political concern for evangelicals during the Nixon and Carter years than it would be for evangelicals in the Reagan era. Nevertheless, historians of evangelical politics have generally underestimated the degree of evangelical opposition to abortion in the 1970s because they have misunderstood its framework, and as a result, they have overlooked evangelical political mobilization on the issue in the 1976 presidential election. In this essay, I argue that a large number of evangelicals did care about the abortion issue in 1976, but they did not yet treat it as a political litmus test. Yet the events of the election season prompted them to give increased attention to abortion and laid the groundwork for abortion to become a partisan litmus test for evangelicals in future elections.

When the 1976 presidential election season began, neither the Democratic nor the Republican Party had an official position on abortion. Nor did evangelicals. In the late 1960s and early 1970s, evangelicals had expressed a variety of positions on abortion, ranging from opposition to nearly all abortions to a belief that abortion was morally permissible in many circumstances and that the law should not prohibit it. The general consensus among the nation's most popular evangelical magazines in the late 1960s—including *Christianity Today, Eternity,* and *Christian Life*—was that abortion was morally problematic because, at the very least, it destroyed a "potential" life but that it was probably morally acceptable in cases of medical necessity, which included cases when a pregnancy endangered a woman's health and in cases of rape or incest. Evangelicals moved toward a more conservative position on the issue in the early 1970s, after several states, including New York, removed nearly all restrictions on abortion during the first two trimesters of pregnancy. In 1971, New York doctors were performing 200,000 legal abortions per year in the state's hospitals, and in 1972, more than a half-million legal abortions were performed nationwide. *Christianity Today* responded with a forceful critique. "The War on the Womb," a two-page editorial published in June 1970, ended the magazine's three-year quest for a centrist position on the issue and, instead, endorsed the view of a minority of evangelical theologians, including John Warwick Montgomery, who argued that human life began at conception and that Christians had a duty to defend the unborn in the political sphere. "For the biblical writers personhood in the most genuine sense begins no later than conception," Montgomery wrote, in a statement that *Christianity Today* quoted with approval.[2] Other pro-life articles followed over the next few months. In June 1971, L. Nelson Bell published an antiabortion editorial in which he lamented that the current push toward legalization of "abortion on demand" "evidence[d] a callous disregard for the realities of the unwarranted termination of life, which sears the souls of all concerned."[3] *Eternity,* another popular evangelical magazine of the time that positioned itself slightly to the left of *Christianity Today* on some political issues, also joined the campaign against abortion in February 1971 with an editorial by Carl F. H. Henry titled "Is Life Ever Cheap?"[4]

Evangelicals who spoke out against abortion in the early 1970s were not yet ready to say that all abortion was wrong. "As a physician I well know that there are times when abortion is necessary," Bell wrote. In fact, he admitted, he had even performed a few abortions himself. "But the reasons then are basically medical," he wrote, "and it is physicians in consultation who alone are competent to determine the matter."[5] This view explained why no major evangelical magazine of the late 1960s had been willing to endorse the right-to-life cause—which at the time was led almost entirely by Catholics—and yet at the same time had expressed grave concern about abortion on demand. It also explains the timing of evangelical expressions of opposition to abortion. Evangelical magazines became more forceful in their opposition to abortion as soon as states began legalizing elective abortion in 1970. Before then, they had been willing to cautiously endorse modest liberalization of abortion laws that dated back to the late nineteenth century and that allowed abortion only in cases when a woman's life was in danger. But as soon as a modest liberalization effort gave way to a demand for outright repeal of all restrictions on abortion, evangelical magazine editors balked. This repeal effort was an attack on human life, and it was linked to the culture of sexual promiscuity, they charged. A consensus gradually emerged that evangelicals should oppose abortion on demand.

Some evangelicals, especially among Southern Baptists, believed that continued promotion of modest abortion liberalization laws would provide an effective deterrent against the campaign to legalize elective abortion. In 1971, the Southern Baptist Convention (SBC) passed a resolution declaring that "society has a responsibility to affirm through the laws of the state a high view of the sanctity of human life, including fetal life, in order to protect those who cannot protect themselves," while nevertheless calling for states to allow for abortion in cases of "rape, incest, clear evidence of severe fetal deformity, and carefully ascertained evidence of the likelihood of damage to the emotional, mental, and physical health of the mother."[6] This resolution reflected the views of the vast majority of the denomination's ministers. A *Baptist Viewpoint* poll that was conducted in 1970 revealed that 71 percent of Southern Baptist pastors and Sunday school teachers believed that abortion should be legal in cases of rape and incest, and 70 percent favored legalizing it for cases in which a pregnancy endangered a woman's health. But 80 percent also opposed the legalization of elective abortion.[7] The 1971 SBC resolution was thus neither a fully pro-life nor a completely pro-choice resolution (to use modern terminology somewhat anachronistically) but, rather, an attempt to affirm the value of fetal life and protect against the legalization of abortion on demand while also allowing for cases of perceived medical necessity. Instead of locating the decision to have an abortion solely with a woman, these evangelicals, like L. Nelson Bell, wanted to give the decision to physicians, and they wanted to make sure that the law still provided tight safeguards to protect fetal life.

Other evangelicals—especially those associated with national parachurch ministries—favored a somewhat more restrictive stance. In 1972, Billy Graham declared that he opposed abortion in all cases except in cases of rape and in instances when a pregnancy endangered a woman's life. This became perhaps the most common evangelical position on abortion in the 1970s. Carl Henry espoused it, as did the National Association of Evangelicals (NAE).[8]

Roe v. Wade therefore fell well to the left of mainstream evangelical opinion. While there were a few evangelical outliers who endorsed the decision—including the staunchly conservative Dallas pastor W. A. Criswell (who later reversed his position and embraced an antiabortion view by the end of the 1970s) and several politically progressive Southern Baptists associated with either the Christian Life Commission or the Baptist Joint Commission on Religious Liberty—most Southern Baptist pastors and other evangelicals did not.[9] Criswell, who had warned against John F. Kennedy's Catholicism in 1960, may have endorsed *Roe* because of a residual suspicion of Catholic political power, while most of the Christian Life Commission and Baptist Joint Commission leaders who favored the ruling did so for the same reasons that mainline Protestant denominational leaders did—namely, that it prevented the imposition of a particular sectarian religious view in politics and protected the liberty of women to make decisions about pregnancy termination that accorded with their own individual consciences. This was a liberal Protestant value, and it was shared by several in the Christian Life Commission and the

Baptist Joint Commission. But most evangelicals did not share it. And in fact, some in the Southern Baptist Convention who were most vocal about abortion rights—such as Christian Life Commission leader Foy Valentine—insisted (perhaps with good reason) in the 1970s that they were not evangelicals.[10] They envisioned the Southern Baptist Convention as a centrist, mainline denomination, not as a participant in a culturally conservative evangelical movement. But for most of those who did identify with evangelicalism, *Roe* was an unwelcome development.

Christianity Today responded to the decision with a forcefully worded editorial that not only denounced the Court but also warned that the decision may have ushered in a changed relationship between evangelicals and the state. "In arriving at this decision, the majority of the Supreme Court has explicitly rejected Christian moral teaching," the magazine declared in a February 1973 editorial. "Christians should accustom themselves to the thought that the American state no longer supports, in any meaningful sense, the laws of God, and prepare themselves spiritually for the prospect that it may one day formally repudiate them and turn against those who seek to live by them."[11]

The National Association of Evangelicals likewise condemned *Roe*. "We deplore in the strongest possible terms the decision of the U.S. Supreme Court which has made it legal to terminate a pregnancy for no better reason than personal convenience or sociological considerations," the NAE resolution declared in 1973. "We reaffirm our conviction that abortion on demand for social adjustment or to solve economic problems is morally wrong." However, the NAE also added, in a reflection of widespread evangelical beliefs at the time: "We recognize the necessity for therapeutic abortions to safeguard the health or the life of the mother, as in the case of tubular pregnancies. Other pregnancies, such as those resulting from rape or incest, may require deliberate termination, but the decision should be made only after there has been medical, psychological and religious counseling of the most sensitive kind."[12]

Southern Baptists also expressed more concern about *Roe* than historians have usually recognized. Robert Holbrook, a Texas pastor, organized Baptists for Life in 1973 and began working to try to convince his fellow Southern Baptists that abortion was the "killing of human life." At the 1974 Southern Baptist Convention, Holbrook, along with Oklahoma messenger Hugo Lindquist, introduced motions to affirm opposition to all abortions and to endorse an antiabortion constitutional amendment. The proposals were defeated, but the messengers at the convention nevertheless registered their concern about *Roe* by voting to reaffirm their 1971 resolution, which had posited a "high view of the sanctity of human life." While recognizing the "complexities of abortion problems in contemporary society," the convention sought what it called a "middle ground between abortion on demand and the opposite extreme of all abortion as murder."[13] For many Southern Baptists, this centrist position was still too liberal. Several state conventions passed resolutions endorsing stricter abortion laws. The Texas Baptist Convention adopted an antiabortion resolution in 1974, and the Ohio and New York conventions followed suit two years later. Oklahoma and Arkansas had already adopted resolutions cautioning against liberalization of state abortion laws in 1972.[14] This unease about abortion was reflected in state Baptist newspapers, which became increasingly critical of abortion after *Roe.* The *Baptist Standard,* the state paper of the Texas convention, ran a moderately critical article on *Roe* in January 1973 but issued a much more direct denunciation in May, when it published an editorial by Holbrook, along with another article warning that legalized abortion might lead to euthanasia—an argument that pro-life Catholics had been making for more than a decade.[15]

Despite this growing discomfort with abortion, few evangelicals joined pro-life organizations. The nation's largest pro-life group, the million-member National Right to Life Committee, was 70 percent Catholic as late as 1980, and it was probably even more heavily Catholic in the mid-1970s.[16] At the time, its board members included several mainline Protestants but only one woman—Judy Fink, an independent Baptist from Pennsylvania—who could be labeled "evangelical." In the summer of 1975, however, Ruth Graham and Trinity Evangelical Divinity School professor Harold O. J. Brown decided to remedy that by convening a meeting of twenty-five evangelicals to form what they considered the first explicitly evangelical Protestant organization designed to repeal *Roe v. Wade.* Fink attended the founding meeting, as did Holbrook.[17] The real stars of the show, though, were largely unknown in pro-life circles but household names among evangelicals. The Christian Action Council, as the new organization called itself, grounded its mission in the historic teaching of Christianity. "Virtually all Christians from the beginning have been against permissive abortion and for the protection of human life," the Christian Action Council declared. Abortion was a problem that threatened "the whole of Western civilization."[18]

And yet for most evangelicals, the abortion issue was only one facet of the larger problem of the sexual revolution and national moral decline, and for that reason, few wanted to make it a litmus test in the 1976 election. By that year, it was nearly impossible to find evangelical publications that endorsed a pro-choice point of view. Even *Sojourners,* the nation's most left-leaning evangelical publication, published a moderately critical article on abortion in December.[19] But even if hardly any evangelical publication was willing to endorse abortion rights, many were still not ready to join the pro-life cause. Several Southern Baptist state papers ignored abortion entirely. A subscriber to the *Arkansas Baptist Newsmagazine* in 1976, for instance, would have encountered one editorial against gambling, one against divorce, one against the Equal Rights Amendment, two against pornography, one against "homosexuality on TV," and several explicitly endorsing Christian principles in the public school and in politics—but no editorials on abortion. On the other hand, readers of numerous other state Baptist papers—including Alabama, Tennessee, and Texas, among others—would have seen several articles discussing the growing opposition to abortion among some Southern Baptists, especially those galvanized by Robert Holbrook. And a reader of the conservative *Southern Baptist Journal* would have seen an occasional pro-life editorial by Holbrook himself.[20] Of all the national evangelical publications, *Christianity Today* was the most outspoken against abortion. It discussed abortion nearly every other month during 1976—and invariably condemned it as a grave evil—and endorsed the Human Life Amendment in one of its editorials that year. The magazine even went so far as to publish a graphic account of an abortion in a two-page spread titled "What I Saw at the Abortion," which ran in the January 16, 1976, issue. In this article, a doctor who became repulsed by the procedure recounted that when he had performed an abortion, he saw a "fetus struggling against the needle."[21] There was no doubt that the nation's largest evangelical magazine was firmly pro-life in its politics by the mid-1970s.

Many evangelicals thus entered the 1976 presidential election season with concerns about abortion. But even those who were strongly opposed to it were not yet ready to make the issue a political litmus test, nor did they treat it as their highest political priority. This differentiated them from pro-life organizations, which encouraged their members to vote against any candidate who did not support a Human Life Amendment. As a result, some pro-life activists moved freely from the Left to the Right, voting for any candidate who was willing to support their desired constitutional amendment. Marjory Mecklenburg, who had served on the board of the National Right to Life Committee and had then founded her own national pro-life organization, American Citizens Concerned for Life, began the 1976 presidential election season working on the advisory committee for the liberal Catholic Democratic candidate Sargent Shriver, whose wife, Eunice Kennedy Shriver, was a nationally known spokeswoman for the pro-life cause. When Shriver did not win the Democratic presidential nomination, Mecklenburg then ended the season as a volunteer for the Ford campaign, after the Republican Party officially endorsed the constitutional amendment that pro-lifers favored.[22] But most evangelicals, unlike their counterparts in the pro-life movement, were not yet single-issue voters. They viewed abortion not as a deciding factor in a presidential election but, rather, as a component in a much larger campaign against the sexual revolution and the decline of Christian values in American life. Most evangelicals therefore were more interested in finding a candidate who shared their Christian faith and moral values than in electing someone who endorsed a particular set of issues. The opposite would be true of the Christian Right when it emerged as a political force in 1980. But in 1976, the overwhelming majority of evangelical leaders who spoke about politics refused to make a litmus test of any particular issue (including abortion) and, instead, spoke about the need for a true Christian leader in the White House.

In January 1976, *Eternity* magazine published an "Open Letter to President Ford" by Carl Henry, which briefly mentioned abortion but devoted most of its space to the evangelical theologian's concerns about Ford's abdication of moral leadership. Henry wanted a president who demonstrated "political competence coupled with devotion to truth and right and justice." Like other evangelicals, he worried about national decline and wanted a "prophetic politician" who would be able to arrest the nation's moral slide. "The worst crime rate in civilizational history, the evident breakup of the American home, the selfish abortion of unwanted fetuses, the crippling curses of alcoholism, drug and cigarette-addiction, the flagrant schemes of welfare opportunists, the degrading moral permissiveness of visual and printed arts characterize a hell-bent if not hell-destined generation," Henry wrote. "Despite the tolerant mood of the times, these are not mere matters of private morality."[23]

Henry's letter was important not only because it was the work of one of the most influential evangelical theological writers of his time but also because it offered a significant indicator of evangelical political priorities that were shared by a large swath of evangelical leaders. Henry had spoken out against abortion for years, so the inclusion of this issue in his open letter to the president came as no surprise, but unlike pro-life activists, neither Henry nor most other evangelicals believed that a constitutional amendment against abortion would solve the nation's core moral problems. Instead, they favored a bevy of moral legislation on issues ranging from homosexuality to alcohol and substance abuse, but even more, they wanted a change in the nation's moral culture that could come only from moral leaders. In the aftermath of Watergate, they were especially wary of politicians whose behavior did not match their deeds. Most of them had voted for Richard Nixon because they believed that he would restore moral order in the nation, and like Billy Graham, they had been badly disappointed. They were critical of President Ford for refusing to take the strong moral stands that they felt were warranted. Henry criticized Ford for pardoning Nixon—an action that many non-evangelicals found equally troubling—and for refusing to criticize his wife's statements in support of premarital sex. Next to these issues, the problem of abortion ranked only as a priority in between the "breakup of the American home" and "the crippling curses of alcoholism" and drug addiction.[24] In other words, the issue was important for Henry but important only as part of a larger package of national moral revival.

Nearly all other evangelicals who spoke out on political issues in the 1976 election made a similar declaration: they refused to make any single issue a political litmus test, and they insisted that presidential candidates' personal moral behavior and faith commitments were far more important than their policy positions. Even Campus Crusade founder Bill Bright, who was more active than most other evangelicals in conservative political organizing, insisted that his real objective was not the enactment of any particular policy but the election of "men and women of God" to Congress and the White House. He conceded that Christians who pursued this goal would likely work with both political parties and would not necessarily confine themselves to a particular set of issues. "I think it is conceivable that the Lord would lead some Spirit-filled people to support one candidate, other Spirit-filled people to support the other," Bright told *Christianity Today* in September 1976. Bright was not speaking from a position of indifference; he had embarked on a massive campaign, in concert with conservative Republican representative John Conlan of Arizona, to promote conservative Christian principles in government. As he said: "America is in grave trouble. . . . Our entire society is becoming increasingly secular, humanistic, and materialistic. Anti-God forces largely control education, the media, entertainment, and government. . . . What happens in this country this year will in my opinion determine whether or not we remain free."[25] But in spite of Bright's dire warnings, he thought that a national turnaround would be accomplished not through a successful political lobbying effort but through a national spiritual revival coupled with the election of people of "integrity and principle" to positions of high office.

Christianity Today concurred. Although the magazine had repeatedly published antiabortion editorials in the months leading up to the 1976 election and although the magazine had warned in December 1975 about politicians who expressed personal opposition to abortion while refusing to endorse an antiabortion constitutional amendment, *CT* editors continued to insist that a candidate's personal faith and integrity superseded all policy positions. "Christians in particular ought to be concerned about the ethical and religious convictions of those who aspire to the presidency," *Christianity Today* declared in April 1976. "The basis upon which a leader makes his decisions is more important than what side he takes in current transient controversies."[26]

For this reason, most of the evangelical commentary in the 1976 presidential election centered not on the policy positions of the major presidential candidates but on their character and faith. At first, this focus seemed especially advantageous to Jimmy Carter's campaign, which did its best to capitalize on it. The Christian book publisher Logos International released *The Miracle of Jimmy Carter,* a book about Carter's faith that sold more than 1.5 million copies. Advertisements for the book appeared shortly before the election in major evangelical publications, including *Christianity Today* and *Eternity,* where readers would have also encountered ads for a book by Carter's sister, the faith-healing minister Ruth Carter Stapleton, titled *The Inner Gift of Healing.*[27] The evangelical organization Citizens for Carter likewise ran a full-page ad in *Christianity Today* in July 1976 that asked, "Does a dedicated evangelical belong in the White House?"[28] As Oklahoma Baptist megachurch pastor (and future SBC president) Bailey Smith famously said at the 1976 Southern Baptist Convention, the United States needed a "born-again man in the White House," and "his initials are the same as our Lord's!"[29] A Gallup poll at the time showed that Carter would likely receive 75 percent of the Southern Baptist vote.[30]

Northern evangelicals were never as excited about Carter, but strikingly, their criticism of the candidate in early 1976 focused not so much on his policy positions but on his authenticity as an evangelical. Fundamentalists criticized his "social drinking."[31] Liberal evangelicals, such as John F. Alexander, editor of *The Other Side,* were critical of what they called Carter's "duplicity" on race relations. When campaigning for governor of Georgia, Alexander said, Carter "allowed (and probably encouraged) people to imagine he was a racist, and then, as soon as he took office, he came out strongly for integration. We should be thankful that he is not a segregationist, but we must demand a level of integrity that requires politicians to state their views openly before election time."[32] Carter, in other words, may have had the right policy positions for this evangelical, but could he be trusted to be a man of integrity? In the aftermath of Watergate and a new skepticism about politicians' character, evangelicals of all political stripes wanted, above all, to elect moral people to Washington. For many, this amounted to a direct declaration that they intended to vote only for true Christians. As the editor of the *Arkansas Baptist Newsmagazine,* the official paper of the Arkansas Baptist Convention, wrote in an editorial shortly before the 1976 election, "Christians can influence our country for right . . . by supporting those people who are Christian candidates."[33]

It was for that reason that evangelical news profiles of Carter and Ford gave little attention to policy issues but, instead, focused largely on their personal faith. When *Eternity* magazine published a two-page interview with Carter in September 1976, the magazine focused its questions not on Carter's politics but on the way that his faith affected his life. The first question was on Carter's "Christian convictions," and the next was on the way that his political career affected his "family life" and "church life." The interview concluded with a question about how he would "use the office of President to demonstrate [his] Christian convictions." In the course of the interview, Carter mentioned that he had received more questions about his position on abortion than on any other moral issue, but *Eternity* did not press him on his position or ask him to elaborate. In an interview in which six out of seven questions focused on Carter's faith rather than his policies, the magazine apparently felt no need to discuss abortion or any other political issue with the candidate.[34]

Perhaps it was not surprising, then, that the one issue that damaged Carter most severely in the eyes of his fellow evangelicals was not a policy position but, rather, his decision to agree to an interview with *Playboy* magazine. After that interview, some of his most enthusiastic Southern Baptist backers, including Bailey Smith, announced that they were no longer sure that they would vote for him, and some evangelicals who had been skeptical about him from the start now began to openly denounce him in the press or preach against him from their pulpits. Evangelicals had supported Carter primarily because they believed his profession of faith, but for many of them, his *Playboy* interview, which included language they found objectionable, called his religious credentials into question. "Here's a man, who like us, professes to be a Christian," *Christianity Today* editor Harold Lindsell declared. "And then he gets himself all tied up in speaking words which at best are most questionable. How can the words he speaks be consistent with the Christianity he professes?"[35] Jerry Vines, an Alabama Baptist pastor who would later serve as president of the Southern Baptist Convention, likewise said that the *Playboy* interview raised doubts about whether Carter was really an evangelical. "A lot of us are not convinced that Mr. Carter is truly in the evangelical Christian camp, and this tends to indicate to us that he isn't," Vines said.[36]

When evangelicals did begin to discuss the issue of abortion in the presidential campaign, they approached it not as an isolated policy position but as a window into the candidates' personal moral commitments. They were often disappointed by what they found. *Christian Life,* a charismatic magazine, was typical in this regard. It followed other evangelical publications in devoting the bulk of its space in its November 1976 article on the presidential candidates to a detailed examination of Ford and Carter's personal faith and individual moral behavior. But when the article did introduce the policy issues of concern to Christians, it devoted more than a page to abortion, which it treated as the issue of first priority. Nevertheless, like other evangelicals, the magazine found it difficult to differentiate between the candidates on abortion. Both candidates, the magazine pointed out, claimed to oppose abortion personally, but neither had shown much interest in legislating their beliefs. "There seemed to be hypocrisy or double talk on all sides," the magazine declared. "Ford has been president two years, but never pushed for a constitutional amendment, and as head of the executive branch, he presided over the funding of 300,000 abortions last year." But Carter's stance was equally problematic, *Christian Life* writer Wesley Pippert believed, because it was difficult to square the former Georgia governor's personal opposition to the procedure with his stated opposition to a constitutional amendment protecting unborn human life. "If Carter felt abortion was morally wrong, why didn't he oppose abortion for the population?" Pippert asked.[37]

Christian Life was perhaps typical in viewing political policy positions primarily as reflections of a candidate's personal beliefs, not as issues of party policy. But for those few evangelicals who paid more attention to political party platforms than to candidates, the choice between the Republicans and Democrats seemed clearer. This was the stance that *Christianity Today* took. Unlike most other evangelical magazines (including *Eternity, Christian Life,* and *Moody Monthly,* along with most Southern Baptist publications), *Christianity Today* ran feature-length articles on both the Republican and Democratic national conventions, and it drew a clear distinction between the two. The magazine's three-page feature article on the Democratic National Convention included extensive commentary on Carter's personal faith and evangelical support, but it also devoted several paragraphs to the party's adoption of a platform statement opposing an antiabortion constitutional amendment—an action that the magazine seemed to think outweighed Carter's expression of personal opposition to abortion. "For someone to say that he is morally opposed to abortion and then that he is against doing anything to stop the current flood of abortions is rather like Pontius Pilate's action in washing his hands at the trial of Jesus," the article quoted Harold O. J. Brown as saying.[38] *Christianity Today's* coverage of the Republican National Convention was somewhat more positive. While the magazine noted that evangelical influence at the convention was muted in comparison to the Democrats'—"Little of the overt spiritual that crept into Baptist Sunday-school teacher Jimmy Carter's campaign found its way into Kemper Arena at the Republican National Convention in Kansas City," the article declared—it nevertheless commended the GOP for choosing the correct stance on moral issues in its platform. The GOP platform "endorsed the adoption of a constitutional amendment 'to restore protection of the right to life for unborn children,' asked that non-sectarian prayers be allowed in public schools, favored tax credits for parents of children in non-public schools, and opposed forced busing," the *CT* article noted.[39] And of these issues, the magazine reported, it was abortion that especially energized some of the organizers of an evangelical prayer breakfast at the convention, an event sponsored by Campus Crusade for Christ and headlined by Pat Boone and Bill Bright. Not all evangelical Republicans agreed with this set of priorities. *Christianity Today* noted that evangelical congressman John Anderson, who would later run against Ronald Reagan as a third-party candidate in 1980, wanted to keep abortion out of the platform and that even Carl Henry's son, Paul Henry, a Calvin College political science professor and Republican convention delegate who believed that abortion was "killing," argued that in some cases the procedure was "justifiable" and that evangelicals should therefore be wary of giving too much weight to the issue.[40]

But if Henry and Anderson were wary about making too much of the Republican Party's stance on abortion, they were the exception among evangelical Republicans rather than the rule. When framing President Ford's stance on abortion, Ford's campaign advisors had noted that although the Republican Party's newfound pro-life stance was likely to have its greatest appeal to Catholics, it would likely help them pick up votes among evangelicals too. For most of his presidency, Ford had said nothing about abortion. He privately favored a "states' rights" approach that would give state legislatures the power to set their own abortion policy, but he had filled his administration with strong supporters of abortion rights, including his vice president, Nelson Rockefeller. When Ronald Reagan began picking up votes among some pro-life Republicans after endorsing an antiabortion constitutional amendment, Ford moved slightly to the right on the issue, a stance that seemed even more politically advantageous after the Democratic Party adopted a platform statement in June 1976 endorsing *Roe v. Wade.* Ford's advisors met with Reagan delegates and pro-life activists to create a Republican antiabortion platform statement that would help them pick up votes among socially conservative Catholics—a group that normally voted Democratic but that had little affinity for Carter. Although they designed the platform plank primarily with pro-life Catholics in mind, they thought that it might help them with a few conservative Protestants, especially in northern swing states. "Many Protestants, particularly of the older generation, view abortion with horror—though not in so uncompromising a way as the official Catholic position," Ford campaign advisor Jim Reichley told Dick Cheney in a memo in June 1976. "The President's position on abortion does not satisfy the extremes on either side, but I think it seems basically right to most people who take some kind of religious view on the subject."[41]

In smaller evangelical denominations that had taken an early lead in the fight against abortion, the Republican Party's pro-life stance probably helped Ford. This was certainly the case among Missouri Synod Lutherans, who had been the first Protestant group to mobilize against abortion in the mid-1960s, years before most other evangelicals joined the cause. Eugene Linse, chair of the Department of Social Sciences at Concordia College and a future executive director of the Lutheran Church—Missouri Synod's Board for Social Ministry Services, sent a letter to nearly fifteen hundred pastors of his denomination in October 1976, urging them to vote for the pro-life candidate. "One candidate for the presidency has enunciated his position clearly in support of the right to life, in support of the right of parents, and in support of the family as historically considered in the Judeo-Christian heritage," he declared. "The other has not. The significance of these distinct positions should not pass unnoticed."[42] And Pat Boone, who had served as a delegate for Ronald Reagan at the Republican National Convention, made a radio advertisement for Gerald

Ford one week before Election Day to highlight the Republican Party's stances against abortion and for school prayer. "President Ford has said he is against abortion on demand and he is willing to do something about it," Boone said. "President Ford believes that children who are encouraged to pray at home should be allowed to pray in school. He wants to do something about that too. Just what is it that Mr. Carter wants to do about these questions? He just hasn't made that clear. These values are too precious to leave them ambiguous and unsettled. Our concerns for life and for our children deserve a clear response."[43]

By the time of the election, some evangelicals had become newly attentive to the abortion issue because of the consideration that it received in Francis Schaeffer's book and film documentary *How Should We Then Live?* published in 1976. Schaeffer connected *Roe v. Wade* and the legalization of abortion to a decades-long rejection of moral absolutes in Western culture. Yet by the time of the election, even the very small number of evangelicals who wanted to make abortion a litmus test lamented their limited options. In October, Harold O. J. Brown sent a letter to Ford, urging him to "clearly articulate as an ethical priority the necessity of overturning the atrocious and evil decision, *Roe v. Wade*." "We know Carter is effectively pro-abortion," he wrote, but "frankly your occasional moralistic comments on the issue are not such to inspire confidence in you." "Perhaps many of us will vote for you anyway as the lesser of two evils," Brown declared, speaking on behalf of his fellow pro-life activists. "But you need enthusiastic support, not just 'lesser of two evils' votes.... If we can trust no one, we will vote for no one."[44]

In the end, as *Christianity Today* noted, northern evangelicals indicated a slight preference for Ford, while those in the South were more likely to vote for Carter. Nationwide, the two candidates split the white evangelical vote almost evenly.[45] The candidates' personal positions on abortion were barely distinguishable, and it was unclear whether abortion was a decisive issue for more than a small number of evangelicals. For most evangelicals, personal professions of faith and general moral concern still mattered more than policy positions. But even those evangelicals who made their choice primarily on the basis of the candidates' religious faith and ethical records still expected substantive action on policy issues. And for many of those evangelicals, abortion was an increasingly important concern. When *Christianity Today* published its list of policy priorities for newly elected President Carter in January 1977, abortion headed the list. "Abortion is now the leading cause of death in America, and forthright action is sorely needed," *Christianity Today* declared. "If he [Carter] is to keep his promise to be responsive to the rank and file, he will take strong steps to put back into American legal codes the right of the fetus to live."[46] In fact, Carter did not take these "strong steps" on behalf of fetal rights. Instead, he brought Sarah Weddington, the leading abortion rights attorney in *Roe v. Wade,* into his administration, and he continued the Democratic Party's pro-choice stance, despite his stated personal discomfort with abortion.[47] By 1980, many conservative evangelicals had decided that candidates' personal professions of faith were no guarantee of right policies; what they needed, instead, was a party platform guaranteeing certain policy goals. And because of the 1976 Republican Party platform, the GOP was already committed on paper to many of their causes, including opposition to abortion. In 1976, that platform statement had attracted the support of only a few evangelicals because although many evangelicals cared about abortion, most of them had not yet decided that that issue superseded all others, nor did they believe that a right stance on the abortion question could make up for a lack of faith or morality in a candidate's personal life. After 1980, their attitude would be different. The Republicans lost approximately 50 percent of the evangelical vote in 1976 because policy positions alone were not yet sufficient to win evangelical support. But after the early 1980s, the GOP would discover that it could appeal to evangelical voters based largely on one specific policy pledge—a promise to end legal abortion. The benefits of that strategy would not become fully evident for several years, but the groundwork for it was laid in the 1976 election.

NOTES

1. Randall Balmer, *Evangelicalism in America* (Waco, TX: Baylor University Press, 2016), 109–21.

2. "Legal Abortion: Who, Why, and Where," *Time,* September 27, 1971; "The War on the Womb," *Christianity Today,* June 5, 1970, 24–25. For a sampling of evangelical articles proposing a cautiously moderate position on abortion in the late 1960s, see Nancy Hardesty, "Should Anyone Who Wants an Abortion Have One?" *Eternity,* June 1967, 32–34; S. I. McMillen, "Abortion: Is It Moral?" *Christian Life,* September 1967, 50, 53; Robert D.

Visscher, "Therapeutic Abortion: Blessing or Murder?" *Christianity Today*, September 27, 1968, 6–8.

3. L. Nelson Bell, "An Alternative to Abortion," *Christianity Today*, June 18, 1971, 17.

4. Carl F. H. Henry, "Is Life Ever Cheap?" *Eternity*, February 1971, 20–21.

5. Bell, "Alternative to Abortion," 18.

6. Southern Baptist Convention, Resolution on Abortion, June 1971, http://www.sbc.net/resolutions/13/resolution-on-abortion.

7. Paul L. Sadler, "The Abortion Issue within the Southern Baptist Convention" (Ph.D. diss., Baylor University, 1991), 25–26.

8. Billy Graham, "Any Abortion Method Violation of God's Law," *Atlanta Constitution*, November 27, 1972; National Association of Evangelicals, Resolution on Abortion, 1973.

9. For Criswell's initial endorsement of *Roe v. Wade*, see Religion News Service, "The Supreme Court's Decision on Abortion: Dr. Criswell Says He Agrees with It," *Baptist Bible Tribune*, February 16, 1973, 1. For his later change of thinking on abortion, see David Roach, "How Southern Baptists Became Pro-Life," *Baptist Press*, January 16, 2015, http://www.bpnews.net/44055/how-southern-baptists-became-prolife. For an example of more liberal Baptist endorsements of *Roe*, see Robert O'Brien, "Abortion Decision Leaves Moral Responsibility to Individual," *Baptist Standard*, January 31, 1973, 4.

10. Barry Hankins, *Uneasy in Babylon: Southern Baptist Conservatives and American Culture* (Tuscaloosa: University of Alabama Press, 2002), 17.

11. "Abortion and the Court," *Christianity Today*, February 16, 1973, 33.

12. National Association of Evangelicals, Resolution on Abortion, 1973. Much of the language for this resolution was borrowed from an earlier abortion resolution adopted by the NAE in 1971. See "Evangelicals See Religious Revival," *Long Beach (CA) Independent Press-Telegram*, April 24, 1971.

13. "Baptists for Life," *Southern Baptist Journal*, May 1974, 12; *Annual of the Southern Baptist Convention, 1974* (Nashville: Southern Baptist Convention, 1974), 74.

14. *Proceedings of the 1974 Annual Session of the Baptist General Convention of Texas* (Dallas: Baptist General Convention of Texas, 1974), 25; *Annual Convention of the State Convention of Baptists in Ohio, November 1976* (Columbus: State Convention of Baptists in Ohio, 1976), 26; *Annual and Minutes of the 1976 Baptist Convention of New York* (Syracuse: Baptist Convention of New York, 1976), 34–38; W. Barry Garrett, "Questions Were Raised When Abortion Laws Were Struck Down," *Religious Herald*, February 22, 1973, 9; Joe L. Ingram to Bob Holbrook, March 4, 1974, folder 79.1: Abortion: 1974–1975, box 79, Southern Baptist Convention Christian Life Commission Resource Files, Southern Baptist Historical Library and Archives, Nashville.

15. "Baptist Abortion Stand Unclear," *Baptist Standard*, January 31, 1973, 4; Robert Holbrook, "Court Ruling Forces Issue," *Baptist Standard*, May 16, 1973, 13; T. B. Maston, "Some Guidelines," *Baptist Standard*, May 16, 1973, 13.

16. Donald Granberg, "The Abortion Activists," *Family Planning Perspectives* 13 (1981): 158–60.

17. "Aids 'Defense of Life,'" *Baptist Standard*, September 3, 1975, 4.

18. RNS, "Protestants v. Abortion," *Catholic Voice*, August 18, 1975, 7.

19. Charles Fager, "The Abortion Impasse: A Way Out," *Sojourners*, December 1976, 10.

20. Dennis M. Dodson, "Till Death Do Us Part?" *Arkansas Baptist,* January 22, 1976, 22–23; Harry N. Hollis Jr., "Legalized Gambling: An Exercise in Self Delusion," *Arkansas Baptist,* March 25,1976, 16; Harry N. Hollis Jr., "Pornography, a Cancer That Plagues America," *Arkansas Baptist,* April 1, 1976, 20; Daniel R. Grant, "When There Ought Not to Be a Law," *Arkansas Baptist Newsmagazine,* September 16, 1976, 4; Charles H. Ashcraft, "The Pig-Sty in the Parlor," *Arkansas Baptist Newsmagazine,* September 23, 1976, 2; J. Everett Sneed, "Homosexuality on TV," *Arkansas Baptist Newsmagazine,* October 7, 1976, 3; J. Everett Sneed, "Christians Should Vote," *Arkansas Baptist Newsmagazine,* October 28, 1976, 3; Baptist Press, "Pastor Sends 15,000 Letters Urging SBC Abortion Action," *Alabama Baptist,* June 3, 1976, 9; Baptist Press, "Pastor Sends 15,000 Letters Urging SBC Action on Abortion," *Baptist and Reflector,* June 3, 1976, 9; W. Barry Garrett, "Abortion Issue Looms Large in Rising Religious Fight," *Rocky Mountain Baptist,* February 13, 1976, 1, 4, 6; "Pastor Pushes Abortion Stand," *Baptist Standard,* May 26, 1976, 3; Bob Holbrook, "Why the 1971 Abortion Resolution Should Be Replaced," *Southern Baptist Journal,* May–June 1975, 7.

21. Richard Selzer, "What I Saw at the Abortion," *Christianity Today,* January 16, 1976, 11–12. For other statements against abortion in *Christianity Today,* see "Personally Opposed," *Christianity Today,* December 5, 1975, 24; "Three Years Is Too Long," *Christianity Today,* February 13, 1976, 38–39; "The Politics of Abortion," *Christianity Today,* April 23, 1976, 48–49; "Abortion: No Adjustment," *Christianity Today,* August 27, 1976, 21; "Decision '76: What Stand on Abortion?" *Christianity Today,* September 24, 1976, 54.

22. Marjory Mecklenburg to Larry De Santo, October 28, 1975, folder: ACCL Admin File: Kennedy Foundation Proposal—Shriver Campaign Committee (1), box 30, American Citizens Concerned for Life Records, Gerald R. Ford Presidential Library, Ann Arbor, MI; Marjory Mecklenburg to Bill Russo (1976), folder: Abortion Issue (1), box C25, President Ford Committee Papers, 1975–76, Gerald R. Ford Presidential Library.

23. Carl F. H. Henry, "An Open Letter to President Ford," *Eternity,* January 1976, 23.

24. Ibid.

25. "Yoking Politics and Proclamation—Can It Be Done? An Interview with Bill Bright," *Christianity Today,* September 24, 1976, 20–22.

26. "Carter's Credibility," *Christianity Today,* April 9, 1976, 31.

27. Advertisements, *Eternity,* October 1976, 58, 73.

28. Advertisement, *Christianity Today,* July 16, 1976, 43.

29. Myra MacPherson, "Evangelicals Seen Cooling on Carter," *Washington Post,* September 27, 1976.

30. Ibid.

31. Ibid.

32. John F. Alexander, in "How I Think I'll Vote," *Eternity,* September 1976, 30.

33. J. Everett Sneed, "Christians Should Vote," *Arkansas Baptist Newsmagazine,* October 28, 1976, 3.

34. "Jimmy Carter Explains His Faith," *Eternity,* September 1976, 80–81.

35. MacPherson, "Evangelicals Seen Cooling on Carter."

36. Michael Satchell, "'Barnyard Language' Denounced," *Washington Star,* September 21, 1976.

37. Wesley G. Pippert, "Where Do They Stand? Issues Significant to Christians," *Christian Life,* November 1976, 97–98.

38. Edward E. Plowman, "The Democrats: God in the Garden?" *Christianity Today,* August 6, 1976, 24.

39. Tim Miller and Tonda Rush, "God and the GOP in Kansas City," *Christianity Today,* September 10, 1976, 59.

40. Ibid., 59–60.

41. Jim Reichley to Dick Cheney, June 25, 1976, folder: Constituency Analysis, box 2, A. James Reichley Files, Gerald R. Ford Presidential Library.

42. Eugene Linse, direct mail to pastors of the Lutheran Church–Missouri Synod, October 25, 1976, and Marjory Mecklenburg to Bill Russo (October 1976), folder: Abortion Issue (1), box C25, President Ford Committee Papers, Gerald R. Ford Presidential Library.

43. Pat Boone Statement (November 1976), folder: ACCL Political File '76 Pres. Camp.—Memos, box 45, American Citizens Concerned for Life Records, Gerald R. Ford Presidential Library.

44. Harold O. J. Brown to Gerald R. Ford, October 22, 1976, folder: Abortion-General (1), box 1, Sarah C. Massengale Files, Gerald R. Ford Presidential Library.

45. "The Political Peak Is Also the Brink," *Christianity Today,* November 19, 1976, 33–34; Lyman Kellstedt et al., "Faith Transformed: Religion and American Politics from FDR to George W. Bush," in *Religion and American Politics: From the Colonial Period to the Present,* ed. Mark A. Noll and Luke E. Harlow, 2nd ed. (New York: Oxford University Press, 2007), 272–73.

46. "If I Were President," *Christianity Today,* January 7, 1977, 26.

47. For Carter's nuanced stance on abortion and his tense relationship with some conservative evangelicals, see J. Brooks Flippen, *Jimmy Carter, the Politics of Family, and the Rise of the Religious Right* (Athens: University of Georgia Press, 2011).

Dwelling in the Shelter of the Most High

RONALD REAGAN AND THE RELIGIOUS RIGHT

J. BROOKS FLIPPEN

Every day commentator Bryan Fischer opens his show on American Family Radio with a quotation from Ronald Reagan. Every year Regent University, founded by the evangelist Pat Robertson, hosts a Reagan Symposium to highlight the former president's legacy. Today one does not have to look far to ascertain the modern Religious Right's opinion of Ronald Reagan, best summed up by the founder of the Moral Majority, Jerry Falwell Sr., just before his death in 2007. Reagan, Falwell stated, was our "beloved president." While there are of course dissidents who cite shortcomings in Reagan's legacy, such as Mark Tooley of the conservative Institute of Religion and Democracy, who noted that Reagan "wasn't consistently a saint," the populism inherent in the Religious Right sees no such ambiguity.[1] In fact, as scholars note, Reagan's true legacy was much different. Reagan largely appeased his conservative theological followers to keep them under the umbrella of the so-called New Right. He offered them access and rhetoric they had never enjoyed before but generally ignored their policy demands. At the time, a number of evangelical leaders protested. Only later, given the context of late-twentieth-century liberalism, did this respect prove enough. Framed by the disappointments of Jimmy Carter and George Bush and, subsequently, the tumultuous challenges posed by Bill Clinton, the Reagan administration never looked so good to the Religious Right. The movement needed a hero, and despite his true record, Reagan fit the bill.

Let me dispense at the outset here with what I mean by *Religious Right,* which, of course, is a nebulous term. I will refer to the movement as a loose coalition of religiously minded activists opposed to cultural liberalism. It certainly incorporates many fundamentalists and evangelicals, but of course, both are themselves diverse, and many do not consider themselves part of the Religious Right. Not all members of the movement are born-again Christians, and in fact, there are even elements who are not Christian at all. All share, however, conservative theological beliefs and a sense that God needed to exert his law into the public sphere. In this sense, Christian Reconstruction theology was influential. Spread in large part by the efforts of Rousas John Rushdoony in the years after World War II, this movement took from Genesis a mandate for Christians to have dominion over all aspects of life, government included. "As implausible as a vision of a reconstructed United States might seem," author Michael J. McVicar concludes," such "dominionism" had "steadily crept into America's popular and religious consciousness." By Reagan's election, *Newsweek* had even characterized Rushdoony's Chalcedon Foundation as "the think tank of the Religious Right."[2]

Many theological principles influenced the growth of the Religious Right, not just dominionism, and as such, it remained fluid, often driven by individual charismatic leaders or the emergence of new controversial issues. While scholars have characterized the Religious Right in terms of race, class, partisanship, and denomination, among others, there is nevertheless enough overlap that I will use the terms *conservative Christians* and *evangelicals* in the broadest sense for simplicity.[3]

In any event, it was Carter that was the impetus for it all. The cultural liberalism of the 1960s, including feminism, abortion rights, sexual liberation, and homosexual rights, constituted to many conservative Christians a direct threat to the divinely ordained foundation of society, the nuclear family. Carter, who professed his born-again faith, appeared to these conservatives the perfect antidote. What these hopeful new activists did not understand, however, was that Carter embodied the traditional Baptist faith in the separation of church and state. He shared their beliefs that such things as abortion and homosexuality were sinful but rejected the idea that it was the government's role to intervene. Moreover, Carter had emerged as the standard-bearer of the Democratic Party with its liberal coalition near fracture. Emboldened by their success, party liberals rejected any compromise. Caught in the middle, Carter pleased few.[4]

Even as he expressed his own belief that much of cultural liberalism was ungodly, Carter allowed his liberal aides to host that first White House reception for gay rights advocates. While he supported the new Hyde Amendment prohibiting federal funds for abortion, he did nothing to challenge the *Roe v. Wade* decision and ultimately rejected a constitutional amendment to overturn it. When Carter encouraged a White House Conference on Families, an attempt in part to acknowledge conservative concerns, the conference broke down in bickering over what constituted a true family. Carter supported ratification of the Equal Rights Amendment and the teaching of evolution in schools, the latter a catalyst for Rushdoony's activism.[5] He appeared weak on the godless communism of the Soviet Union. These concerns were too much for many of the same activists who had put such faith—pun intended—into Carter in 1976. With Falwell's newly minted Moral Majority leading the way, the table was set for Ronald Reagan.

Reagan appeared an odd champion of the Religious Right. Despite the fact that he had been baptized a Disciple of Christ and attended the denomination's Eureka College, little suggests that Reagan shared the views of the new movement. He did not attend church regularly and divorced his first wife. He worked in Hollywood, that bastion of cultural liberalism despised by conservatives since the days of the Hollywood Ten. Although he later claimed it was a mistake, he signed the Therapeutic Abortion Act as California governor. When he ran for president, he selected George Bush as his running mate. Bush had previously campaigned as a pro-choice candidate.[6] Early in the campaign, when asked if he, like Carter, was born-again, Reagan stumbled, offering a rambling reply that suggested that he did not understand what the term meant.[7] Several of the new leaders of the Religious Right, including not only Falwell but Paul Weyrich, Phyllis Schlafly, and Howard Phillips, sensed Reagan's true beliefs as well, warning him that if he did not more forcibly reflect their concerns, he risked endangering their vote.[8] Certainly not all antiabortion activists accepted Reagan as a fellow traveler. One, Ellen McCormack, thought Reagan insincere and ran her own campaign as the Right-to-Life Party. The idea of Reagan running as a champion of the religious conservatives both infuriated and amused Carter's staff, who viewed Reagan as opportunistic.[9]

Reagan knew the politics. Nixon's famed "Southern Strategy" had shown that white working-class voters, many of whom held conservative theological beliefs, were open to the Republican Party. Richard Wirthlin, Reagan's pollster, lobbied Reagan that he could keep Carter from "cornering the market" on the born-again Protestant vote, which he explained was significant not only in the South but in key electoral college states such as Ohio.[10] Seeking to stimulate the economy by weakening environmental regulations, Reagan's advisors also understood that while Christian traditions had stressed the protection of God's creation, many, such as the Baptists—strong in the South—saw such a mandate as individual and less collective. The environmental justice movement was only beginning, and Pope John Paul II had remained relatively quiet on the issue. In fact, the Vatican would not address environmental protection until 1990. In short, Reagan was free to deregulate without much impact on his religious outreach.[11] Moreover, while the Catholic Church had long been opposed to abortion, the archbishop of Boston had taken the unprecedented step of releasing a letter urging all Catholics to vote for the candidate who was strongest against abortion.[12] Reagan had all the political incentives he needed, any personal conversions aside.

What followed was a well-scripted Reagan campaign to win the new Religious Right. As he quietly assured moderates at the convention that he shared their concerns, he embraced a public platform that reflected the concerns of the religious conservatives in a way it never had before. Reagan now spoke of opposition to the ERA, whereas before he had been vague, and for the first time he came out in support of the Human Life Amendment. At the convention Reagan, in an emotion-filled voice, called for a moment of silent prayer, concluding with "God bless America."[13]

Reagan pressed his case in both private and public. In the middle of the convention season, Reagan agreed to address a large group of evangelical leaders in Dallas organized by the Religious Roundtable. There Reagan remarked to much applause—and publicity—that while the crowd could not endorse him, "I endorse you."[14] He encouraged the teaching of creationism alongside evolution, which he had never done before. Later in the campaign, he met privately with a group of evangelical ministers in

Washington, DC. Asked what he had done to enter heaven, Reagan no longer fumbled his reply. He could not give God any reason for letting him in, Reagan humbly answered, but would simply beg for mercy. Later still, in New Orleans, Reagan invited Falwell to travel with him in his limousine. Falwell was impressed, remembering that the two had prayed together. Howard Phillips, who earlier had questioned Reagan's commitment, was impressed as well. Reagan's personal overtures surpassed anything Carter had done.[15]

Reagan continued to shore up his support among the Religious Right, his campaign hiring Robert Billings, an associate of Falwell, and coordinating with Morton Blackwell, an associate of Weyrich and Richard Viguerie, a Republican activist who was a leading advocate of incorporating conservative Christians into the Republican fold. At the same time, Reagan adeptly sidestepped a controversy when Bailey Smith, president of the Southern Baptist Convention, stated that God did not hear the prayers of Jews. In trying to explain Smith's comments, Falwell then threw gas on the fire by claiming that while God heard the prayers of Jews, he did not always answer them. Reagan refused to condemn either man while subtly distancing himself. Christians and Jews prayed to the same God, Reagan remarked, but everyone was free to "make his own interpretation of the Bible."[16]

The coordination between the Religious Right and the Reagan campaign was to Robert Maddox, Jimmy Carter's liaison to religious groups, terribly frustrating. Even as the conservative pastors remarked that they were not officially endorsing Reagan, which could threaten their tax-exempt status, they "always portrayed Reagan as this paragon of Christian virtue and Carter as sort of an anti-Christ."[17] As Reagan focused on ongoing inflation and the Iranian hostage crisis, a group known as Christians for Reagan mailed pro-Reagan pamphlets to the thousands of Moral Majority members and churches around the nation, having obviously acquired Falwell's mailing list.[18] Another group, Christian Voice, mailed a packet dubbed *Make Your Christian Voice Count* that declared bluntly, "The American Christian community must support Ronald Reagan for president."[19] For its part, the Religious Roundtable's newsletter, the *Roundtable Report,* was less overtly partisan but left little doubt that Carter had failed Christians. Similarly, Pat Robertson's Christian Broadcasting Network, Falwell's *Old Time Gospel Hour*, and the conservative psychologist James Dobson's radio program, *Focus on the Family*, all left little doubt who Jesus Christ would favor.[20]

Given their participation, it was not surprising that the leaders of the Religious Right claimed credit for Reagan's overwhelming victory. The landslide was obviously due to much more than the Religious Right, but its influence was part of the picture, certainly to Carter and his wife, Rosalynn. The Religious Right, Carter concluded, had a "very profound impact." Rosalynn agreed, recalling dozens of women shouting at her that she did not love Jesus. According to one of Falwell's colleagues, the attitude among the Moral Majority was "Can you believe what we just did?"[21] As Falwell, Weyrich, Schlafly, Robertson, Viguerie, and others all took very public victory laps, evangelist Tim LaHaye summed up the mood. God, he declared, "saw thousands of us working diligently to awaken his sleeping church to its political responsibilities."[22]

Of course, they expected results—and fast. Blackwell, now working in the White House, saw trouble looming. "I knew that there was going to be great tension, that there would be a lot of people who would be disappointed when not everything they wanted was achieved at once," Blackwell remembered.[23] Indeed, just after the election, Senate Majority Leader Howard Baker announced that social issues would have to wait until the economy recovered. This was intolerable, Weyrich told his colleagues. "If the idea that economic issues are more important than moral ones takes hold, then it says something about what we stand for."[24] Soon members of the Religious Right complained that Reagan had made too few evangelical appointments. They applauded antiabortion C. Everett Koop as surgeon general and James Watt as secretary of interior. Watt had stated publicly that God's judgment was imminent.[25] They welcomed Billings as an assistant education secretary, which Falwell took credit for. Blackwell remained an obvious connection, but otherwise, the only true ally they saw was the evangelist Gary Bauer, appointed as a low-level domestic policy advisor, and the evangelist Jerry Reiger, selected to lead the new Office of Families.[26] Blackwell tried to explain without much success that many religious leaders lacked sufficient managerial experience and expertise.[27]

As Blackwell calmed nerves, Reagan snubbed the annual Washington convention of the National Religious Broadcasters, who had been so confident of his attendance they had printed his name on the program. When the Religious Roundtable attempted a repeat of its successful Dallas convention the previous year, no one from the administration attended. The press quoted Reagan's aides as saying that abortion and the issue of school prayer were "no-win issues," while top advisor Michael Deaver reportedly stated that evangelicals would have to come "through the back door." The press began to speculate publicly that Reagan had simply used the Religious Right, an infuriating conclusion to Falwell and the others.[28]

Once again, to calm tensions, the White House invited Falwell for a meeting, and as Falwell later acknowledged, his first trip to the grandeur of the Oval Office did wonders. It was humbling, Falwell recalled, agreeing to mute public criticism. Reagan agreed to meet with members of his Family Policy Advisory Board, including the advocate of the traditional family Connie Marshner. The ambitious Marshner left unimpressed, however, and wrote a memorandum implying that if Reagan did not more forcibly push conservative social legislation, the Religious Right might not support Reagan's budget efforts.[29] Sensing that a direct meeting with key Religious Right leaders might be necessary, Blackwell and his boss, Elizabeth Dole, met with Weyrich to plan a meeting. Soon, however, much to the chagrin of the evangelical community, the White House delayed the date and ultimately canceled the meeting. Blackwell protested, noting that the conservative religious community demanded respect.[30]

As the administration unfolded, Robert Maddox perceived a clear strategy. Reagan would appease the Religious Right while distancing himself from its more extreme elements and doing little of substance legislatively on its behalf, lest risking the vote of social moderates. Reagan would meet informally with key leaders, giving them the attention and respect they craved.[31] As one example, the administration allowed Dobson to broadcast one of his radio shows from the White House. Dobson later proudly pronounced himself one of Reagan's regular consultants. Falwell enjoyed more visits with Reagan, who also agreed to appear three times on Pat Robertson's television show, *The 700 Club*. For his part, Robertson had begun both to enjoy the access to power and a belief that politicians—even Reagan—would always let him down. Forming the Freedom Council in 1981, Robertson was clearly envisioning his own political career. In fact, Robertson would run unsuccessfully against George Bush for the Republican nomination in 1988.[32]

Reagan also kept up the rhetoric that so pleased the Religious Right, not only frequent references to the Almighty but language that evangelicals understood. The Soviet Union, for example, was not just a geopolitical rival but an "Evil Empire." Most notably, Reagan published an impressive lament on abortion in the journal *Human Life Review* to mark the tenth anniversary of the *Roe* decision, an article that elated many in the Religious Right. In the words of one, "Until now, Reagan had not gone much beyond code words fit for poster."[33]

Indeed, Reagan remained largely quiet when a Human Life Statue and a Family Protection Act, both key policy goals of the Religious Right, were introduced early in his administration. The Religious Right clearly applauded his military buildup, but that already constituted a cornerstone of the Reagan agenda, any evangelical support aside. The same was true for his domestic cuts, which activists like Marshner believed strengthened the family unit and the conservative publication *Pro-Family Forum* described as commendable. Reagan gave credence to proposals to extend tax credits to private schools and to advance school prayer, the latter including a proposed constitutional amendment, but his administration applied little pressure within the Halls of Congress for passage, viewing both proposals as disruptive to the broader economic agenda.[34] Reagan's nomination of Sandra Day O'Connor was perhaps a reflection of Reagan's true sentiments. While clearly an overture to female voters, O'Connor ultimately the first female justice, she was no antiabortion activist. Falwell admitted that he had never heard of her. When Reagan told Falwell that he would just have to trust him, Falwell agreed. Marshner, however, complained that the Senate Judiciary Committee had learned nothing about her position on abortion and began to rally pro-life groups against the nomination.[35] In the end, of course, O'Connor did in fact prove a relative moderate. Weyrich complained that religious leaders should have joined Marshner but did not want to jeopardize "their pleasure in being able to get in even the back door of the White House."[36]

When it came to ERA ratification, a similar dynamic was at play. Reagan had come out against the amendment but, once in office, remained relatively quiet. Opponents such as Schlafly welcomed Reagan's opposition but quietly complained that he needed to do more to ensure its defeat.[37] Reagan certainly tried to avoid the issue of homosexuality. On one hand, conservative religious leaders demanded a more active stance against gay rights. One wrote asking for an FBI investigation. Blackwell and Dole found many of the letters troubling. In the words of one publication, "Almost all gays ingest significant amounts of fecal material every week of their sexually active lives."[38] At the same time, however, the National Gay Task Force requested a meeting similar to the one Carter had allowed. Ultimately, the White House granted a meeting with a low-level staffer but no one else. Dole suggested stalling and finding a "polite way" to say no.[39]

When the AIDS crisis hit, Reagan famously said nothing. He did not endorse the harsh proposals of conservatives such as William F. Buckley, including quarantines of high-risk groups such as the gay community, nor did he support Falwell's outrageous claims that the virus was divine retribution for sinful behavior. On the other hand, he did virtually nothing to combat its spread. It was five years before Reagan even mentioned the term *AIDS,* and even then the government allocated only thirty-three million dollars to combat the growing epidemic. Despite over ten thousand calls a day, the Department of Health and Human Services AIDS hotline employed only six people. Groups such as the AIDS Coalition to Unleash Power (ACT UP) formed, pressing the White House to do more, but Reagan remained mostly mute.[40]

First Lady Nancy Reagan's reported belief in astrology, which some conservative pastors associated with witchcraft, did not help. It all was just not what many in the Religious Right had anticipated. In time, the movement's foremost advocate in the White House resigned. Morton Blackwell insisted that the reason for his departure was a desire to return to his activist origins, but he acknowledged that "some people have been disappointed."[41] Perhaps given their initial optimism, disappointment was inevitable. Membership in the Moral Majority dropped, the organization officially dissolving before the end of Reagan's term. One of its former executives wrote a book concluding that all the efforts had "brought us nothing." Other leading Religious Right groups suffered as well. The Religious Roundtable lost income, while the Christian Voice, having failed to promote school prayer, drifted away from direct-issue advocacy.[42]

One can debate the causes of the Religious Right's struggles at the end of the Reagan administration. The continued growth of Christian Reconstruction had inevitably challenged America's constitutional framework, and Reagan had no intention of ever establishing a theocracy. He might mimic the importance of God in government, but he well understood the legal and cultural opposition he would engender by completely breaching the wall of separation between church and state. In fact, perhaps a product of its success, Christian Reconstruction had begun to fracture by the end of Reagan's term, its extreme elements now as obvious as its internal divisions. When, for example, Reagan declared 1983 the "Year of the Bible," leaders of the movement had fought bitterly over a publication, *Power for Living,* that was to accompany the declaration. It was obvious that if Christian Reconstruction were to establish God's dominion, exactly what that dominion meant was still a cause for conflict.[43]

Without a doubt, the antics of certain pastors contributed to tarnishing the Religious Right. While the televangelist Jim and Tammy Bakker had not engaged in politics to the extent of Pat Robertson, who had helped launch their broadcasting career, their sex and fraud scandal as Reagan left office hardly helped the broader movement. Likewise, evangelist Oral Roberts, also suffering from declining revenue, pronounced that God would call him home if he did not raise sufficient funds to keep his ministry afloat. Evangelist Jimmy Swaggart, caught in his own sex scandal, famously went on air crying that he had sinned. To couch the failures of these few as representative of a movement that still captivated millions is, of course, grossly unfair and inaccurate, but nevertheless, it undoubtedly still had an impact.[44]

There is, of course, another interpretation of the Religious Right's struggles in the late 1980s. While Reagan had not lived up to the expectations of many of the Religious Right's leaders, the administration's apparent embrace of their movement ironically hampered fundraising by removing a sense of urgency and crisis. In fact, groups in opposition to the ruling party usually find their membership growing. Reagan, for example, weakened environmental protections and attacked environmentalists as liberal extremists. In turn, groups such as the Sierra Club and the National Resources Defense Council saw their fundraising explode during the Reagan years—the exact opposite of the Religious Right organizations.[45] Similarly, groups opposed to the Religious Right were the ones that grew during the Reagan administration. Membership in the American Civil Liberties Union grew, and new organizations such as People for the American Way formed, organized at the dawn of the Reagan administration explicitly to oppose the Moral Majority.

In this sense, what the Religious Right needed was a fearsome opposition. While as noted it is difficult to define the Religious Right, some have suggested the movement was dynamic, best characterized by periodic causes it supported or opposed. In the words of one writer, "The identity of the Religious Right is determined by the specific for or against campaigns it wages."[46] As Reagan left office, it simply needed more to be against.

Reagan's successor, George Bush, was at least something. Many Religious Right leaders saw Bush's attempts to embrace their constituency as simple expediency. Bush did not get the benefit of the doubt as Reagan had. Indeed, a sense that Bush was not one of their own led many in the Religious Right to support the failed candidacy of Pat Robertson in 1988. Robertson was, in fact, one of the first to lionize Reagan, attempting to run under his mantle and airing television commercials that cast his administration as a hero, the former president's shortcomings already forgotten.[47] Indeed, Bush, the perceived Brahman Episcopalian who described his faith as "quiet," was hardly similar to those who inherited the fire-and-brimstone traditions of the Great Awakening.[48] Perhaps still smarting over his loss, Robertson warned his followers just after Bush's election to be wary of the new president. Soon Robertson declared that "evangelical Christians have virtually been excluded from any meaningful position in the government." When Bush agreed to meet with Robertson, Falwell, and other leaders in 1989 to soothe over tensions, Bush's director of personnel told the group that it was illegal to count people according to their religion. Robertson replied sarcastically, "You have no difficulty identifying evangelicals and their allies during the campaign."[49] For the remainder of Bush's term, Religious Right leaders supported Bush because, as Robertson believed, they had nowhere else to go. Bush saw himself as so popular after the liberation of Kuwait, Robertson assumed, that he did not need to cater to the boisterous and sometimes unseemly Religious Right. Even when Bush appointed Clarence Thomas, an ideological ally to the Religious Right on many issues, to the Supreme Court, Bush still did not receive tremendous credit. Having just left the Reagan administration, Gary Bauer fought for Thomas's nomination and later lamented that too many conservative Christians had not stood up for him during the contentious Senate hearings.[50]

It was perhaps no coincidence that during the presidency of George Bush, both Reagan's reputation grew among the Religious Right and the movement itself resumed its growth. In fact, it was at Bush's inaugural dinner where Robertson met the young political activist Ralph Reed. Soon the two coordinated the launch of a new powerful Religious Right organization, the Christian Coalition. Designed to learn from the flaws of the Moral Majority, the Christian Coalition thrived during Bush's presidency. In the words of one scholar, "The immediate concern of the Christian Coalition was the new Bush administration." By the end of Bush's presidency, the Christian Coalition had grown to more than a quarter-million members.[51]

If Bush was an incentive for the Religious Right, the presidency of Bill Clinton was a boon. In the words of one observer, Clinton served as "an enormous bull's eye for the arrows of the Christian Right."[52] From his early order to allow homosexuals in the military in his controversial Don't Ask, Don't Tell policy to his affair with Monica Lewinsky, Clinton enraged conservative Christians and served as the perfect foil. First Lady Hillary Clinton did her part as well, representing the feminism that had spurred on the early Religious Right activists during the Carter administration.[53] The Christian Coalition continued its growth. New organizations such as Promise Keepers formed. The Religious Right found new focus—for example, protesting what it termed partial birth abortions and initial efforts to promote gay marriage. The Religious Right was back enough that bumper stickers appeared on cars proclaiming that God was not a Republican.

By this point, Ronald Reagan was a staple of Religious Right rhetoric. Any earlier criticism had long passed, his legacy airbrushed for the masses. By the end of Clinton's presidency, every Republican presidential aspirant came to the Christian Coalition's Road to Victory Conference. There every would-be nominee cited Reagan to the cheers of the crowd. Gary Bauer, the Reagan veteran, was a featured speaker and evoked fond images of his political mentor. According to one, "Reagan was a ghost whose image and ideas permeated the entire weekend."[54] Reagan evoked an image of American rebirth, which for many in the Religious Right meant a rebirth of faith, wholesomeness, and the American family.[55] The Religious Right, of course, was not alone in viewing Reagan in this light. Today if one does a Google search for the terms *Reagan* and *icon,* almost a million hits come up. *Time,* for example, lists Reagan as one of the top political icons in American history.[56] Reagan has become a popular name for children, and Republican legislators name building after building in his honor, the most noteworthy being Washington's Reagan National Airport.

In the end, of course, the ebb and flow of history continued. The Christian Coalition, like the Moral Majority of the Reagan years, faded. Clinton won reelection before the tides shifted again and George W. Bush entered the White House to the cheers of the Religious Right. Reagan succumbed graciously to Alzheimer's disease, citing his faith in the process and reaffirming his iconic status among conservative Christians. As the details of Reagan's presidency faded, the mythology of Reagan continued to grow. Pundits speculated whether the Baptist minister and champion of the Religious Right Michael Huckabee would prove to be the "next Ronald Reagan," the very real differences in their respective records and positions lost in the mythology.[57] Michael Reagan, the adopted son of the former president, bemoaned in 2015 how groups such as the Religious Right molded the memory of his father to their own ends. "It is interesting to see how many of them recreate my father in their image and likeness instead of his," Reagan stated.[58] Going forward, the Religious Right will undoubtedly find much to be against, but one thing is certain: it has created an exemplar of what to be for—Ronald Reagan.

NOTES

1. Jerry Falwell, "Our Christian Hero," Beliefnet, http://www.beliefnet.com/news/2004/06/ronald-reagan-my-christian-hero.aspx; Mark Tooley, "Ronald Reagan's Legacy and the Religious Right," Patheos, http://www.patheos.com/blogs/philosophical fragments/2014/02/10/ronald-reagans-legacy-the-religious-right.

2. Michael J. McVicar, *Christian Reconstruction: R. J. Rushdoony and American Religious Conservatism* (Chapel Hill: University of North Carolina Press, 2015), 4–6, quotation on 5.

3. See, for example, Matthew Moen, *The Christian Right and Congress* (Tuscaloosa:

University of Alabama Press, 1989), 4; Simon Hill and Dennis Owen, *The New Religious Political Right* (Nashville: Abington, 1982), 15–16; Clyde Wilcox, *God's Warriors: The Christian Right in 20th-Century America* (Baltimore: Johns Hopkins University Press, 1992), 65–69; Michael Lienesch, *Redeeming America: Piety and Politics in the New Christian Right* (Chapel Hill: University of North Carolina Press, 1993), 10; Lowell Streiker and Gerald Strober, *Religion and the New Majority: Billy Graham, Middle America, and the Politics of the 1970s* (New York: Association Press, 1972), 141–44; Gabriel Fackre, *The Religious Right and the Christian Faith* (Grand Rapids, MI: William Eerdmans, 1982), xi, 6.

4. For a full discussion of Carter, see J. Brooks Flippen, *Jimmy Carter, the Politics of Family, and the Rise of the Religious Right* (Athens: University of Georgia Press, 2011).

5. Julie J. Ingersoll, *Building God's Kingdom: Inside the World of Christian Reconstruction* (New York: Oxford University Press, 2015), 97.

6. Andrew E. Busch, *Reagan's Victory: The Presidential Election of 1980 and the Rise of the Right* (Lawrence: University of Kansas Press, 2005), 82.

7. Elizabeth Drew, *Portrait of an Election: The 1980 Presidential Campaign* (New York: Simon & Schuster, 1981), 173.

8. Dinesh D'Souza, *Falwell, before the Millennium: A Critical Biography* (Chicago: Regnery Gateway, 1984), 126.

9. *New York Times*, August 27, 1980, 17; interview, author with Robert Maddox, December 2, 2009.

10. Drew, *Portrait*, 172.

11. Mark R. Stoll, *Inherit the Holy Mountain: Religion and the Rise of American Environmentalism* (New York: Oxford University Press, 2015), 243, 275.

12. *New York Times*, September 18, 1980, 31.

13. *New York Times*, July 9, 1980, 1, and July 10, 1980, 10; interview, author with Howard Phillips, December 6, 2009; 1980 Republican Party Platform, American Presidency Project, University of California, Santa Barbara, http://www.presidency.ucsb.edu/ws/index.php?pid=25844.

14. Interview, author with Jerry Falwell, July 24, 2003; Karen O'Connor, *No Neutral Ground: Abortion Politics in an Age of Absolutes* (Boulder: Westview, 1996), 87; Reagan, quoted in William Martin, *With God on Our Side: The Rise of the Religious Right in America* (New York: Broadway, 1996), 216–17.

15. Quoted in Martin, *With God on Our Side*, 209; interview, author with Jerry Falwell, July 24, 2003.

16. Interview, author with Jerry Falwell, July 24, 2003; quoted in William Goodman and James Price, *Jerry Falwell: An Unauthorized Profile* (Lynchburg, VA: Paris and Associates, 1981), 3; D'Souza, *Falwell*, 122–23.

17. Exit interview, Robert Maddox, Jimmy Carter Presidential Library, Emory University, Atlanta.

18. *New York Times*, August 18, 1980, 11; interview, author with Jerry Falwell, July 24, 2003.

19. Quoted in Hill and Owen, *New Religious Political Right*, 59–60.

20. See William Chasey, *The Legislative Scenario* (Washington, DC: Religious Roundtable, 1980); David Snowball, *Continuity and Change in the Rhetoric of the Moral Majority*

(New York: Praeger, 1991), 43; Gill Alexander-Moegerie, *James Dobson's War on America* (Amherst, NY: Prometheus Books, 1997), 42.

21. Quoted in Martin, *With God on Our Side*, 220.

22. Quoted in Randall Balmer, *God in the White House: How Faith Shaped the Presidency from John F. Kennedy to George W. Bush* (New York: HarperCollins, 2008), 119.

23. Exit interview, Morton Blackwell, Ronald Reagan Presidential Library (RRPL), Simi Valley, CA.

24. Quoted in Balmer, *God in the White House*, 121–22.

25. *New York Times*, August 22, 1981, 6.

26. Interview, author with Jerry Falwell, July 24, 2003.

27. Blackwell exit interview, RRPL.

28. *Conservative Digest* 8 (February 1982): 11; Martin, *With God on Our Side*, 223; interview, author with Jerry Falwell, July 24, 2003.

29. Interview, author with Connie Marshner, December 4, 2009; memo, Richard Williams to Lyn Nofziger, March 5, 1981, folder "Pro-Family Activists (1)," OA12450, Morton Blackwell Files (MBF), RRPL.

30. Memo, Morton Blackwell to Red Cavaney, April 30, 1981; Schedule Proposal, Elizabeth Dole, May 5, 1981; memo, Morton Blackwell to Elizabeth Dole, June 11, 1981, all in folder "Pro-Family Activists (1)," OA 12450, MBF, RRPL.

31. Interview, author with Robert Maddox, December 2, 2009.

32. Robert Boston, *The Most Dangerous Man in America? Pat Robertson and the Rise of the Christian Coalition* (Amherst, NY: Prometheus Books, 1996), 29; Martin, *With God on Our Side*, 235; David John Marley, *Pat Robertson: An American Life* (New York: Rowman & Littlefield, 2007), 45–47, 79, 82.

33. Wilbur Edel, *Defenders of the Faith: Religion and Politics from the Pilgrim Fathers to Ronald Reagan* (New York: Praeger, 1987), 193; Ronald Reagan, "Abortion and the Conscience of a Nation," *Human Life Review* 9, no. 2 (1983): 7–16.

34. Memo, Connie Marshner to Morton Blackwell, February 4, 1982; memo, Morton Blackwell to Elizabeth Dole, August 20, 1982, both in folder: "Pro-Family Activists (3)," OA 12450, MBF, RRPL; interview, author with Connie Marshner, December 4, 2009; Gary Scott Smith, *Faith and the Presidency: From George Washington to George W. Bush* (New York: Oxford University Press, 2006), 349; William Willoughby, *Does America Need the Moral Majority?* (Plainfield, NJ: Haven Books, 1981), 76–78.

35. D'Souza, *Falwell*, 133; *Family Protection Report* 3, no. 9 (1981): 4.

36. Quoted in Balmer, *God in the White House*, 122.

37. Interview, author with Phyllis Schlafly, December 4, 2009.

38. *Newsletter of the Institute for the Scientific Investigation of Sexuality* 1, no. 1 (1983): 1.

39. Quoted in *Texas Tribune*, June 9, 1983, 20.

40. John Gallagher and Chris Bull, *Perfect Enemies: The Religious Right, the Gay Movement, and the Politics of the 1990s* (New York: Crown, 1996), 21–22; Rachel Kranz and Tim Cusick, *Gay Rights* (New York: Facts on File, 2000), 41; William Turner, "Mirror Images: Lesbian/Gay Civil Rights in the Carter and Reagan Administrations" in *Creating Change: Sexuality, Public Policy, and Civil Rights*, ed. John D'Emilio, William B. Turner, and Urvashi Vaid (New York: St. Martin's Press, 2000), 21.

41. Blackwell exit interview, RRPL.

42. Cal Thomas and Ed Dobson, *Blinded by the Might: Can the Religious Right Save America?* (Grand Rapids, MI: Zondervan, 1999), 24.

43. McVicar, *Christian Reconstruction,* 178–81.

44. Interview, author with Jimmy Allen, December 4, 2009.

45. Samuel Hays, *Beauty, Health, and Permanence: Environmental Politics in the United States, 1955–1985* (New York: Cambridge University Press, 1987), 491–92; Kirkpatrick Sale, *Green Revolution: The American Environmental Movement, 1962–1992* (New York: Hill & Wang, 1993), 33, 53.

46. Fackre, *Religious Right,* 7.

47. Marley, *Pat Robertson,* 118, 130.

48. D. Michael Lindsay, *Faith in the Halls of Power: How Evangelicals Joined the American Elite* (New York: Oxford University Press, 2007), 20.

49. Quoted in Marley, *Pat Robertson,* 207.

50. Gary Bauer, "The Politics of Destruction," Patriot Post, https://patriotpost.us/opinion/45375; Miranda Blue, "Gary Bauer: Christians Should Have Supported Clarence Thomas Even if They Believed Anita Hill," Right Wing Watch, People for the American Way, http://www.rightwingwatch.org/post/gary-bauer-christians-should-have-backed-clarence-thomas-even-if-they-believed-anita-hill/.

51. Marley, *Pat Robertson,* 206, quotation on 207.

52. Sara Diamond, *Not by Politics Alone: The Enduring Influence of the Christian Right* (New York: Guilford Press, 1998), ix.

53. Interview, author with Howard Phillips, December 6, 2009; interview, author with Phyllis Schlafly, December 4, 2009.

54. Marley, *Pat Robertson,* 239.

55. Jules Tygiel, *Ronald Reagan and the Triumph of American Conservatism* (New York: Pearson, 2006), 250.

56. Dan Fastenburg, "Top 25 Political Icons," *Time,* February 4, 2011, http://content.time.com/time/specials/packages/article/0,28804,2046285_2045996_2046088,00.html.

57. Timothy Stanley, "Is Huckabee the Next Reagan?" CNN, January 6, 2015, http://www.cnn.com/2015/01/06/opinions/stanley-huckabee-2016/index.html.

58. Elizabeth Ralph, interview with Michael and Ronald Reagan Jr., September 16, 2015, *Politico,* http://www.politico.com/magazine/story/2015/09/reagan-sons-interview-donald-trump-213149.

End of a Life Cycle

THE DECLINE AND FALL OF SOUTHERN EVANGELICAL
POLITICAL AUTHENTICITY

JEFF FREDERICK

In 1976, Americans, frustrated by the casual embrace of truth and apparent moral ambiguity of former president Richard Nixon and his credibility-challenged predecessor Lyndon Johnson, elected a one-term governor whose career had spanned the United States Navy, southwest Georgia agribusiness, and the Peach State's legislature. By inauguration—January 20, 1977— perhaps the only element more famous than Jimmy Carter's trademark toothy grin, the peanuts he raised, or the emerging pop culture identity of brother Billy or mama Miss Lillian was the new president's public, and near universally acknowledged as authentic, Baptist faith.

As a Christian, the president sure appeared to the American people as the real deal. Born in tiny Plains, Georgia, Carter, nicknamed "Hot Shot," was straight out of evangelical central casting. The thirty-ninth president grew up on an unelectrified farm, was public school educated, drove other kids to church as early as age twelve, married a local girl, served his country with distinction, and resigned his commission to return home to the family business when his daddy died of cancer. He even magnanimously thanked Gerald Ford for helping to heal the nation in the first line of an inaugural address the *Washington Post* called "like a sermon." In that speech, the new president waited a grand total of three sentences before invoking the Bible and then proceeded to refer to the Old Testament prophet Micah and the admonition to "do justly, and to love mercy, and to walk humbly with thy God." Then, finishing the remarks, he lived them by setting a standard for humility that began with walking from the inaugural reviewing stand to the White House and included carrying his own luggage and minimizing the pomp and circumstance of the office.[1]

None of this means that the Carters weren't a bundle of contradictions. Father Earl, briefly a member of the state house, cut his political teeth on the local school board, though he had not finished high school. Jimmy, the image of the New South to many northerners, won the 1970 gubernatorial election over Carl Sanders at least in small part due to segregationist appeals by some supporters and the circulation of racially loaded photographs. Jimmy, a lifelong Baptist first at Plains and then Maranatha, married Rosalynn in a Methodist church. A conservative Democrat by comparison to other national figures in his times, Carter's political opponents often reduced him to a Great Society liberal and a feckless one at that. With a long and well-regarded postpresidential tenure, Carter is seen as a humanitarian by many, a naive do-gooder by others; in fact, he was deeply ambitious as any person seemingly must be to rise to the ranks of governor and president, once noting of Senator Ted Kennedy that he didn't feel it necessary to "kiss his ass." Carter didn't always love his enemies, but even those who interpreted their politics or their piety differently did not suggest that the president was a pretender.[2]

All of this is simply a method of introducing the reality that ironies abound in the study of Carter and the labeling of evangelicals, as the discussion of both has evolved significantly since *Newsweek* responded to the rise of the Georgian by naming 1976 as the "Year of the Evangelicals." In the decades since then, Carter, who much of America greeted in the mid-1970s with bewilderment over his "born-again" statements of faith and admission to *Playboy* magazine that "I've looked on a lot of women with lust. I've committed adultery in my heart many times," has been widely derided by a portion of the Southern Baptist Convention (SBC) as insufficiently evangelical. Nevertheless, in the moment of his national emergence, few questioned his evangelical bona fides. His confession to *Playboy* that he had lusted in his heart generated full-throated guffaws from some, but to authentic evangelicals, it was a statement that the candidate had read Matthew 5, that he had pondered the Sermon on the Mount, and more to the point, that Jimmy Carter had wrestled with the goal of applying the words of Christ in his own life. He was the real deal—a Bible believer and a Bible practitioner.[3]

Even so, after winning a majority of Baptist votes in 1976, Carter saw Ronald Reagan, a non-evangelical, carry the denomination in 1980, in part because of the emergence of more overtly political national religious figures such as Pat Robertson and Moral Majority leader Jerry Falwell Sr. It wasn't as if Carter renounced his faith over the course of his first term either. The Carter administration sponsored three White House Conferences on Marriage and the Family, and a 1980 campaign commercial featured an open Bible with clear wording that this was a trusted source for difficult presidential decisions. Carter split from the SBC two decades later, in 2000, though he had supported the less rigid Cooperative Baptist Fellowship since 1993. "Evidently," then SBC president James Merritt noted of the decision, "[he] has a set of personal convictions that are at odds with what we believe as Southern Baptists. . . . We felt the need to turn our denomination back to a more conservative theology, and for whatever reason, the president did not agree with that." It was almost as if Carter had become George McGovern, the South Dakota senator, failed 1972 Democratic presidential candidate, and mainline Methodist Episcopal whose politically progressive faith failed to catch fire with evangelicals. For some, then, Carter had ceased to remain sufficiently Baptist, a term substantially easier to define than *evangelical* or, as Barry Hankins and others have demonstrated, *inerrantist.*[4]

The historian Randall Balmer notes that *evangelical* is a term wrapped in theological, soteriological, cultural, and historical trappings that foster a belief in faith, not works, and a "sudden, instantaneous, datable experience of grace." No matter its central components, evangelicalism is increasingly organic, perhaps even evolutionary in its ability to adapt in response to cultural change. For Balmer, evangelicals comprise a competitive and distinctly American subculture, responding to incursions as needed. In her description of evangelicalism, sociologist Lydia Bean has used the metaphor of a fleet of ships that turn somewhat slowly but visibly in different directions over different eras. Turning the ships was no easy feat given the denominational and doctrinal differences in American Protestantism as well as the regional, economic, and racial identities that separated northern and southern evangelicals. Changes in technology, shared narratives of Christian nationalism, and a belief that the predominant culture was under attack united different factions from time to time, creating momentum for the ships to sail in common directions.[5]

Throughout the last quarter of the twentieth century and well into the next, political actors have embraced voters and values by identifying themselves or their beliefs to be in keeping with contemporaneous understandings of evangelicalism. Some, like Carter, expressed themselves as evangelicals who happened to be running for office. To most, Carter was an authentic man of faith, different from the mainstream culture in how he thought and acted. Most Americans understood him to be authentic and genuine in the way he applied the values of his faith to his life and work. More than forty years after Carter's election, public perceptions of evangelicalism have changed. Increasingly, Americans no longer see much difference between evangelicals and the unchurched. Faith, in the minds of an ever-growing number of Americans, has become a means to a political end, devoid of sincerity and characterized as a vote-gathering and fund-raising mechanism. Candidates, then, are often seen by voters as politicians who merely happen to be Christian, a complete reversal of the identity Carter presented as he campaigned in 1975 and 1976. Why has this changed so sharply?

All of these changes related to authenticity are replete with various shades of gray. Carter himself was not immune to highlighting one set of faith-grounded concepts or another based on the audience that was in front of him. Conservative audiences, as historian Brooks Flippen has noted, heard about Carter's status as born-again and his beliefs that certain emerging social issues—homosexuality and abortion—were sinful. Other more progressive groups in the context of the rapidly changing 1970s heard him testify to the needs for access, rights, and equality for those who were gay or pro-choice. If as theologian Reinhold Niebuhr has argued, "the sad duty of politics is to establish justice in a sinful world," then Carter surely straddled certain lines carefully. The president, in fact, quoted this familiar Niebuhr maxim in a 1978 speech to a conclave of lawyers in Los Angeles. The point of all of this, as Flippen argues, is that it was sometimes "easier to be vague when all sides were just beginning to flesh out their political positions."[6]

A starting point for determining how public perception of evangelicals in politics changed might be tracing Jimmy Carter's transition from evangelical role model to untrustworthy liberal Christian. Equally important and interesting is the broader question of what to make of evangelicals who over four decades went from occasional political actors to a functioning interest group. In fact, these transitions should be placed in an even larger context. Early-twentieth-century Southern Baptists and evangelicals were likely to advocate varying degrees of separation between church and state, with some preachers even recommending against the faithful venturing into politics. Alabama Baptists in the 1940s cautioned preachers not to run for office and remained hesitant to embrace public school teaching of Christianity for fear that certain heretical Protestant theologies might be included or, worse yet, other faiths might be included in the name of equal time and fairness. And some twentieth-century southern politicians, such as North Carolinian Frank Porter Graham, were politically and theologically liberal. "Whites and Blacks," Graham declared in a 1938 speech in Birmingham, Alabama, "have joined hands here to go forward by way of interracial cooperation toward the Kingdom of God." According to various polling and survey instruments, evangelical Christians were actually less likely to vote than other groups up to 1984.[7]

To be sure, evangelicals throughout American history jumped into the political process as issues of temperance, immigration, nativism, prohibition, evolution, civil rights, and school prayer took public prominence. Sometimes these political issues allowed Catholics and Protestants to join forces, sometimes not. Many Christians organized within and across denominations in response to these social or cultural issues, only to recede back into daily life as change was either muted or gradually accepted. Balmer has characterized the half-century between the Scopes Trial and the Carter presidency as a period when "evangelicals largely steered clear of politics." Seminaries, he notes, taught future preachers to avoid politics lest their comments unnecessarily cloud their pastoral authority or confuse their congregants. But by the mid-1970s and with television accessible to over 90 percent of Americans, activism, protest, reactions, and counterreactions made faith and politics increasingly intertwined, especially if the evening news kept such matters within the daily discourse.[8]

The environment of television and the utility of cultural warring transformed the landscape and eventually gave rise to the belief that Jimmy

Carter was not evangelical enough. Jerry Falwell Sr., Pat Robertson, Paul Weyrich, James Dobson, Phyllis Schlafly, Anita Bryant, and others were excellent fundraisers and committed to keeping their messages on radio and across the ever-expanding platforms of cable television. Homosexuality and the proper definition of the family were centerpiece issues in the conceptualization that the occupant of the Oval Office needed to be sent packing. "This so-called born again Christian President is not acting very born-again," Bob Jones III, president of his eponymous university, blasted. "God's judgement is going to fall on America as on other societies that allowed homosexuality to become a protected way of life." Falwell's liberties with a conversation in which Carter indicated nonverbally that a committed gay relationship would constitute a family further cemented the sense that Carter had to go. The Georgian was now too liberal for evangelicals while simultaneously too conservative for mainline Protestants. George McGovern, as historian Mark Lempke notes, thought "Carter's Christianity began and ended with his own born-again experience and was devoid of larger social responsibilities." His reelection hopes, mired as well in economic underperformance and foreign policy complications, collapsed. Evangelical groups embraced Ronald Reagan, a divorcé from California, as their own, though eight years later his support for their intentions had proven to be lukewarm as well. Even so, evangelicals became a political interest group at the national and state level, and their influence grew exponentially.[9]

By the end of the twentieth and start of the twenty-first centuries, Southern Baptists and other evangelicals placed voting guides in the church narthex, railed against theological and political liberals, depicted a nation and its Christians pitted in a culture war that threatened to call down the wrath of God, and encouraged pastors to preach on politics and run for office if called. Voting guides were not entirely new, but they were now ubiquitous. "A religious right activist group from Washington placed them in our church's vestibule," Russell Moore remembered, "outlining the Christian position on issues. Even as a teenager, I could recognize that the issues just happened to be the same as the talking points of the Republican National Committee. With many of these issues, there did seem to be a clear Christian position—on the abortion of unborn children, for instance, and on the need to stabilize families. But why was there a 'Christian' position on congressional term limits, a balanced budget amendment, and the line item veto? Why was there no word on racial justice and unity for those of us in the historical shadow of Jim Crow?"[10]

More recently, evangelicals have become immersed in campaigns and policy. First Baptist Church, Dallas, senior pastor Robert Jeffress argued in the 2016 presidential election that voting was critical for stopping evil. "Over the last eight years," Jeffress announced, in making clear his 2016 candidate of choice, "the Obama administration has launched an all-out attack on religious liberty in America by suing the Little Sisters of the Poor Catholic charity, forcing Christians schools to allow men in women's locker rooms under Title IX requirements for transgender rights, and being a willing accomplice in bankrupting Christians who try to exercise their faith through their businesses. This war against religious liberty will only escalate under Hillary Clinton."[11]

But for all of these changes taking evangelicals from bystander to active and partisan participant, one net result is the decline of authenticity for evangelicals. As historian Kevin Kruse has demonstrated, the rise of a suburban South, which occurred concomitant to the rise of a political evangelical culture, is an important factor. Suburban southern whites—suspicious of modernity, integration, busing, abortion, crime, and paying taxes for public schools they deemed underperforming and perhaps unnecessary—and rural southern whites, concerned about Second Amendment incursions, the decline of industrial and agricultural ways of life, and cultural expressions they found antithetical to their own traditions, made common cause in a culture war that was wrapped several inches deep in Protestant Christianity. Clearly, some of these political cleavages among suburban and rural whites included notions of race. Historian Mark Newman has shown that some Southern Baptist churches by 1980 were still officially excluding racial minorities, and others, having passed open-door policies, were hedging their bets, believing that no black worshippers would actually seek attendance or membership.[12]

"We have lost our moral consensus," Southern Baptist Convention president Adrian Rogers warned in 1993. "You can see it in education, the killing of the unborn, the move toward euthanasia, prevalence of teenage pregnancy, breakup of the home, proliferation of sexual perversion, pornographic explosion, the drug culture. I think it's a crisis. I think our society is decadent." Agree or disagree with Rogers, a complicated figure and one of the more prominent actors in reshaping the SBC to a more stridently conservative theological and political role at the end of the twentieth century, there was little doubt that he was devout in his own sense of faith.[13]

Abortion was a central organizing piece to the rise of a Religious Right that saw elections and policy as critical to its mission of political engagement. While Jimmy Carter straddled the gray area between seeing abortion as sinful but understanding access was guaranteed by the courts, others were taking a harder line. Nationally, Francis Schaeffer and others sought to unite Catholics and Protestants in opposition to abortion and created films and other mechanisms of response to *Roe v. Wade* until, as journalist Ross Douthat argues, "the fate of the unborn had become perhaps the animating issue driving evangelical political mobilization." In states like Iowa with their own Right to Life Committees, activists such as Sarah Leslie kept the issue front and center. "First, we had abortion," a Leslie radio commercial declared, "and they said that was all they wanted. Twenty million babies ago." Local preachers and local candidates across the country wove stories of the unborn into so many sermons and stump speeches that even folks running for offices for which abortion would not be even tangentially attached to their job description were asked to take a side.[14]

Such complex and controversial social issues were often weighed through the prism of actual Scripture. In response to the killing of physicians who provided abortion services, a group assembled in Tennessee drafted a thoughtful and scripturally laced response on the topic of abortion (against) and violence against providers (also against). "We realize that what is legal and what is moral are not always identical," the 1994 Nashville Statement of Conscience read. "Where they diverge, Christians bear a dual responsibility, first to act in accordance with the moral law, and second to respect and obey the legitimate authority of government. So long as a government retains legitimacy, and so long as opportunities for reform remain, individuals and groups must work within the democratic process and must resist the temptation to take the law into their own hands." The entire document is grounded in a patient, thorough, measured, conservative interpretation of both scripture and constitution.

Even as Jim Bakker, Jimmy Swaggart, and others watched their ministries rise with modern broadcasting possibilities and fall to time-tested temptations of lust and money, Americans derided the individual actions of charlatans without dismissing the authenticity of rank-and-file evangelicals. Despite the peccadilloes of televangelists—famously called "electronic soul molesters" by Will Campbell, a different sort of evangelical—a 1987 Pew Research poll found only 8 percent of respondents identified as atheist, and 88 percent stated their belief in God has never wavered. Equally elevated into popular culture as Bakker and Swaggart but unsaddled by sexual scandal, James Dobson and Jerry Falwell faced varying degrees of scrutiny for intemperate comments, but comparatively few except their harshest critics doubted that they actually believed in Christianity and were attempting to live out their own interpretation of it. Hate the sin, love the sinner, as the old saw goes, was still a reasonable assumption about evangelical Christianity.[15]

Of course, not every social conservative calling themselves evangelical in the 1980s and 1990s was practicing what they preached." "All his life," Ernest Furgurson, biographer of North Carolina senator Jesse Helms, noted, "he has done and said things offensive to blacks and to anyone sensitive to racial nuance.... He either denies his action or its racial intent. But he never says he is sorry." Historian Sam Hill, in a retrospective to his 1966 work *Southern Churches in Crisis,* argued that 1990s religious-political culture was about purity. "I do judge," Hill wrote, of the last decade of the twentieth century, "the enforcement of rational purity to be new, though not an unheard of consideration, for the large, popular, mainstream southern perspective." But not all evangelicals were necessarily always socially conservative or pure, at least not on every issue. In the 1990s, much of Alabama was affiliated with one evangelical denomination or another, and yet polling suggests nearly two-thirds of the state approved of both abortion and an education lottery. Legislators (136, of 140, of whom self-identified as Christian) did not pass new legislation on either front or reform the state's regressive tax code, according to historian Wayne Flynt, because for them "Christian ethics consisted of private moral actions, not the creation of a just society."[16]

In fact, the notion of private moral actions being the hallmark of an evangelical continues to evolve. In a September 1998 letter to his friends and ministry partners written partially in response to Bill Clinton's improprieties, Focus on the Family's James Dobson averred: "As it turns out, character DOES matter. You can't run a family, let alone a country, without it. How foolish to believe that a person who lacks honesty and moral integrity is qualified to lead a nation and the world! Nevertheless, our people continue to say that the President is doing a good job even if they don't respect him personally. Those two positions are fundamentally incompatible. In the Book of James the question is posed, 'Can both fresh water and salt water flow from the same spring' (James 3:11 NIV). The answer is no." Eighteen years later, the issue of character had been reformatted. "First, I do not condone nor defend Donald Trump's terrible comments made 11 years ago," Dobson argued, referring to Trump's recorded comments on grabbing the genitalia of women. "They are indefensible and awful. I'm sure there are other misdeeds in his past, although as Jesus said, 'Let him who is without sin cast the first stone.' I am, however, more concerned about America's future than Donald Trump's past. . . . Donald Trump is pro-life. Clinton and his wife disrespect the Constitution of the United States, although Trump has promised to protect it, especially the First Amendment. Shall I go on?"[17]

The transition from "character is everything," in response to the Clinton scandals, to "policy is what truly matters," in the age of Trump, is striking. "Jimmy Carter sat in the pew with us. But he never fought for us," Ralph Reed, chairman of the Faith and Freedom Coalition, told the *Washington Post*. "Donald Trump fights. And he fights for us." The commingling of faith and politics in the twenty-first century has made each virtually inseparable from the other to both evangelical and non-evangelical observers alike, albeit sometimes for completely different reasons. Polling is one place to see these thought transitions come to life. Among Republicans convinced President Trump did little or nothing wrong in his dealings with Ukraine, two groups, according to the nonpartisan Public Religion Research Institute (PRRI), emerged as most vigilant in their support of the president. In the fall of 2019, 99 percent of white evangelical Protestants and 98 percent of Republicans whose primary source of information is Fox News believed that the president should not be impeached and removed.[18]

Robert Jones, author of *The End of White Christian America* and CEO of the PRRI, quantifies the changing nature of personal morality belief among evangelicals. In a *Time* magazine column, Jones identified that in 2011, 30 percent of evangelicals surveyed believed a politician who had been caught in a messy and public sin could still be an effective public leader. In 2016, 72 percent responded that such a "moral wall" between the public and private could be built. "White evangelicals," Jones concludes, have gone from the least likely to the most likely group to agree that a candidate's personal immorality has no bearing on his performance in public office." Evangelicals have even surpassed those with no religious affiliation in their full-throated defense of the morally ambiguous in elected office. This is a major change, indicating that personal moral character or reputation is now subservient to party and policy in the minds of most evangelical voters. In 2017, as Republican Senate candidate for Alabama and "Ten Commandments" judge Roy Moore was alleged to have dated teenagers as a thirty-two-year-old and inappropriately touched a fourteen-year-old, some Alabamians responded that such actions, if they occurred, might even be scriptural. "He's as clean as a hound's tooth," state auditor John Zeigler said of Moore, who carried strong support among many of the state's evangelicals. "Take the Bible—Zachariah and Elizabeth, for instance. Zachariah was extremely old to marry Elizabeth. . . . Also, take Mary and Joseph. Mary was a teenager. . . . There's just nothing immoral or illegal here. Maybe just a little bit unusual."[19]

Clearly, not all evangelicals responded in the same way to reporting about Moore and other public disclosure and investigations of wrongdoing. Plenty believed the allegations, responded with outrage, and made immediate calls for the twice-removed former Alabama Supreme Court justice to step aside. But the direct connection between evangelicals and conservative politics created a bond so tight that denouncing the four accusers of Judge Moore was an involuntary reflex for American Family Association president Tim Wildmon and Liberty University president Jerry Falwell Jr. "This does not change our support for Roy Moore," Wildmon announced. "I don't think this kind of story will change support for him among Christians since he has categorically denied it." Falwell Jr. identified the accusers as less credible than Judge Moore in his full-throated defense of the candidate. Others, like Marion County, Alabama, GOP chair David Hale found the passage of time to be the defining factor. "It was 40 years ago," he noted. "He was 32. She was supposedly 14. She's not saying anything happened other than they kissed." No matter the reaction, the former insistence that private conduct and character mattered had simply vanished in the minds of many. For non-evangelicals, the insistence by evangelicals that either Moore was innocent or that his guilt was of no consequence strained credibility. What could be authentically Christian about sweeping aside such allegations, given the lack of repentance?[20]

Increasingly, Americans view evangelicalism through the eyes of Roy Moore or others such as Houston, Texas, megachurch pastor Joel Osteen, not Habitat for Humanity house–building former presidents. Osteen, a best-selling author and televangelist whose net worth likely tops fifty million dollars, advocates the prosperity ethos—a philosophy that God is ready to heap literal riches on Christians if they will only step out on faith. Surely, half a millennium after Martin Luther kick-started the Reformation, folks interpret the Bible differently, but Osteen's painfully slow response in making his massive Lakewood Church available for storm refugees seemed stark and indifferent after Houston was lashed by Hurricane Harvey in August 2017. The piety and practice of sharing, ministering to the poor, and serving others was abundant all over Houston. Yet the takeaway for many was the relative indifference of some who seemed unwilling to give of their abundance. "Osteen embodies a shift," journalist Ross Douthat suggests, "of very different sorts—the refashioning of Christianity to suit an age of abundance, in which the old war between monotheism and money seems to have ended, for many believers, in a marriage of God and Mammon."[21]

Carter is no pauper; *USA Today* estimates his net worth at $8.1 million, with landownings of some twenty-five hundred acres. Yet he left the presidency cash poor, a million dollars in debt, having left his business in a blind trust and returning to a Georgia home that had barely been lived in for years. For money, he started writing what would eventually become some two dozen books, and for storage, he and Rosalynn installed a new wood floor in the house's attic, by themselves.[22]

If, as in a previous decade, evangelicals in fact were still focused on a candidate's "private moral actions," perhaps not engaging in social change would be a defensible intellectual position. However, polling data from the last decade and a half suggests that evangelicals do not act demonstrably different from the rest of the population. In a 2005 article in *Christianity Today,* Ronald Sider reaches this very conclusion, noting that evangelicals divorce, engage in premarital sex, and sample pornography at approximately the same rate as the general population—though each are either forbidden or frowned upon by pastors of most born-again denominations. "Gallup and Barna," theologian Michael Horton summarizes of the conclusions reached by most pollsters, "hand us survey after survey demonstrating that evangelical Christians are as likely to embrace lifestyles every bit as hedonistic, materialistic, self-centered, and sexually immoral as the world in general." Religious intermarriage between a Christian and non-Christian, formally taboo among some denominations, is on the rise and defines nearly 20 percent of marriages today, four times as many as in 1960. Behavior, then, as extrapolated into an evangelical moral economy, has become less critical for political and personal lifestyle choices. To crudely summarize, the polling indicates that do as I say has increasingly replaced do as I do and certainly do as Jesus would do.[23]

In a separate question-and-answer piece in *Christianity Today,* Sider delves deeper into the congruence of behaviors and actions between evangelicals and the general population. "A Gallup study," he notes concerning beliefs about race, "discovered that when they asked the question, 'Do you object if a black neighbor moves in next door?' the least prejudiced were Catholics and non-evangelicals. The next group, in terms of prejudice, was mainline Protestants. Evangelicals and Southern Baptists were the worst." So, in a general sense and while exceptions are certainly present in every church, town, and state, evangelicals have lost their authenticity. The rest of the population no longer sees them as different because in many ways they are not. Encouraged by Christ to be salt and light—useful and self-evident, easily identifiable—twenty-first-century southern evangelicals have fallen short, becoming culturally Christian in political expressions but indistinguishable otherwise. The contrast with Carter, whom Balmer describes as "driven—almost obsessed—by a kind of works righteousness," is striking.[24]

Even more specifically, Carter's faith stands in contrast to the twenty-first-century impulse to compare and judge the actions of others. "In His day," he told the *New York Times* in April 2017, "Jesus broke down walls of separation and superiority among people. Those (mostly men) who practice superiority and exclusion contradict my interpretations of the life and teachings of Jesus, which exemplified peace, love, compassion, humility, forgiveness and sacrificial love." When the thirty-ninth president suggested that the forty-fifth might have won the 2016 election due to Russian assistance, President Trump was unable to remain silent. "He's a nice man," Trump responded to reporters while in Japan in June 2019. "He was a terrible president. . . . He's been trashed within his own party. He's been trashed."[25]

Political scientists Marc Hetherington and Jonathan Weiler attribute the political and cultural changes leading to the divide between Americans to a hardening of worldviews into two types, fixed or fluid. A fixed worldview, home to most contemporary evangelicals, is characterized by an affirmation of statements like "Our lives are threatened by terrorists, criminals, and illegal immigrants, and our priority should be to protect ourselves." Those with a more fluid worldview adopt a preference for seeing the best in each other, embracing differences, and connecting one to another. For evangelicals with a fixed worldview, immigration is something that merits suspicion, and Carter-style appeals to embrace and advocate for human rights is a recipe for welcoming more decline. Biblical passages about being a Good Samaritan fade from view, as do Christ's teachings from Matthew 25: "For I was hungry and you gave me something to eat, I was thirsty and you gave me something to drink, I was a stranger and you invited me in, I needed clothes and you clothed me, I was sick and you looked after me, I was in prison and you came to visit me."[26]

A higher percentage of evangelical respondents to a recent LifeWay study viewed immigrants as an economic drain than as a pool of people to be brought to Christ. While the majority agreed that both enhanced border security and a path to citizenship were good ideas, respondents noted they were more likely to get their views on immigration from friends, family, or the media than from Scripture. Surely, evangelicals who don't seek their guiding principles from within the sixty-six books of the inerrant Bible don't seem much like evangelicals in the traditional sense of the word. In fact, a *Washington Post* analysis of a 2016 American National Election Studies Pilot Study found a curious tidbit: "Trump does best among evangelicals with one key trait. They don't really go to church. In short, the evangelicals supporting Trump are not the same evangelicals who have traditionally comprised the Christian Right." Other polling by Pew indicates that after the 2016 Republican primary season, Trump fared best among evangelicals who did regularly attend. Evangelicals offered President Trump high marks for job performance after assuming office. Even acknowledging pre-inauguration survey differences on whether churchgoing evangelicals or nonchurchgoing evangelicals burn with the most intensity for President Trump, it remains clear that his support among any who identify as evangelicals remains robust.[27]

Liberty University, founded by the late Jerry Falwell and run today by his namesake son, built a one million–dollar gun range for students and faculty. All are encouraged to take a free concealed carry course and pack while on campus to be ready for an active shooter or terrorist scenario. Home to the school's shooting sports team as well, the Liberty Mountain Gun Club also serves as a public monument of the culture war. "Because of political correctness, most college campuses are running away from the shooting sports and running away from giving their students a chance to properly use and enjoy a firearm," Liberty official Brad Butler announced. "President Falwell is boldly standing up and saying, 'We're not going to just say we support the Second Amendment, we're going to boldly illustrate it by building one of the most beautiful, competitive and safe gun ranges on any college campus.'" This, of course, is an institutional prerogative and constitutionally protected. It just seems to be a stark departure from the more Habitat for Humanity–centric understanding of a Christianity that turns the other cheek and blesses both the peacemakers and the meek.[28]

Biblical illiteracy is decried from pulpits across America—*Christianity Today* called it an epidemic—but not much is being done about it. A Life-Way survey suggests that the number of Christians who regularly read the Bible is roughly equal to the number of believers who report they rarely do. Old-timers complain that their grandkids aren't memorizing Scripture and are spending so much time being entertained in family life centers. Kids today, some grandparents aver, don't know much other than God wants you to be happy and good people go to heaven. Scholars Christian Smith and Melinda Lundquist Denton have termed this phenomenon "moralistic therapeutic deism."[29]

For many evangelicals, biblical illiteracy is but one symptom of cultural decay. The American Family Association, the Family Research Council, the Richard Land Center for Cultural Engagement, and a cottage industry of televangelists and prosperity end-times prognosticators and soothsayers have proclaimed the Fall of Rome over and over again. Meetings were scheduled; conferences held; conversations initiated; declarations published. "The institution of marriage, already buffeted by promiscuity, infidelity, and divorce," the signatories of the Manhattan Declaration of 2009 observed, "is in jeopardy of being redefined to accommodate fashionable ideologies."[30]

Both Richard Land—president of Southern Evangelical Seminary and a signer of the Manhattan Declaration—and former speaker of the House Newt Gingrich have heeded a call to return to 1955 or thereabouts. "These people want safety," Gingrich, the Georgian who ran for president in the 2012 Republican primaries, explained of suburban southerners, "and they believe big cities have failed and are controlled by people who are incapable of delivering goods and services." Robert Jones, the pollster, now refers to evangelicals as "nostalgia voters, who are looking back to this golden age where they were more of the demographic center of the country, and their values were more the center of the country. Make America Great, the last word in that slogan 'again,' is probably the most powerful word in that slogan for white evangelicals."[31]

Returning the country to a previous social order is a critical concept for many older, white evangelical voters, who equate that bygone era with unlocked doors, crime-free streets, and no government agencies telling their kids to wear a helmet when they hop on their bikes. More to the point, for many the past has become a mythical golden age when school prayer was legal and abortion was not, when towns could place Nativity scenes on the courthouse lawn and nobody prevented you from offering a Merry Christmas greeting. The sentiment is strong but clearly problematic. For starters, the golden age of 1955 was plenty tarnished for groups whose numbers among the American population are now on the rise. Minorities, women, the disabled, LGBTQ+, and plenty of other Americans see the social empowerment movements of the civil rights era as a positive and necessary change. And the next great academic study on the sinister plot against Christmas will be the first. Even so, the return to the good ol' days sentiment evoked by Trump and many of the evangelicals who support him includes an ample dose of disdain, perhaps anger, for the cultural changes of recent decades. "He was as angry as they were," author Stephen Mansfield has argued. "He was as fed up with talking heads and indecisive politicians and traitorous corporations as they could ever be. He might not be the kind of man they would want their daughters to date, but he would give them back their nation."[32]

The hand-wringing and doomsday predicting has had a chilling effect on evangelical identity among younger Americans, who don't seem to have much affinity for the idea of living in 1955. "The Christian share of the U.S. Population," the Pew Research Center declared in 2016, "is declining while the number of U.S. adults who do not identify with any organized religion is growing." This group is sometimes referred to as the "nones," as they have no clear religious affiliation. Black teenagers, unlikely to identify as future Republican voters, are significantly more likely to profess religious belief than white members of what psychologist Jean Twenge calls the "I-Generation," those born from 1995 to 2012. In fact, the Republican Party, home of evangelicals since Ronald Reagan defeated Carter in 1980, is now older, whiter, and more partisan. The GOP is also losing traction, comparatively, with Millennials (age 18–33), Generation Xers (34–49), and Boomers (50–68). Younger voters, Pew notes, are more likely to be "turned off by the cage match of modern politics." The news is only somewhat better for Democrats, as younger voters seem collectively disinterested in party identity.[33]

While this changing dynamic does not portend immediate changes in heavily conservative, largely evangelical Red southern states—Alabama, Mississippi, South Carolina, and Texas, for example—it does suggest that evangelicals may be nearing the end of a political life cycle, at least as the body politic is currently constructed. Admittedly, this may not seem at first glance to be a reasonable conclusion given that 81 percent of evangelicals voted to elect Donald Trump and with Republicans dominating governorships, state legislatures, and the Congress. But with evangelicals in statistical decline as a percentage of the population, with young people less likely to see faith in the same manner or with the same importance as their parents or grandparents, with the minority percentage of the total American population growing, and with conservative ideas about social issues such as gay marriage, immigration, and to some extent abortion less resonant with younger voters, it could well be that evangelicals, the South, and presidential voting patterns are poised to be redefined significantly in the next decade.

Like the Carter family, the study of evangelicals in politics is replete with ironies. As noted earlier in this essay and by so many elsewhere, the very term *evangelical* is hard to define both theologically (white or black? born-again? believer in a certain set of fundamentals?) and politically (why do some self-described evangelicals not vote?). Historian Thomas S. Kidd argued shortly before the 2016 election that the term had lost all or most of its previous meaning, noting that "in American pop culture parlance, 'evangelical' now basically means whites who consider themselves religious and who vote Republican." The Pew Research Center has concluded that nearly 25 percent of evangelicals are nonwhite or immigrant. This finding led prominent evangelical leaders Russell Moore and Samuel Rodriguez to speculate in a July 2015 *Wall Street Journal* editorial that an "immigrant-basher" could not win the evangelical vote, a prediction that surely fell on rocky ground and gained no purchase.[34]

Some devout Christians, including Moore, see the collapse of evangelical authenticity as more opportunity than threat. "Almost Christianity,'" Moore argues of the watered-down version of faith that has become virtually indistinguishable from secularism, "looks in the mainline like something from Nelson Rockefeller to Che Guevara at prayer. Almost Christianity in the Bible Belt looks like a God-and-Country civil religion that prizes cultural conservatism more than theological fidelity." Applied by Moore to contemporary evangelicals who identify as Christian but don't actually practice the faith of their founder, *Almost Christianity* seems ironic as a term. Essentially, it was suggested that Carter himself was almost but not quite a true Christian because of his failure to meet the strict standards of his theologically conservative critics. Criticism was nothing new for Carter; he had faced a boycott of his farm products after refusing to join the White Citizens' Council during the civil rights era and received some wayward looks in 1965 when he voted to open Plains Baptist Church to African Americans. The irony is that Carter's knowledge of the Scriptures is virtually encyclopedic, the result of a lifetime of consulting the Bible and teaching Sunday school. The civil religion of Almost Christianity, by comparison, seems at times to be an inch deep, a mile wide, and fashioned one bumper sticker at a time.[35]

All of which is to say the current life cycle of southern evangelicals as an *authentic* political presence is reaching an end, or perhaps more accurately a point of reconfiguration or maybe even a potential new or reimagined awakening. Faith, culture, and southern politics have been reformulated before: in response to abolition and emancipation; in the context of modernity; in light of the Cold War, civil rights, women's empowerment, and at other historical moments. What it means to be an evangelical is in flux nationally as well as in the South. What it means to be a southerner is also in transition as ethnic, racial, economic, and cultural transformations are reshaping expectations and assumptions. As those changes become clearer, a new life cycle of southern evangelical political influence may emerge, more authentic and perhaps more relevant in its quest to refashion society in a more Christlike image.

In December 2019, *Christianity Today* published an editorial by retiring editor Mark Galli, calling for the removal of recently impeached President Donald Trump from office. Echoing an argument the theologically moderate to right-of-center publication made two decades earlier—the editorial is subtitled "It's time to say what we said 20 years ago when a president's character was revealed for what it was"—Galli called Trump "a leader of such grossly immoral character." Three days after Galli's blast, *Christianity Today* president and CEO Timothy Dalrymple doubled down in tone and sentiment, not from a political but from a spiritual perspective. "Out of love for Jesus and his church," Dalrymple wrote, "not for political partisanship or intellectual elitism, this is why we feel compelled to say that the alliance of American evangelicalism with this presidency has wrought enormous damage to Christian witness. . . . It has harmed African American, Hispanic American, and Asian American brothers and sisters. And it has undercut the efforts of countless missionaries who labor in the far fields of the Lord. While the Trump administration may be well regarded in some countries, in many more the perception of wholesale evangelical support for the administration has made toxic the reputation of the Bride of Christ."[36]

The two commentaries and sympathetic support from other evangelical quarters made the argument that evangelicals had changed in part because of compromises born of political expediency. Evangelicals, in the minds of some, had become political actors who trafficked in religious lexicon, rather than deeply committed spirit-led believers who thought the political process and civil society would be enriched with a heaping measure of Christian values. Clearly, many politically engaged evangelicals—among them James Dobson, Jerry Falwell Jr., Franklin Graham, Robert Jeffress, Richard Land, Tony Perkins, and Ralph Reed—rejected the *Christianity Today* thesis and published their own strongly worded responses almost immediately. President Trump joined the conversation, averring, "The fact is, no President has ever done what I have done for Evangelicals, or religion itself!" Evangelicals were never monolithic, but the word itself had lost meaning. "The word evangelical has been sullied in a serious way," Christian journalist Peggy Wehmeyer told the *New York Times*. "I don't like to call myself that anymore."[37]

The future offers more gloaming than clarity, a reminder that historians always do better with the past than what lies ahead. Even so, the past is clear. An evangelical, Jimmy Carter, brought a new awareness of how faith might influence elections and policy to the post-Watergate political landscape. Equally true is the fact that Carter's ascension to the national stage marked him, in the perception of most Americans, as different: southern, honest, Bible believing, and genuine in his piety. In the years since, the words, actions, attitudes, and beliefs of some political evangelicals have changed until they no longer seem either different from the mass of Americans or particularly authentic.

NOTES

1. Jimmy Carter, *Turning Point: A Candidate, a State, and a Nation Come of Age* (New York: Times Books, 1992), 6–17; Peter G. Bourne, *Jimmy Carter* (New York: Scribner, 1997), 29–32; *Washington Post*, January 21, 1977; "Inaugural Address of President Jimmy Carter," January 20, 1977, American Presidency Project, University of California, Santa Barbara,https://www.presidency.ucsb.edu/documents/inaugural-address-0.

2. Jeff Frederick, "The Gubernatorial Campaigns of Jimmy Carter" (master's thesis, University of Central Florida, Orlando, 1998), 9–14; Randy Sanders, *Mighty Peculiar Elections: The New South Gubernatorial Campaigns of 1970 and the Changing Politics of Race* (Baton Rouge: Louisiana State University Press, 2002); Bourne, *Jimmy Carter,* 52–54; Carter, *Turning Point,* 3–19; and "Biographical Sketch of the 1977–1978 Georgia Official and

Statistical Register," RG 4-10-74, Georgia Department of Archives and History (GDAH), Atlanta; William E. Leuchtenburg, "Jimmy Carter and the Post–New Deal Presidency," in *The Carter Presidency: Policy Choices in the Post–New Deal Era*, ed. Gary M. Fink and Hugh Davis Graham (Lawrence: University of Kansas Press, 1998)7–20.

3. Interview of Jimmy Carter by Robert Sheer, *Playboy,* November 1976; Wayne Flynt, *Alabama Baptists: Southern Baptists in the Heart of Dixie* (Tuscaloosa: University of Alabama Press, 1998), 585–92.

4. Mark Newman, *Getting Right with God: Southern Baptists and Desegregation, 1945–1995* (Tuscaloosa: University of Alabama Press, 2001), 199–200; Ruth Murray Brown, *For a Christian America: A History of the Religious Right* (New York: Prometheus Books, 2002), 142–44; Randall Balmer and Lauren F. Winner, *Protestantism in America* (New York: Columbia University Press, 2002), 66–67; Beliefnet, October 20, 2000; *New York Times,* October 21, 2000; Mark A. Lempke, *My Brother's Keeper: George McGovern and Progressive Christianity* (Amherst: University of Massachusetts Press, 2017); Barry Hankins, *Uneasy in Babylon: Southern Baptist Conservatives and American Culture* (Tuscaloosa: University of Alabama Press, 2002).

5. Randall Balmer, *Mine Eyes Have Seen the Glory: A Journey into the Evangelical Subculture in America* (New York: Oxford University Press, 2000), xv–xviii, 314–17; Lydia Bean, *The Politics of Evangelical Identity: Local Churches and Partisan Divides in the United States and Canada* (Princeton: Princeton University Press, 2014), 26–34.

6. J. Brooks Flippen, *Jimmy Carter, the Politics of Family, and the Rise of the Religious Right* (Athens: University of Georgia Press, 2011), 61–62; *Washington Post,* May 10, 1978; Randy Sanders, "The Sad Duty of Politics: Jimmy Carter and the Issue of Race in 1970 Georgia Gubernatorial Campaign," *Georgia Historical Quarterly* (Fall 1992): 612–38.

7. Flynt, *Alabama Baptists,* 418–25; Frank Porter Graham, quoted in Rob Christensen, *The Paradox of Tar Heel Politics: The Personalities, Elections, and Events That Shaped Modern North Carolina* (Chapel Hill: University of North Carolina Press, 2008), 123; Glenn H. Utter and James L. True, *Conservative Christians and Political Participation* (Santa Barbara: ABC-Clio, 2004), 117–18.

8. Utter and True, *Conservative Christians and Political Participation,* 6–14; Balmer, *Mine Eyes Have Seen the Glory,* 172–73; Bean, *Politics of Evangelical Identity,* 20–44; Ross Douthat, *Bad Religion: How We Became a Nation of Heretics* (New York: Free Press, 2012), 24–54.

9. Flippen, *Jimmy Carter,* 252–61; Lempke, *My Brother's Keeper,* 174–75; Erling Jorstad, *Evangelicals in the White House: The Cultural Maturation of Born Again Christianity, 1960–1981* (New York: Edwin Mellen Press, 1981), 147–50.

10. Russell D. Moore, "Can the Religious Right Be Saved?" Erasmus Lectures, Institute on Religion and Public Life, *First Things,* January 2017, https://www.firstthings.com/article/2017/01/can-the-religious-right-be-saved.

11. Hankins, *Uneasy in Babylon,* 107–64; Robert Jeffress, "Why Christians Must Vote in This Election (Staying Home Is Not an Option)," Fox News, November 1, 2016, http://www.foxnews.com/opinion/2016/11/01/why-christians-must-vote-in-this-election-staying-home-is-not-option.html.

12. Kevin Kruse, *White Flight: Atlanta and the Making of Modern Conservatism* (Princ-

eton: Princeton University Press, 2005), 234–51, 259–66; Newman, *Getting Right with God*, 191–200.

13. Hankins, *Uneasy in Babylon*, 66–67.

14. Douthat, *Bad Religion*, 122–24; Balmer, *Mine Eyes Have Seen the Glory*, 147–51.

15. Hankins, *Uneasy in Babylon*, 191–95; Nashville Declaration of Conscience, September 1994, printed copy in author's possession, http://old.erlc.com/article/nashville-declaration-of-conscience; *New York Times*, December 18, 2008; *Los Angeles Times*, March 25, 1987; David Horace Harwell, *Walker Percy Remembered: A Portrait in the Words of Those Who Knew Him* (Chapel Hill: University of North Carolina Press, 2006), 150; Tom Rosentiel, "Trends in Attitudes toward Religion and Social Issues, 1987–2007," Pew Research Center, October 15, 2007, http://www.pewresearch.org/2007/10/15/trends-in-attitudes-toward-religion-and-social-issues-19872007.

16. Christensen, *Paradox of Tar Heel Politics*, 265–86; Ernest Furgurson, *Hard Right: The Rise of Jesse Helms* (New York: Norton, 1986); Wayne Flynt, *Alabama in the Twentieth Century* (Tuscaloosa: University of Alabama Press, 2004), 477–81; Samuel, S. Hill, *Southern Churches in Crisis Revisited* (Tuscaloosa: University of Alabama Press, 1999), xxxix.

17. Letter from James Dobson to Supporters, September 1998, printed copy in author's possession, http://ontology.buffalo.edu/smith/clinton/character.html; http://www.charismanews.com/politics/opinion/60502-dr-james-dobson-how-christians-can-support-donald-trump-but-condemn-bill-clinton. Dobson is referring to audio of Donald Trump that references the "grabbing" of women's genitalia.

18. *Washington Post*, November 14, 2017; *Fractured Nation: Widening Partisan Polarization and Key Issues in 2020 Presidential Elections*, report, PRRI, October 20, 2019, https://www.prri.org/research/fractured-nation-widening-partisan-polarization-and-key-issues-in-2020-presidential-elections; *Atlantic*, October 21, 2019.

19. Robert Jones, *The End of White Christian America* (New York: Simon & Schuster, 2016); *Time*, November 19, 2016; *Washington Post*, November 8–12, 2017; *Washington Examiner*, November 9, 2017.

20. *Atlantic*, November 10, 2017.

21. Douthat, *Bad Religion*, 182–86; *UK Guardian*, August 30, 2017.

22. *USA Today*, February 13, 2019; Bourne, *Jimmy Carter*, 474–76.

23. Ronald Sider, "The Scandal of Evangelical Conscience: Why Don't Christians Live What They Preach?" *Christianity Today*, 2005, "The Evangelical Scandal," interview of Ron Sider by Stan Guthrie, *Christianity Today*, April 13, 2005, http://www.christianitytoday.com/ct/2005/april/32.70.html; Ronald J. Sider, *The Scandal of the Evangelical Conscience: Why Are Christians Living Just like the Rest of the World?* (Grand Rapids, MI: Baker Books, 2005).

24. "Evangelical Scandal," Sider interview; Matthew 5:13–16, New International Version (NIV); Ed Stetzer, "The Epidemic of Bible Illiteracy in Our Churches," *Christianity Today*, July 6, 2015, http://www.christianitytoday.com/edstetzer/2015/july/epidemic-of-bible-illiteracy-in-our-churches.html; Randall Balmer, *Redeemer: The Life of Jimmy Carter* (New York: Basic Books, 2014), 164–69.

25. *New York Times*, April 15, 2017; *Politico*, June 29, 2019.

26. Marc Hetherington and Jonathan Weiler, *Prius or Pickup: How the Answers to Our*

Simple Questions Explain America's Great Divide (New York: Houghton Mifflin Harcourt, 2018), x-xii, 79–82; Matthew 25:35–36, NIV.

27. LifeWay Research, *Evangelical Views on Immigration,* report, February 2015, http:// lifewayresearch.com/wp-content/uploads/2015/03/Evangelical-Views-on-Immigration -Report.pdf; Gregory A. Smith, *Among White Evangelicals, Regular Churchgoers Are the Most Supportive of Trump,* report, Pew Research Center, April 26, 2017, https://www .pewresearch.org/fact-tank/2017/04/26/among-white-evangelicals-regular-churchgoers -are-the-most-supportive-of-trump; *Foreign Policy,* October 29, 2018.

28. *Washington Post,* December 15, 2016; Ryan Klinker, "New Liberty Gun Club Opens," *Liberty Champion,* April 9, 2018, https://www.liberty.edu/champion/2018/04/ new-liberty-mountain-gun-club-opens/.

29. Jeff Frederick, "The Shadow Remains: Victimization, the Gospel of Decline, and Other Southern Ingredients in the Twenty-First Century Political Culture," *Alabama Review* (October 2016): 321–34; Stetzer, "Epidemic of Bible Illiteracy"; Christian Smith and Melinda Lundquist Denton, *Soul Searching: The Religious and Spiritual Lives of American Teenagers* (Oxford: Oxford University Press, 2009); *Christianity Today,* July 6, 2015.

30. "Manhattan Declaration: A Call of Christian Conscience," *First Things,* November 20, 2009, https://www.firstthings.com/web-exclusives/2009/11/manhattan-declaration -a-call-of-christian-conscience.

31. Newt Gingrich, quoted in Kruse, *White Flight,* 260; *Hill,* September 12, 2018.

32. Stephen Mansfield, *Choosing Donald Trump: God, Anger, Hope, and Why Christian Conservatives Supported Him* (Grand Rapids, MI: Baker Books, 2017), 161; *Rolling Stone,* December 2, 2019; *New York Times,* December 19, 2016.

33. Paul Taylor, "The Demographic Trends Shaping American Politics in 2016 and Beyond," Pew Research Center, January 27, 2016, https://www.pewresearch.org/fact -tank/2016/01/27/the-demographic-trends-shaping-american-politics-in-2016-and -beyond/; Jessica Martínez and Gregory A. Smith,

"How the Faithful Voted: A Preliminary 2016 Analysis," Pew Research Center, November 9, 2016, https://www.pewresearch.org/fact-tank/2016/11/09/how-the-faithful-voted -a-preliminary-2016-analysis/; Jean Twenge, *I Gen: Why Today's Super-Connected Kids Are Growing Up Less Rebellious, More Tolerant, Less Happy, and Comparatively Unprepared for Adulthood* (New York: Atria, 2017), 132–42.

34. Thomas S. Kidd, "Polls Show Evangelicals Support Trump, but the Term 'Evangelical' Has Become Meaningless," *Washington Post,* July 22, 2016, https://www .washingtonpost.com/news/acts-of-faith/wp/2016/07/22/polls-show-evangelicals -support-trump-but-the-term-evangelical-has-become-meaningless/; "America's Changing Religious Landscape," Pew Research Center, May 12, 2015, https://www.pewforum .org/2015/05/12/americas-changing-religious-landscape/; *Wall Street Journal,* July 16, 2015.

35. Russell Moore, "Is Christianity Dying?" blog post, May 12, 2015, http://www .russellmoore.com/2015/05/12/is-christianity-dying; Flippen, *Jimmy Carter,* 344–45; Newman, *Getting Right with God,* 160. Some use the terms *cultural Christianity* or *nominal Christianity* to describe those who identify as Christians but have little or no understanding of the elements of the faith.

36. *Christianity Today,* December 12, 22, 2019; "An Open Letter from Friends of *Christi-*

anity Today Affirming Mark Galli's Editorial," Religious News Service, December 24, 2019, https://religionnews.com/2019/12/24/an-open-letter-from-friends-of-christianity-today -affirming-mark-gallis-editorial/.

37. *Washington Post,* December 20, 24, 2019; *Christian Post,* December 22, 23, 2019; *New York Times,* December 20, 2019.

A Question of Emphasis?

EVANGELICALS, TRUMP, AND THE ELECTION OF 2016

R. WARD HOLDER

N*ewsweek* proclaimed 1976 the "Year of the Evangelicals."[1] The emergence of Jimmy Carter and his forthright presentation of his "born-again" Christianity had placed evangelical Christianity in the spotlight. The next forty years were fraught with evangelical political moments. From the formation of the Moral Majority, spearheaded by Rev. Jerry Falwell, to the consideration of the impeachment of President Bill Clinton that was accompanied by the chorus of evangelical calls for morality from elected leaders, the path of evangelicals and political power that struck public consciousness in 1976 grew beyond anything the editors of *Newsweek* could have imagined. But in 2016, a new challenge for evangelicals who wished to exercise their political influence arose.

In the election of 2016, American evangelicals were faced with three choices.[2] Vote for Hillary Clinton and continue the legacy of President Barack Obama, which for many represented an unthinkable abrogation of their values. Vote for Donald Trump, who had frequently shattered Christian sensibilities with his language, his personal history, and his inability even to speak in Christian terms—but who was seen as the standard-bearer of the social programs with which evangelicals had become identified. Finally, evangelicals could stay home and leave the electoral levers in other hands. Numerous thinkers suggested that this was an unpalatable situation that could lead to a variety of outcomes that were negative for the Republican Party, for the social conservative agenda, for American Christian evangelicals, or for Donald Trump.

While the final numbers are still being analyzed and it will never be fully clear what the turnout for evangelicals was, exit polling points to white evangelicals voting for Trump by a four to one margin.[3] Although that four in five, or 80–81 percent, figure is sometimes attacked, there is little doubt that among white evangelicals who chose to vote, Trump was the overwhelming favorite.[4] The white evangelical vote was an enormously important part of Trump's electoral math to get to the White House and, as part of the ongoing Trump base, has continued its fervor. The Public Religion Research Institute published the results of a poll in March 2018 that demonstrated the staying power of the Trump brand with white evangelicals, noting that 75 percent of them had a favorable view of the president.[5]

It's legitimate to ask what happened. Progressive Christian analysts and many secular voices on the left, and even some voices on the right, have suggested that this was simply a matter of enormous hypocrisy. The Moral Majority that believed Bill Clinton could not be trusted with the affairs of state because of the affairs of the bedroom had demonstrated that it was never about morality and was always about power. Far too much of what passes for religious and political "analysis" made that simple calculation and turned away, as if an article claiming religious and moral hypocrisy mattered in this political moment.[6] Was this an example of evangelical social witness overwhelming evangelical morality? Or is something more significant at stake? Did white evangelical fealty to the Republican Party crush any doubts that evangelicals might have felt?[7] Does evangelicalism actually have an institutional issue that promotes support for authoritarian government?[8]

To examine this dynamic, this essay will examine two important Southern Baptist leaders and their different reactions to the choice that evangelicals faced. Rev. Robert Jeffress, pastor of First Baptist Church, Dallas, became a strong Trump supporter. Rev. Russell Moore, president of the Ethics and Religious Liberty Commission of the Southern Baptist Convention, was a firm critic of Trump who called him a lost soul in need of forgiveness. The comparison of the two men's theological and cultural positions will reveal that while it seemed necessary for Jeffress-type Baptists and other evangelicals to make some accommodations to support Trump, this was not the case. Instead, Trump's authoritarianism and racism fit white evangelicalism's historical model and suggested the possibility of a return to an earlier time in which races and religions knew their true place in the social order.

ROBERT JEFFRESS: THE QUESTION OF EMPHASIS

In August 2015, Frank Bruni of the *New York Times* wrote an op-ed entitled "Trump-ward, Christian Soldiers?" In it, the author raised the obvious questions sparked by the widespread Christian evangelical support of Donald Trump. Bruni wrote, "If I want the admiration and blessings of the most flamboyant, judgmental Christians in America, I should marry three times, do a queasy-making amount of sexual boasting, verbally degrade women, talk trash about pretty much everyone else while I'm at it, encourage gamblers to hemorrhage their savings in casinos bearing my name and crow incessantly about how much money I've amassed?" Bruni went on the offensive, suggesting that the evangelical support for Trump demonstrated the selectivity and incoherence of the religiosity of American evangelicalism.[9]

One would think that the opinions of an Italian, openly gay, New York–residing columnist for one of the most openly liberal papers in America, the *New York Times,* would not really catch the attention of Christian evangelicals, especially Southern Baptists, who are concentrated, not surprisingly, in the South. But such was not the case. Rev. Robert Jeffress, pastor of one of the largest Southern Baptist churches in America, First Baptist in Dallas, answered Bruni in an opinion piece published on the Fox News website on September 8, 2015. Jeffress turned Bruni's characterization of evangelical religiosity as "selective and incoherent" into "ignorant or hypocritical," words that Bruni never used. Jeffress argued that Bruni had failed to recognize the real issue for evangelicals, which was Barack Obama. He wrote, "There is a palpable feeling among many Christians (as well as non-Christians) that our nation has been in a downward death spiral during the last seven years of President Obama's administration." Faced with that reality, Jeffress reasoned, evangelicals were willing to accept the flawed candidate with the necessary leadership capabilities. Jeffress claimed that evangelicals had changed, that they no longer required a candidate who was one of them as their standard-bearer.

Rather, in a shocking statement for which he gave no particular supporting facts, Jeffress wrote that "seven years of Barack Obama have drasti-
cally lowered the threshold of spiritual expectations Evangelicals have of
their president. No longer do they require their president to be one of
them. Evangelicals will settle for someone who doesn't HATE them like
the current occupant of the Oval Office appears to." Jeffress concluded
his editorial with a non-prediction that stated only God knew who would
win the nomination, that evangelical support would clarify when other
evangelical-friendly candidates dropped out, and that in the meantime
the election was fascinating and fun to watch.[10]

Jeffress accomplished several things in his op-ed. First, he answered
Bruni's charges. Second, he divorced Trump's shaky evangelical Christian credentials from his suitability for receiving evangelical support by
arguing that the issue of leadership no longer could be tied to religious
orthodoxy. The pragmatic choice to support a leader in no way cast doubt
upon the coherence of evangelical religion or theology, because the two
were separable, and in Donald Trump's case necessarily separated, given
his sinful and unrepentant biography. Third, he made the case that Barack
Obama was a person filled with hatred for evangelicals. In the mirror re-
verse of Donald Trump, it would make no difference that Obama fulfilled
many of the qualifications that traditional evangelicals had wanted from
their national and spiritual leaders. Married only once in a marriage that
seemed quite strong, Obama was clearly devoted to his family, and there
was not a whiff of scandal about his personal sexuality.[11] That was the
ideal for evangelical Christian thinkers in the Bush years and especially
in the Clinton years. But in both Trump and Obama, Jeffress argued that
character did not count but only the positions that were taken. Obama's
personal story of Christian conversion should not be counted in light
of his support for LGBTQ+ rights, his support for legal abortion, and
his efforts to support young undocumented immigrants, brought to the
United States by their parents, frequently called "Dreamers."

In February 2016, faced with growing support by evangelicals nationwide for Donald Trump and divisions between supporters of Texas senator Ted Cruz and those who supported Trump even in his own congre-
gation, First Baptist Church in Dallas, Jeffress was again in the national
spotlight, interviewed by National Public Radio's Audie Cornish. Jeffress

again described evangelicals as being divided between pragmatists and idealists, a question of emphasis and strategy, not a question of the differentiation between faith positions. He said: "But evangelicals are divided between what I call the idealist and the pragmatist. The idealist are the ones who are supporting Ted Cruz and would say if we could just get a strong Christian in the White House, perhaps we could return our nation to its Judeo-Christian foundation. But then there are the pragmatists who say as much as we would like to have a faith-centered candidate, perhaps our country has moved too far to the left for that to happen, and so let's get the most conservative candidate who is electable. And many of those are going for a Donald Trump." In response to Cornish's question about "faith no longer being the ultimate litmus test in terms of casting the ballot," Jeffress gave the example of 1980, when the choice was between a born-again Christian married to one wife and a twice-married movie star whose wife practiced astrology. Evangelicals voted not for the most religious candidate but for the one who they believed had the most significant quality, that of leadership.[12] Late in the campaign, after the exposure of the tapes of Trump bragging about assaulting women and his performance in the second presidential debate, *All Things Considered* interviewed Jeffress again about Trump.[13] In an interview with Michel Martin, Jeffress stated that politically, Trump had redeemed himself after the debacle of the leaked tape and that his performance showed resiliency, a good reason to vote for him as president in a dangerous world. Jeffress was clear that the appropriate candidate to vote for was the one who would put the right policies in place and not the one with the right morals. Jeffress even went so far as to say: "When I'm looking for a leader who's going to fight ISIS and keep this nation secure, I don't want some meek and mild leader or somebody who's going to turn the other cheek. I've said I want the meanest, toughest SOB I can find to protect this nation."[14] This was extraordinary because Jeffress explicitly rejected someone who would follow the commands of Jesus in favor of national protection.

In all three media appearances, Jeffress sought to create a division between the candidates whom evangelicals support and evangelicals' moral values. In response to a question of whether evangelical backing for Trump was hypocritical because of his rejection of so many evangelical moral values, Jeffress consistently argued that the issue was not whether a candidate was moral but whether the candidate supported the correct policies. For Jeffress, the issue seemed only to be a question of where to put the emphasis. In choosing a pastor, that emphasis was clearly on finding a moral guide. In the new millennium, the point was to find a strong leader who supported Christian and evangelically supported positions, even if he were not himself a strong Christian.

One of the key examples has been on the issue of the appointment of judges. During the campaign, Trump had said in a televised debate that he would appoint pro-life judges.[15] He strengthened that promise by the seemingly unprecedented release of a list of judges he would consider as candidates for the Supreme Court. His original list was released in May 2016, and an updated list came out that September.[16] It was compiled by Don McGahn, at the time one of the Trump campaign's lawyers, with significant input from the Federalist Society.[17]

On assuming the presidency, Trump immediately appointed Neil Gorsuch to the vacant seat on the Supreme Court and then nominated Brett Kavanaugh to the second vacancy. The Supreme Court justice nominations are an important consideration when attempting to parse out whether evangelicals were being hypocritical or pragmatic in their support for Trump. With the nomination of two staunchly conservative and pro-life candidates, Trump has kept his side of the bargain between himself and evangelicals.

RUSSELL MOORE: THE QUESTION OF CHARACTER

If Robert Jeffress could be said to hold up the wing of evangelicalism that supports Trump for his policies though not his personal proclivities, Rev. Russell Moore is his diametrical opposite. Moore is president of the Ethics and Religious Liberty Commission of the Southern Baptist Convention. As early as 2015, Moore was slamming both Trump and evangelicals who supported him. In an op-ed in the *New York Times* published on September 17, 2015, Moore wrote that to back Trump, evangelicals and other social conservatives "must repudiate everything they believe." Moore pointed out that although there was not a requirement of being "born-again" for the office of presidency, it was logical and right for genuine and thoughtful believers to ask about a candidate's character. For that, Moore said, evangelicals needed to look no further than to Trump's own recorded and published comments. He wrote: "His attitude toward women is that of a Bronze Age warlord. He tells us in one of his books that he revels in the fact that he gets to sleep with some of the 'top women in the world.' He has divorced two wives (so far) for other women." Moore pointed out that "in the 1990s, some of these social conservatives argued that 'If Bill Clinton's wife can't trust him, neither can we.' If character matters, character matters." Moore concluded his article with an allusion to Luke 14.27–29 and Jesus's admonition to the disciples that they must count the cost of following him. He went on to write that "we should also count the cost of following Donald Trump. To do so would mean that we've decided to join the other side of the culture war, that image and celebrity and money and power and social Darwinist 'winning' trump the conservation of moral principles and a just society."[18]

Moore's foray into the pages of the *New York Times* was hardly his only effort at criticizing Trump's candidacy and evangelicals who would support it. In January 2016, Moore penned a similar attack for *National Review*. Moore reprised his attack that conservatives had long believed that character mattered—what had changed? He asserted that conservatives had been fighting for religious freedom as a natural right, consistent with the beliefs of the founding fathers. He held up Trump's willingness to ban Muslims, even temporarily, as a grave issue that departed from the insights of Thomas Jefferson, which were supported by Baptists. He raised the specter of a celebrity-driven election, won by a mobocracy, and concluded that "sound moral judgments are displaced by a narcissistic pursuit of power. Social and religious conservatives have always seen this tendency as decadent and deviant. For them to view it any other way now would be for them to lose their soul."[19]

Time and space preclude a fuller consideration of Moore's engagement with Trump throughout 2015 and 2016. Some have rightfully suggested that Moore took an unholy pleasure in baiting Trump, especially when Trump tweeted back.[20] What is important to note is that Moore was setting out a position that denied Jeffress's position. Moore mounted a verbal assault on the position that it could be a Christian conservative choice to vote strategically for a candidate with moral flaws who held the right policy positions. To Moore, this seemed to be an act of surrender in the culture wars, an acceptance of Trump's various moral peccadilloes, and a reversal from the positions staked out during the Clinton presidency that character matters.

THE POLITICS OF EVANGELICALISM

November 8, 2016, came and went, with surprises, worries, jubilation, and everything that normally accompanies an upset win. Russell Moore penned an appropriately chastened piece that appeared in the *Washington Post*, entitled "Why Christians Should Not Succumb to the Apocalyptic Language of the Election." In it, he encouraged Christians to pray for President-Elect Trump, following the demands of Scripture. He called for reconciliation, that the churches could embody the reconciliation of the kingdom of God that is their gift to a broken world.[21] Moore's position had lost, and he knew it.

Robert Jeffress's position, on the other hand, won the day. But did Jeffress really follow the ideal he set out for evangelicals in general, and Baptists in particular, avoiding the issue of whether the candidate was godly in favor of simply voting for the candidate who correctly answered the policy questions? A variety of items suggests otherwise. Jeffress recalled meeting with Trump early in the campaign and telling him that God had called him to lead the country.[22] This was not a flawed candidate but God's chosen instrument. On January 3, 2017, Jeffress tweeted that he had met with Trump and believed the president-elect would be the most faith-friendly president in the nation's history.[23] Then on the morning of the inauguration, Jeffress preached a sermon to Trump, his wife, and the gathered faithful at St. John's Episcopal Church in Washington, DC. In the sermon, Jeffress obliterated the division between a secular candidate and the support of a Christian public by preaching a sermon that made the president-elect into a modern-day Nehemiah. Jeffress preached on the biblical figure of Nehemiah, a leader of the Israelites who had brought them back from Babylon and rebuilt the wall around Jerusalem. He likened Trump to Nehemiah, saying, "God is not against building walls." He instructed Trump not to pay attention to his critics because they would stop him from doing the work that God had intended him to do. And he assured the president-elect that he had reached this height only through the choice of God.[24]

It does not require a seminary degree or a doctorate in theology to engage in the most basic homiletical and exegetical analysis of Jeffress's sermon and to see that no thoughtful reader could examine this sermon and believe that the preacher was not fully supportive of the president-elect. Jeffress's earlier argument that evangelicals could support Trump in spite of his moral failings has been replaced with Trump being set out as a biblical figure, with clear arguments that he has assumed his place at God's will.

Jeffress's ongoing support for President Trump was rock-solid. As further news stories of President Trump's peccadilloes increased, Jeffress remained part of the core Trump support. Published tales of affairs with a pornography star and a Playboy model were followed by discussions of payoffs and who knew what at what point in time.[25] Aside from the allure of prurient tales of public people, questions were also raised about whether the payoffs actually functioned as cash donations to the Trump campaign and were thus violations of federal election regulations.[26] The set of allegations would have been far too much for the old Moral Majority of the 1980s.

Jeffress displayed no consternation about supporting President Trump through the storm of scandal. Instead of attempting a "he-said, she-said" defense, the Dallas pastor seemed to accept that the allegations were true but meaningless. He appeared on Fox News to say that none of it mattered. "Evangelicals still believe in the commandment: Thou shalt not have sex with a porn star," he said. "However, whether this president violated that commandment or not is totally irrelevant to our support of him."[27] Evangelicals were comfortable with Trump because he gave them the policies that they wanted. Whether in judicial appointments, the withdrawal from the Paris Climate Accords, or the harsh enforcement of borders that included separating children from their parents, evangelicals who supported Trump did it because they approved of his policies.

In turn, Trump rewarded Robert Jeffress, making him a member of Trump's evangelical board of advisors. Further, though Jeffress had in the past stated unequivocally that Jews would go to Hell, he was a featured speaker during the festivities that marked the opening of the new American embassy in Jerusalem in 2018.[28] Transported from the largest American stage to a world stage, the pastor's acceptance of Trump as a model president was clear from the beginning of Trump's administration.

Russell Moore? He stands as a cautionary tale. While some Southern Baptists, most notably Al Mohler, president of Southern Baptist Theological Seminary, stood up to criticisms of Moore, those criticisms intensified since Trump's election. Mike Huckabee suggested that it is ridiculous for the denomination to pay someone to attack it.[29] The Christian alt-right sprang up with assaults on Moore that range from the severe to the unprintable.[30] Most significant for a denominational employee, some churches began to vote with their withheld donations.[31] The situation for Moore got so bad that a postelection *Christianity Today* article ran under the headline "Is It Too Late for Russell Moore to Say Sorry?"[32]

CHRISTIAN EVANGELICALISM AND DONALD TRUMP AS THE NEW DAVID

Another contributor to this volume and one of the deans of American political and religious history, Randall Balmer, has been instrumental in unmasking the true facts about the birth of conservative evangelical political power in this country.[33] The American myth of evangelical political power is that evangelicals rose up after a godless liberal Supreme Court unleashed a culture of death in the *Roe v. Wade* decision in 1973. Balmer has argued that the apparent rise of evangelical political organization in response to *Roe v. Wade* is an intentionally false projection. Actually, there is good evidence that the mainstream of evangelicals were originally happy with the *Roe* decision because it kept government out of Christian decisions. W. Barry Garrett, writing in *Baptist Press*, stated that "religious liberty, human equality and justice are advanced by the Supreme Court abortion decision."[34] However, Balmer points out that the worries about abortion were originally a cover to hide the true issue that drove white evangelicals. The real reason behind evangelical Christian organization was the Bob Jones University IRS decision that came about because of the university's discriminatory racial policies. Conservative political activist Paul Weyrich stated clearly that the beginnings of the Religious Right as a political movement in modern America were motivated by the IRS decision concerning Bob Jones University and its tax-exempt status.[35] This decision had been working its way through the courts for years and was not finally decided until Ronald Reagan was in office. But long before that, the writing was on the wall that southern evangelical segregated schools would not receive the preferential treatment that they believed they deserved.

The historical moment marked by Trump's presidency eerily echoes the rise of the Religious Right as a power center in conservative politics. At that moment, a white evangelical base was energized by fears of loss of tax advantages that were held by segregated religious institutions, especially schools. The efforts of Paul Weyrich were concentrated on finding a more palatable cause than segregation to unite white evangelicals behind a set of issues that would clearly benefit their communities and disadvantage minority communities.

In response to the Trump presidency and opportunities it affords, white evangelicalism has exchanged its concern for character, which was its martial cry throughout the Clinton administration, for a concentration on policies. While that seems pragmatic and realistic, it comes with costs. Among those are three significant issues that should not be ignored. First, the Moral Majority headlined a movement that sought to bring the country back to what it believed were its Christian roots. The variety of ways that the Christian Right has sought to portray the founding of the American nation and its ongoing existence as a special act of divine providence are legion.[36] But whether nuanced or blunt, these efforts to set America up as a Christian nation amount to a sense of a special place in America for Christianity and for Christian values, morals, and laws. American jurisprudence, American culture, and what some have called the need for a shared American philosophy were all to be resourced by Christian sources. American laws should be founded upon the Ten Commandments.[37] American culture should be based on biblical mores.[38]

But the effort to bring the country back to Christian roots while unfailingly supporting an American who rejects those mores has opened the door to charges of hypocrisy. It cannot be denied that the Christian evangelical political machine risks winning a Pyrrhic victory. Already, some Christian evangelical groups are abandoning the term *evangelical* because of the toxic nature of the claims that have been made under it.[39]

Becoming a punch line that means hypocrisy cannot help the movement in the culture wars.

Second, evangelicals risk guilt by association in support of Trump. In supporting Trump, they are seen to support the appointment of judges who will overturn *Roe v. Wade.* They are linked to a particular ideal in the culture wars of returning America to a former greatness. Evangelicals are also linked to strong borders and a populist sense of the economic good. With all of these priorities, the great majority of evangelicals would express contentment.

But Trump's presidency is like few others in modern days. In supporting Trump, evangelicals are associated with disgraceful rhetoric about Trump's political opponents, including John McCain. Backing Trump, evangelicals are linked to neo-Nazis and white nationalists. Aiding Trump with their campaign dollars, evangelicals became caught up in the debacle of separating undocumented children from their parents and keeping them in cages or shelters, where they have been involuntarily administered psychotropic drugs.[40] Even though there is a demonstrable consideration of racially tinged policies of which white evangelicals approve, they do not want to be associated with policies and photos that make them seem cruel or outwardly racist.

Third, the effort by evangelicals to pursue pragmatic policies that get their goals approved with no care for their standard-bearer comes with a significant cost. They risk becoming just another interest group. They would be no different from the hog farmers in the Midwest seeking to get relief from the effects of tariffs. They would be no different from the National Rifle Association requesting that senators and representatives enact laws to protect Second Amendment rights. They would be no different from any secular interest group, distinguished only by the policies they support.

But for evangelicals, that is a huge loss. Evangelicals are, if anything, most concerned about their identity. The rhythm of Romans 12:2, "Do not be conformed to this world, but be transformed by the renewing of your mind," is ever before true evangelicals. Becoming simply another interest group is a loss of identity, one that evangelicals believe is found in Christ. Loss of that identity is why the rejection of the term *evangelical* by some of the faithful has been so upsetting to others.

The argument can be made that evangelical pragmatism will never lose its Christian center because of the crucial nature of that link. Evangelicals are first and foremost about Jesus Christ. The 2016 record of Wayne Grudem, a prominent evangelical theologian, suggests otherwise. On July 28, 2016, Grudem published "Why Voting for Donald Trump Is a Morally Good Choice."[41] The article was basically Jeffress's point in a much longer format. Since Donald Trump would deliver many things that evangelicals wanted and Hillary Clinton would not, the moral choice was clear—vote Trump. On October 9, in the wake of the *Access Hollywood* tape scandal, Grudem removed his earlier post and replaced it with "Trump's Moral Character and the Election."[42] In that post, Grudem apologized for having not investigated Trump's character further and openly hoped that Trump would withdraw from the race. But contrition can only last so long in the heat of a presidential race. Ten days later, Grudem reposted his original piece and added a revised post supporting Trump, "If You Don't Like Either Candidate, Then Vote for Trump's Policies."[43] Here Grudem returned to the pragmatism he had displayed earlier. Further, his list of Trump's policies that evangelicals should support went far beyond the normal list of culture war or religious hot-button topics. Yes, judges that would be trusted to overturn *Roe v. Wade* and legal protections for Christian conservative positions, such as denying service to homosexuals, were both there. But so was a call for lower taxes and an effort to withdraw money from public schools as well as expansion of the military. None of those are biblically oriented, especially the desire for a huge military to serve the Prince of Peace. Yet all of these were presented as part of the correct choice for evangelicals. The line between evangelical Christians and mere conservative American voters was blurred, intentionally so.

While Robert Jeffress presented a bifurcated position of moral dismay and policy agreement with Donald Trump during the election, afterward he revealed that he had always believed that God had called Trump to lead the country, identified Trump with a positive biblical figure in Nehemiah, and stated that he believed that Trump would be the most "faith-friendly" president in the history of the United States. Jeffress abandoned his reserve to argue that the president's moral failings were insignificant in the context of his divinely given role. In that move, Jeffress made Trump not into a modern Nehemiah but into a modern David. David, who came to power through a tortuous series of events that even included working for a traditional enemy of the Israelites. David, who had several problems running his own household. David, the adulterer. David, who recognized that Jerusalem was the capital city of Israel.

The David analogy is instructive. The Old Testament looks at David frequently as the model king—he achieved God's purposes. But David was chastised by Nathan when he took Bathsheba and had Uriah the Hittite murdered. David was punished both with the prophet speaking truth to power and with the death of his son.[44] But Jeffress and the other "court evangelicals" did not chide Trump; they did not correct him either with parables of stolen sheep or blatant claims of irresponsibility.[45] Since that is the case, it begins to create a window into the evangelical mind about Trump's policies and why the scandals did not matter.

The scandals did not matter because at their core, the court evangelicals accepted Trump's personal proclivities as the price for achieving policies that they support. As demonstrated in the consideration of Grudem's posts during the campaign, some of those policy priorities were the same positions that evangelicals have supported for decades. But some were simply elements of populist and conservative culture, even to the point of abrogating biblical teaching. Why did they do this? While myriad answers that seek to get behind the psyche of the Trump voter have been offered, Balmer's analysis remains true.[46] The rise of evangelicalism as a modern political force was not ignited by the fires that sparked after *Roe v. Wade*. Instead, they arose in a protective reflex over the right of white Christians to segregate in schools and to have tax advantages, whether such policies flouted federal law or not.

This conclusion is made even clearer by the analysis of John Compton. In Compton's theory of evangelical religious authority, the leaders of evangelical churches do not actually lead. "On the contrary, evangelical elites tend to take their marching orders from the men and women in the pews—men and women who, again, overwhelmingly identify as conservative Republicans."[47] Compton's sociological analysis brings out the manner in which this pattern arose. The highly decentralized structure of many evangelical churches prevented oversight as well as leadership from a top-down perspective. The model of power that depended upon individual congregations created an impossible task for leadership. Leadership in such groups is a matter of divining what the rank and file believe, rather than pointing them in a new direction. The historical anxieties about issues of race and class and the other would be basic to any such churches.

Thus, Trump's continual appeal to racist and authoritarian themes throughout his campaign and presidency—beginning with calling Mexicans rapists to moral equivalency regarding the protests in Charlottesville, Virginia, to calling African countries "shithole countries"—found a ready ear in political evangelicalism. The legions of white evangelicals looked forward to "making America great again" specifically because it harked back to a time when white Protestantism defined the culture and minorities and other religions knew their place.[48] The duel for the heart of political evangelicalism between Russell Moore and Robert Jeffress was over before it began. White political evangelicalism found in Donald Trump the leader to restore them to Zion and to bring back the New Israel in which they believe their parents lived.

Religious language is significant in the public square. The First Amendment's Establishment Clause ensures that religious language will be able to take its place at the center of political and cultural discussions. However, it is worthwhile to ask whether the religious language employed in the Trump era works for the public consideration of questions of morality and law. Kathleen Sands writes that religious speech frequently has been designed to conceal the concerns behind it. "Architecture is artifice, rarely designed to reveal the lives or tangled relations of those who inhabit it. So it has been with American religion-talk, which by its opacity hides speakers from each other, by its absolutism prevents negotiated solutions, and by its manipulability makes it all but inevitable that 'religion' will be used to ratify judgments one has already reached while obscuring the reasons behind those judgments."[49] The example of white evangelicalism and its love affair with Donald Trump provides an instructive case that demonstrates the veracity of this analysis. In political evangelicalism, white evangelicals find the religious answer that will provide the balm that soothes with the knowledge that they are chosen by God for privilege that is their right, and any who would suggest otherwise break not only true religion but also the truth itself.

NOTES

1. Jon Meacham, "The Editor's Desk," *Newsweek,* November 12, 2006, https://www .newsweek.com/editors-desk-106637.

2. The definition of *evangelical* is always difficult, and the present moment has made it more so. The classic definition comes from David W. Bebbington's *Evangelicalism in Modern Britain: A History from the 1730s to the 1980s* (London: Unwin Hyman, 1989), 2–17. The four characteristics were a concentration on the authority of the Bible, frequently read literally; a concentration on the salvific work of Jesus Christ; a concentration on conversion, frequently with a call for a dated moment of "accepting Jesus"; and the belief that the entire world should be brought to Christ. These are termed *biblicism, crucicentrism, conversionism,* and *activism.* While this is useful, it does not cover the breadth of American evangelicalism in the present day.

3. Sarah Pulliam Bailey, "White Evangelicals Voted Overwhelmingly for Donald Trump, Exit Polls Show," *Washington Post,* November 9, 2016, https://www.washingtonpost .com/news/acts-of-faith/wp/2016/11/09/exit-polls-show-white-evangelicals-voted -overwhelmingly-for-donald-trump/.

4. Kate Shellnutt, "Trump Elected President, Thanks to 4 in 5 White Evangelicals," *Christianity Today,* November 9, 2016, http://www.christianitytoday.com/gleanings/2016/ november/trump-elected-president-thanks-to-4-in-5-white-evangelicals.html. Myriam Renaud weighed in with "Myths Debunked: Why Did White Evangelical Christians Vote for Trump?" https://divinity.uchicago.edu/sightings/myths-debunked-why-did-white -evangelical-christians-vote-trump. Joe Carter argued that the majority did not vote for Trump, when one counts the nonvoters, "No, the Majority of American Evangelicals Did Not Vote for Trump," https://www.thegospelcoalition.org/article/no-the-majority-of -american-evangelicals-did-not-vote-for-trump.

5. Tara Isabella Burton, "Poll: White Evangelical Support for Trump Is at an All-Time High," *Vox,* April 20, 2018, https://www.vox.com/identities/2018/4/20/17261726/poll -prri-white-evangelical-support-for-trump-is-at-an-all-time-high.

6. The following is only a tiny sample of the articles, social media posts, and tweets that have been posted. Dick Polman, "Hypocritical Conservative Evangelicals Shelter Themselves from Stormygate," WHYY, January 24, 2018, https://whyy.org/articles/ hypocritical-conservative-evangelicals-shelter-stormygate/. Peter Wehner, "The Heavenly Heights of Evangelical Hypocrisy," *New York Times,* October 9, 2016, https://www.nytimes .com/interactive/projects/cp/opinion/clinton-trump-second-debate-election-2016/ the-heavenly-height-of-evangelical-hypocrisy. Kirsten Powers, "Yes, Liberals Can Be Condescending, but Trump Is Still Conservatives' Fault," *Washington Post,* June 1, 2018, https://www.sltrib.com/opinion/commentary/2018/06/01/kirsten-powers-yes-liberals -can-be-condescending-but-trump-is-still-conservatives-fault/. Ian Schwartz, "Bill Maher: Trump Exposed Evangelicals as the Shameless Hypocrites They've Always Been," *Real Clear Politics,* November 5, 2016, https://www.realclearpolitics.com/video/2016/11/05/maher_ trump_exposed_evangelicals_as_the_shameless_hypocrites_theyve_always_been.html.

7. Thomas S. Kidd, *Who Is an Evangelical? The History of a Movement in Crisis* (New Haven: Yale University Press, 2019), 154.

8. John Compton, "How the Decline of Religious Institutions Fueled the Rise of the Trump-Evangelical Coalition," *Religion in Public,* December 9, 2019, https://religion inpublic.blog/2019/12/09/how-the-decline-of-religious-institutions-fueled-the-rise-of -the-trump-evangelical-coalition/.

9. Frank Bruni, "Trump-ward, Christian Soldiers?" *New York Times,* August 25, 2015, https://www.nytimes.com/2015/08/26/opinion/frank-bruni-trump-ward-christian -soldiers.html.

10. Robert Jeffress, "Why Trump Is Triumphant with Evangelicals . . . for Now," FoxNews.com, September 8, 2015, http://www.foxnews.com/opinion/2015/09/08/why -trump-is-triumphant-with-evangelicals-for-now.html.

11. R. Ward Holder, "Trump, Obama and Christianity," *World Religion News,* May 22, 2017, http://www.worldreligionnews.com/religion-news/trump-obama-christianity.

12. Audie Cornish, "Why Do Evangelicals Support Donald Trump? A Pastor Explains," National Public Radio (NPR), *All Things Considered,* February 25, 2016, http://www .npr.org/2016/02/25/468149440/why-do-evangelicals-support-donald-trump-a-pastor -explains.

13. Michel Martin, "Pastor Robert Jeffress Explains His Support for Trump," *All Things Considered,* NPR, October 16, 2016, http://www.npr.org/2016/10/16/498171498/pastor -robert-jeffress-explains-his-support-for-trump.

14. Martin, "Pastor Robert Jeffress."

15. NBC News, October 20, 2016, https://www.nbcnews.com/video/trump-i-will-be -appointing-pro-life-judges-789632067780.

16. Trump campaign website, https://web.archive.org/web/20170502205549/ https://www.donaldjtrump.com/press-releases/donald-j.-trump-adds-to-list-of-potential -supreme-court-justice-picks. An updated list also resides on the White House website, https://www.whitehouse.gov/briefings-statements/president-donald-j-trumps-supreme -court-list/.

17. Joel Achenbach, "A Look at the List Helping Trump Reshape the Supreme Court," *Chicago Tribune,* July 8, 2018, http://www.chicagotribune.com/news/nationworld/ politics/ct-trump-supreme-court-list-20180708-story.html.

18. Russell Moore, "Have Evangelicals Who Support Trump Lost Their Values?" *New York Times,* September 17, 2015, https://www.nytimes.com/2015/09/17/opinion/have -evangelicals-who-support-trump-lost-their-values.html.

19. Russell Moore, "Donald Trump Is Not the Moral Leader We Need," *National Review,* January 22, 2016, http://www.nationalreview.com/article/430119/russell-moore -trump-symposium.

20. Janet Mefferd, "Russell Moore vs. Conservatives: This Isn't Just about Trump," *One News Now,* January 12, 2017, https://www.onenewsnow.com/perspectives/guest -commentary/2017/01/12/russell-moore-vs-conservatives-this-isnt-just-about-trump.

21. Russell Moore, "Why Christians Should Not Succumb to the Apocalyptic Lan-guage of the Election," *Washington Post,* November 9, 2016, https://www.washington-post.com/news/acts-of-faith/wp/2016/11/09/why-christians-should-not-succumb-to-the -apocalyptic-language-of-the-election/?utm_term=.c41a17f144ae.

22. Sarah Pulliam Bailey, "God Is Not against Building Walls! The Sermon Trump

Heard from Robert Jeffress before His Inauguration," *Washington Post,* January 20, 2017, https://www.washingtonpost.com/news/acts-of-faith/wp/2017/01/20/god-is-not-against-building-walls-the-sermon-donald-trump-heard-before-his-inauguration/?utm_term=.0175aa0b4454.

23. "Robert Jeffress: 5 Fast Facts You Need to Know," *Heavy,* http://heavy.com/news/2017/01/robert-jeffress-donald-trump-inauguration-pastor-inaugural-service-gays-muslims-islam-video-bio-catholics-mormons/.

24. Bailey, "God Is Not against Building Walls."

25. Michael Rothfeld and Joe Palazzolo, "Trump Lawyer Arranged $130,000 Payment for Adult-Film Star's Silence," *Wall Street Journal,* January 12, 2018, https://www.wsj.com/articles/trump-lawyer-arranged-130-000-payment-for-adult-film-stars-silence-1515787678. Joe Palazzolo, Michael Rothfeld, and Lukas I. Alpert, "National Enquirer Shielded Donald Trump from Playboy Model's Affair Allegation," *Wall Street Journal,* November 4, 2016, https://www.wsj.com/articles/national-enquirer-shielded-donald-trump-from-playboy-models-affair-allegation-1478309380.

26. Philip Bump, "How the Stormy Daniels Payment May Have Violated Election Law," *Washington Post,* April 9, 2018, https://www.washingtonpost.com/news/politics/wp/2018/03/09/new-evidence-the-stormy-daniels-payment-may-have-violated-election-law/?utm_term=.8d0c1097cd4e.

27. Tom Steele, "First Baptist Pastor Robert Jeffress: Evangelicals Don't Care if Trump Had Sex with Porn Star," *Dallas News,* March 13, 2018, https://www.dallasnews.com/news/donald-trump-1/2018/03/13/first-baptist-dallas-pastor-robert-jeffress-evangelicals-dont-care-trump-sex-porn-star.

28. Matthew Haag, "Robert Jeffress, Pastor Who Said Jews Are Going to Hell, Led Prayer at Jerusalem Embassy," *New York Times,* May 14, 2018, https://www.nytimes.com/2018/05/14/world/middleeast/robert-jeffress-embassy-jerusalem-us.html.

29. Tom Gjelten, "Evangelical Leader under Attack for Criticizing Trump Supporters," NPR, December 20 2016, http://www.npr.org/2016/12/20/506248119/anti-trump-evangelical-faces-backlash.

30. See, for instance, ADI, "Russell Moore Endorses Idolatry," http://faithandheritage.com/2016/06/russell-moore-endorses-idolatry/.

31. David Roach, *Baptist Press,* in *Christianity Today,* February 17, 2017, http://www.christianitytoday.com/gleanings/2017/february/trump-advisers-church-withholds-donation-sbc-graham-moore.html.

32. Kate Shellnutt, "Is It Too Late for Russell Moore to Say Sorry?" *Christianity Today,* December 21, 2016, http://www.christianitytoday.com/ct/2016/december-web-only/is-it-too-late-to-say-sorry-russell-moore-erlc-sbc-trump.html.

33. Randall Balmer, *Thy Kingdom Come: How the Religious Right Distorts the Faith and Threatens America—An Evangelical's Lament* (New York: Basic Books, 2006). But this has been considered in a variety of articles in the national media, and has become such a commonplace that sometimes Balmer is not even cited. See Sarah Posner, "Amazing Disgrace: How Did Donald Trump—a Thrice-Married, Biblically Illiterate Sexual Predator—Hijack the Religious Right?" *New Republic,* March 20, 2017, https://newrepublic.com/article/140961/amazing-disgrace-donald-trump-hijacked-religious-right.

34. Quoted in Balmer, *Thy Kingdom Come*, 12.

35. Balmer, *Thy Kingdom Come*, 13–15.

36. See especially John Fea, *Was American Founded as a Christian Nation?* rev. ed. (Louisville, KY: Westminster John Knox Press, 2016).

37. An example comes in the person of Judge Roy Moore, who rose to the elected position of chief justice of the Alabama Supreme Court, largely on his reputation as the "Ten Commandments judge," for his habit of posting the Ten Commandments in his courtroom. His most spectacular act in this regard was to have a two and a half–ton block of granite with the Ten Commandments carved on it placed outside the state judicial building on his own authority. Eventually, the case, *Glassroth v. Moore,* proceeded to trial in district court, and the district court ordered the removal of the monument. Moore was eventually removed from office for refusing to obey the order of a federal court. See Leada Gore, "Who Is Roy Moore? Former Alabama Chief Justice, '10 Commandments Judge' Wins GOP Senate Runoff," *AL.com,* September 26, 2017, https://www.al.com/news/index.ssf/2017/09/who_is_roy_moore_former_alabam.html; Jess Bidgood, Richard Fausset, and Campbell Robertson, "For Roy Moore, a Long History of Combat and Controversy," *New York Times,* November 18, 2017, https://www.nytimes.com/2017/11/18/us/roy-moore-alabama.html.

38. The National Association of Evangelicals joined other groups in an amicus curiae brief to the Supreme Court arguing against the idea that the nation should extend protections to homosexuals in their desire to be married. NAE.net, April 3, 2015, https://www.nae.net/obergefell-v-hodges/.

39. Timothy Keller, "Can Evangelicalism Survive Donald Trump and Roy Moore?" *New Yorker,* December 19, 2017, https://www.newyorker.com/news/news-desk/can-evangelicalism-survive-donald-trump-and-roy-moore.

40. Samantha Schmidt, "Trump Administration Must Stop Giving Psychotropic Drugs to Migrant Children without Consent, Judge Rules," *Washington Post,* July 31, 2018, https://www.washingtonpost.com/news/morning-mix/wp/2018/07/31/trump-administration-must-seek-consent-before-giving-drugs-to-migrant-children-judge-rules/?utm_term=.f2e8d3948644.

41. Wayne Grudem, "Why Voting for Donald Trump Is a Morally Good Choice," *Townhall,* July 28, 2016, https://townhall.com/columnists/waynegrudem/2016/07/28/why-voting-for-donald-trump-is-a-morally-good-choice-n2199564.

42. Wayne Grudem, "Trump's Moral Character and the Election," *Townhall,* October 9, 2016, https://townhall.com/columnists/waynegrudem/2016/10/09/trumps-moral-character-and-the-election-n2229846.

43. Wayne Grudem, "If You Don't Like Either Candidate, then Vote for Trump's Policies," *Townhall,* October 19, 2016, https://townhall.com/columnists/waynegrudem/2016/10/19/if-you-dont-like-either-candidate-then-vote-for-trumps-policies-n2234187.

44. 2 Samuel 11–12.

45. See John Fea's use of this term in "Why Won't Most of Trump's 'Court Evangelicals' Publicly Condemn His Border Policy?" *Religion News Service,* June 21, 2018, https://religionnews.com/2018/06/21/why-arent-most-of-trumps-court-evangelicals-publicly

-condemning-his-border-policy/; and "The Court Evangelicals," *Way of Improvement Leads Home*, May 6, 2017, https://thewayofimprovement.com/2017/05/06/the-court -evangelicals/.

46. Morris Fiorina rejects explanations rooted in the rise of racial politics. "The Meaning of Trump's Election Has Been Exaggerated," *RealClearPolitics*, January 10, 2018, https://www.realclearpolitics.com/articles/2018/01/10/the_meaning_of_trumps_ election_has_been_exaggerated__135968.html. Adam Serwer contends, however, that the heart and soul of Trump's support is rooted in racial resentment. See Serwer, "The Nationalist's Delusion," in the *Atlantic*, November 20, 2017, https://www.theatlantic.com/ politics/archive/2017/11/the-nationalists-delusion/546356/. Katherine J. Cramer examined Wisconsin, a key swing state, and found that opinions about social welfare programs are situated in attitudes toward work. Opposition to social welfare is regularly framed as a critique that people don't work hard enough. Cramer, *The Politics of Resentment: Rural Consciousness in Wisconsin and the Rise of Scott Walker* (Chicago: University of Chicago Press, 2016).

47. Compton, "How the Decline of Religious Institutions."

48. Robert Jones, *The End of White Christian America* (New York: Simon & Schuster, 2016).

49. Kathleen M. Sands, *America's Religious Wars: The Embattled Heart of Our Public Life* (New Haven: Yale University Press, 2019), 273–74. In analyzing the "religious freedom" laws that have been passed since the Clinton presidency, Sands notes, "Far from denoting a liberty that is equally available to all, 'religious freedom' has become a code for opposition to laws that protect the equality of women and LGBT people, just as it once served as a code for white Christian opposition to school desegregation" (282).

Framing Faith during the 2016 Election

JOURNALISTIC COVERAGE OF THE TRUMP CAMPAIGN AND THE MYTH OF EVANGELICAL SCHISM

HANNAH DICK

It is no accident that this volume revisits the "Year of the Evangelicals" in the wake of the 2016 election. There are significant parallels between white evangelical support for Donald Trump, even over more obviously religious candidates during the primaries, and shifting evangelical support for a Southern Baptist presidential candidate in 1976 (Jimmy Carter) to a morally ambiguous, multiple-married celebrity (Ronald Reagan) by 1980. However, many mainstream news outlets failed to absorb the historical lessons from the 1976–80 period. Throughout 2016, most major news outlets, such as the *New York Times,* employed a familiar frame when talking about the evangelical vote: Trump was creating an irreparable schism within evangelical communities across the country, and the election would signal the end of political power for the Religious Right. However, 81 percent of white evangelicals voted for Trump, a higher margin of evangelical support than that received by Mitt Romney in 2012, John McCain in 2008, and even George W. Bush in 2004.[1]

In this essay, I want to revisit the historical precedents that help to explain the white evangelical vote for Trump, which were largely ignored in mainstream media reporting during the lead-up to the presidential election in November 2016. Rather than treating evangelical support for Trump as exceptional, I read it as historically embedded in the racialized and gendered politics of the American Religious Right. In general, major news outlets focused on the content of Trump's character but ignored the form his campaign took—a form that is culturally familiar to many values voters. As a result of the focus on content, rather than form, many journalists ended up reproducing the same media frame: that evangelicals were fundamentally divided over support for Trump and that the election would cause an overwhelming schism within evangelical communities, many of whose members would refuse to vote for him. Since the election, it is clear that many white evangelicals remain Trump's staunchest supporters, even when they disagree with the administration's policies. Throughout 2016, however, much of the journalistic coverage of Trump's courtship of evangelicals was framed as an exception rather than the norm. In the first part of the essay, I review major news coverage of Trump and evangelicals, using Todd Gitlin's concept of media frames. In the second part of the essay, I look at the historical precedent for a white evangelical–Trump political alliance. I argue that Trump embodied a cultural form that was familiar to many white evangelicals, even as the content of his character appeared anathema to values voters.

MAINSTREAM PRESS COVERAGE OF EVANGELICALS

I begin with an overview of news coverage of evangelicals and Trump throughout 2016. For the purposes of this essay, I am only looking at news coverage from early March, following Trump's enormous Super Tuesday gains, up until the election on November 8, in a variety of nationally circulated newspapers (the *New York Times* and the *Washington Post,* for example) and news websites (CNN.com, RollingStone.com, and others). While it is impossible to carry out a comprehensive survey of all news coverage of Trump and evangelicals throughout 2016, I employ Todd Gitlin's concept of media frames to draw out central themes in the coverage across news outlets.

According to Gitlin, media frames are familiar narratives that journalists draw on when facing the increasingly hurried demands of the news cycle.[2] Complex issues are necessarily simplified, conflict is emphasized, and assessment of events relies on the opinions of institutional "experts." In Gitlin's original discussion of framing, he points to the ways that journalists represented student protest movements of the American New Left in the late 1960s. Gitlin explains that journalists draw on "little tacit theories" about how the world works in writing about a phenomenon and these theories tend to be consistent across news platforms.[3] Media frames spread both vertically (within news organizations) as well as horizontally (across different news outlets).[4] They can thus be observed from a variety of vantage points. Ultimately, media frames are tendencies of journalistic discourse that recur, over and over again, legitimizing their own circular logic. "In the end, a story is a continuing national story because it has been made a continuing national story," explains Gitlin.[5]

Media frames emphasize conflict and controversy. When framing marginal or minority groups, journalists often overemphasize the role of detractors, downplay the group's effectiveness or reach, and tend to marginalize supporters or adherents. Controversy also helps to legitimize the continual production of news: national media attention to an issue or event verifies the importance of reporting on it in the first place. In turn, media frames can have substantial material consequences, illustrated by the example of Park51 in New York City.

When news outlets first reported on a proposal to erect an Islamic cultural center in Lower Manhattan during the summer of 2010, journalists quickly latched onto polarizing language describing Park51 as a "Ground Zero mosque." Even news outlets that did not condone the terminology—pointing out that the proposed building was actually a thirteen-story, multi-use community center—reproduced this language.[6] In doing so, journalists repurposed the frame of controversy and amplified the opinions of detractors. Very quickly the story gained national media attention, with politicians weighing in on the so-called controversy.[7] The backlash from the American public (although notably, not denizens of Manhattan) was forceful and swift, resulting in a much more modest building proposal. Since then, the project aimed at building a multi-use community center has been abandoned; by 2017, the project developer, Sharif El-Gamal, announced that the site would be used for a forty-three-floor condominium.[8] Media frames thus not only describe phenomena; they also shape our social, cultural, and political realities.

The frame that surrounded stories about evangelicals and Trump throughout 2016 was one that focused on the content of his personal character and its potential for divisiveness within evangelical communities. As

I will argue, the emphasis on *content* obscured the fact that the *form* his campaign took was historically legible to many white evangelical voters.

MEDIA FRAMES SURROUNDING THE TRUMP CAMPAIGN

Long before Trump secured the GOP nomination, much of the journalistic coverage of the Republican contest underscored the importance of shoring up the evangelical vote. In the lead-up to Super Tuesday, the *Washington Post* described Ted Cruz's "evangelical problem."[9] Cruz was having to compete with Trump in his courtship of evangelicals, who were defecting from the Cruz campaign. In the *New York Times,* Trip Gabriel reported this dynamic under the headline "Donald Trump, Despite Impieties, Wins Hearts of Evangelical Voters."[10] The article includes extensive quotes from Bob Vander Plaats, who is referred to as "a leader of the Christian right in Iowa" along with cochairmen of Cruz's campaign. Vander Plaats "expressed frustration that so-called values voters were giving Mr. Trump a pass on issues about his character, such as his mocking of women, as well as his conservative credentials. Mr. Vander Plaats suggested that they were 'either hypocritical or uninformed or maybe not interested.'"[11] While Gabriel briefly mentions the origins of the Moral Majority in the 1970s, he posits that evangelicals for Trump are of a different sort: these "grass-roots Trump supporters ... identify as evangelical, though they may not be regular churchgoers." Even before Super Tuesday, when Trump effectively clinched the GOP nomination, journalists were looking for reasons to explain away white evangelical support for the candidate. What's more, none of these articles mentions the racialized history of the Religious Right, nor clarifies that evangelicals backing Trump are overwhelmingly white. This is significant because as Penny Edgell and Eric Tranby have shown, faith intersects with race in a way that dramatically affects political attitudes.[12]

In March 2016, CNN religion editor Daniel Burke declared Super Tuesday a death knell for the Religious Right as Trump made significant gains over more obviously religious candidates such as Ted Cruz and Ben Carson. According to Burke, evangelical support for Trump signaled the end of a religiously motivated conservative movement. He noted that evangelical support for Trump was "a direct repudiation of the message Christian leaders have been shouting from the rooftops: *The thrice-married mogul more at home in casinos than churches is not one of us!*[13] This familiar refrain, in which the moral character of Trump is positioned as inevitably at odds with a Christian voting bloc, gets repurposed in most articles about evangelical politics throughout 2016.

Following his de facto win of the GOP nomination, mainstream news outlets began to develop the narrative of evangelical schism. According to this media frame, Trump would cause irreparable divisions within the Religious Right. On March 15, Michelle Boorstein wrote a piece in the *Washington Post* outlining "why Donald Trump is tearing evangelicals apart."[14] Boorstein opens by deferring to the authority of Baptist pastor Rick Scarborough, an evangelical leader whose career has been dedicated to shoring up a politically active Religious Right. Boorstein explains: "The Texas Baptist says he's never witnessed the bitter divisions among evangelicals that this GOP primary season has unleashed."

In June 2016, Trump continued his courtship of the Religious Right and met with evangelical leaders in New York. After the meeting, Focus on the Family founder James Dobson claimed that Trump had been born again and was now a "baby Christian." The *Washington Post* embedded the conversion news within an opinion piece about the Trump campaign's firing of Corey Lewandowski, effectively relegating it to an issue of secondary importance.[15] The *New York Times* deferred to Dobson but noted that he had "conceded that Mr. Trump did not exactly fit the typical mold of an evangelical."[16] Kurtis Lee, writing in the *Los Angeles Times,* couched the news within the broader frame of evangelical division, reporting on the conversion news and then offering this caveat: "Despite winning over the support of a majority of evangelicals throughout the Republican primary, many remain divided and are concerned about the depth of [Trump's] faith."[17] Most journalists heavily qualified the growing alliance between white evangelicals and Trump; an op-ed in the *Washington Post* asserted that "evangelical Christians are selling out faith for politics."[18]

Lincoln Mullen, a historian writing for the *Atlantic,* offered a counterpart to the predominant media frame. Mullen explained that the conversion news, regardless of its verifiability, helped to establish the candidate within the broader cultural framework of the evangelical "redemption narrative," making Trump legible to evangelical voters who "are trying to steel themselves to vote for Trump in the fall."[19] He explained the significance of the "baby Christian" remark: "Regardless of its truth, the claim seems like an attempt to make Trump more palatable to conservative Christian voters and re-secure their now-tenuous grasp on political power. Many evangelicals will be unable to cast a vote for the Republican presidential candidate with an untroubled conscience. If trusted leaders like Dobson can convince them that Trump is born again, some may find it easier to vote for him in November." While Mullen contextualized the significance of Trump's born-again narrative to an evangelical audience, he still repurposed the frame of schism by referencing the inner turmoil of many values voters. This frame suggests that Trump's character would provide a major hurdle for his conservative Christian supporters.

Stories around the evangelical vote for Trump circulated throughout the summer, repeating the same refrain. Even the inclusion of staunch pro-life conservative Mike Pence on the ticket was couched in terms of schism. In mid-July, the *Washington Post* reported that the inclusion of Pence sends "conservative evangelicals a mixed message."[20] Pence's concessions on an Indiana religious freedom bill cast doubt on his conservative credentials, which *Time* also pointed out at the time.[21]

Meanwhile, the Pew Center reported that four out of five evangelicals were backing Trump.[22] Yet in articles reporting this statistic, journalists could not resist pointing out the contradiction between Trump's moral character and his support from values voters.[23] The underlying media frame in these articles is an assumption that this hypocrisy would not hold by November. *Rolling Stone* published a long form piece by Sarah Posner in July with the headline "How Donald Trump Divided and Conquered Evangelicals."[24] Using Jerry Falwell Jr. as a foil to the growing contingent of "Never Trump" evangelicals, Posner dismisses the historical precedent for backing an explicitly nonreligious candidate by contextualizing this precedent in the words of an outspoken Trump detractor, Liberty University graduate (and Jerry Falwell Sr.'s chief of staff) Mark DeMoss: "DeMoss has no patience . . . for Falwell [Jr.]'s claim that his father's endorsement of the divorced Ronald Reagan over Baptist Sunday school teacher Jimmy Carter in the 1980 election, and of George H. W. Bush over Christian right activist Pat Robertson in 1988, is evidence that the supposedly obvious evangelical candidate isn't always the best choice. 'Oh, please,' says

DeMoss. 'Both Reagan and Bush in my opinion exhibited more character and integrity and certainly civility than does Donald Trump.'"[25] Posner's piece traces Trump's courtship of evangelicals back to 2011, but she ultimately employs the frame of evangelical schism to make sense of his support from the Religious Right. Near the end of the article, Posner explains: "Trump has provoked the most significant shake-up of the religious right in nearly 40 years. . . . He divided and conquered the movement as an influencer of Republican presidencies, neutered kingmakers who wouldn't get behind him and, once he clinched the nomination, humiliated evangelical leaders with an impossible set of choices: join the Never Trump camp, and risk losing influence with a mercurial President Trump, or be seen as jettisoning sacrosanct religious principles by caving to him." This frame suggests that religious support for Trump is inherently contradictory and ultimately theologically disingenuous.

By the fall of 2016, mainstream news outlets verified that Trump was causing an irreconcilable schism within evangelical communities. After the release of the Access Hollywood video in which Trump boasts about sexually harassing women, the *Washington Post* reported that "some evangelicals still back Trump despite lewd video."[26] CNN provided a less restrained assessment, with a headline declaring, "Evangelicals 'Disgusted' by Trump's Remarks, but Still Backing Him."[27] Posner also wrote a piece for the *New York Times* with the headline "The Religious Right's Trump Schism," published two weeks before the November election.[28] *New York Times* religion reporter Laurie Goodstein's final piece on Trump and evangelicals before the election, published on October 15, summed up the general consensus: "Donald Trump reveals evangelical rifts that could shape politics for years."[29] In the days leading up to the election, both the *New Yorker* and NPR's *All Things Considered* ran stories on Russell Moore, the president of the Ethics and Religious Liberty Commission of the Southern Baptist Convention, who had spoken out forcefully against evangelical support for Trump throughout 2016.[30] Reports that Liberty University was divided over Falwell Jr.'s endorsement of the GOP candidate further advanced this narrative of schism.[31]

Just three days after the election, Goodstein wrote an article with the headline "Religious Right Believes Donald Trump Will Deliver on His Promises";[32] Goodstein's disbelief is palpable. She begins the piece with the now-familiar refrain: "Donald J. Trump rarely goes to church, said he's never sought forgiveness for his sins, and in his acceptance speech early Wednesday morning, never mentioned God." Goodstein continues to explain that while Trump was not the first choice for many evangelical voters, he did a better job courting their votes than his competitor, Hillary Clinton. This, combined with a recent transition away from values-based voting toward strategic voting among the evangelical electorate, helped to consolidate his win, according to Goodstein.

In his discussion of media frames, Gitlin explains that one of the ways the news gets simplified in order to meet the demands of the genre is by focusing on moments of conflict. It is true that evangelicals were divided over Trump, many of whom circulated the #NeverTrump hashtag on social media. However, the focus on dissensus may have been exaggerated given how many white evangelicals voted for him. An overemphasis on dissension resulted from two features of mainstream news coverage. First, news outlets continue to rely on the authority of evangelical leaders to speak for the community (or communities) as a whole. Deferring to the authority of evangelical leaders, journalists repurposed the language of turmoil and schism coming from the leadership. Focus on religious authorities does not capture the breadth of evangelical sentiment across a huge diversity of grassroots and institutional religious contexts and fails to account for the sentiments of "ordinary" evangelical voters. In fact, the disparity between values voters and evangelical leadership can be traced back to the early days of the Moral Majority, when leaders such as Paul Weyrich struggled to consolidate grassroots evangelical support into a cohesive political movement.[33] Second, the frame that underscored the contradiction between Trump's moral character and his would-be support base focused primarily on the content of his character. Instead, paying attention to the form of Trump's 2016 run can shed light on the ways he became a viable, if not always desirable, candidate for many white evangelicals.

THE HISTORICAL PRECEDENT

During the late 1970s and 1980s, Rev. Jerry Falwell Sr. mobilized many evangelicals under the banner of the Moral Majority. Throughout its tenure, from 1979 to 1989, the Majority lobbied across several fronts: against passage of the Equal Rights Amendment; for overturning the *Roe v. Wade* (1973) decision on abortion; and for a general return to moral traditionalism via the patriarchal, heteronormative family. However, the main and overarching goal of the organization was to register millions of morally conservative Americans to vote. Conservative Catholic strategist Paul Weyrich had been looking for a way to shore up a unified evangelical voting bloc since the 1960s, but he recognized the need to couch it in nonspecific language. It was not until the late 1970s that he and Falwell were able to mobilize political fervor against incumbent Democrat—and fellow evangelical—Jimmy Carter.[34]

A number of cultural factors coalesced in the formation of the Moral Majority. As Randall Balmer argues, the Majority was initially consolidated not in reaction to the *Roe v. Wade* decision but, rather, in response to the IRS rescinding tax exemptions for fundamentalist Christian schools that maintained segregationist policies. Before the late 1970s, many evangelicals saw abortion as a Catholic issue.[35] Meanwhile, President Carter became identified with the IRS decision (even though it was passed during Nixon's tenure), fueling the flames of evangelical resentment against one of "their own."[36] Falwell's call to political action was also an outgrowth of his own Sunbelt politics, which were strongly anti-regulatory and both socially and economically conservative. As Daniel K. Williams argues, Falwell's approach rallied the Religious Right not only on social and cultural issues but also around Republican economic and military policy.[37] Finally, Julie Ingersoll and Michael McVicar both argue that the Moral Majority was influenced by the growing Christian Reconstructionism movement led by R. J. Rushdoony and its attendant "biblical worldview" centered on a patriarchal family order and Dominionist theology.[38] Dominionism calls for Christians to harness control over all institutions within the state and, in doing so, erect a theocracy based on biblical law.

In the American context, then, there has been a specific historical alignment between white evangelicalism as a cultural framework, a religious affiliation, a class-based category, and a political orientation. It is notable that 81 percent of white evangelicals voted for Trump, while Black and Hispanic evangelicals tended to support Clinton.[39] In the wake of the election, sociologist of religion Penny Edgell has rightly called for increasing intersectionality in the study of religion, acknowledging the deep political differences between white evangelicals and white Catholics, on the one hand, and Black and Hispanic members of these traditions, on the other.[40] Edgell also points out that much of the mainstream news coverage of values voters throughout 2016 conflated *evangelicals* with *white evangelicals,* without clearly distinguishing between these categories: "Coverage like this implies—and sometimes states directly—that White evangelicals voted for Trump primarily because their religious beliefs about abortion influenced them to place potential Supreme Court nominations over other considerations in their vote. The implication is that, while other parts of Trump's coalition may have voted based on racism, xenophobia, or economic interests, 'the evangelical vote' was a moral one."[41] The problem is that the predominant media frame describing "evangelicals" has assumed that voters are influenced by only one dimension of their identity—in this case religious belief—while ignoring the intersections between faith, race, gender, class, and politics.

As Elizabeth Castelli demonstrates, the American Religious Right has long espoused a rhetoric of persecution in order to curtail political debate.[42] This "Christian persecution complex" was deployed with particular fervor in the wake of 9/11 and was redoubled during the Obama era, when many white evangelicals described a sense of real existential threat.[43] In particular, expanded rights for LGBTQ+ communities, including the repeal of "Don't Ask, Don't Tell" and the federal legalization of same-sex marriage, left many conservative evangelicals reeling. Explaining evangelical support for Trump in the lead-up to the election, prominent Dominionist thinker Lance Wallnau described Trump as a flawed vessel of God who would "deliver us from Hillary."[44] And as one evangelical writer explained immediately after the election: "Donald Trump may well prove to be [a] destructive force. Time will tell. But for many people, he is currently destroying *all the right things.*"[45] In contrast, he said about Clinton: "Christians are having conversations around the dinner table about what do if the government forces curricula on them that they cannot accept, because their own government is increasingly indicating that Christian parents are too homophobic and too hateful to teach their own children. Can you understand how terrified mothers and fathers are at the prospect that those in power want to actively prevent them from passing their beliefs on to their own children?" In a context in which the expressions of white evangelical Christians have long been privileged in the American public sphere, these expansions of rights are read as a real threat. Indeed, within evangelical media circles, the mainstream treatment of the evangelical outsider is well known. Alex Wilgus, writer for the Christian journal *The Common Vision,* explains that "religion, to mainstream media, is a ghost."[46] He suggests that the dominant media frame around evangelicals is one of controversy. "Rarely do evangelicals occasion a story in a mainstream press outlet unless they have angered someone or have been caught in scandal," he points out.[47] These scandals, more often than not, center on evangelical resentment toward LGBTQ+ rights and access to reproductive health services.

It is possible that many evangelicals ended up voting for Trump despite his egregious character flaws and boisterous presentation style, not because of them. But we also need to recognize the ways that Trump provided a familiar cultural "fit" for some white evangelicals experiencing a feeling of disenfranchisement. Trump's proximity to white supremacy makes him culturally familiar to a Religious Right born in the context of disputes over desegregation. The nostalgic slogan "Make America Great Again" signals a return to some imaginary past for many values voters.[48] At the same time, it repurposes a discourse of the founding of America on (white) Christian principles—a historical revisionism popular among members of the Moral Majority during the 1970s and 1980s.

Wilgus elaborated on the tripartite structure of Trump's appeal for some evangelicals in January 2016. First, he explained in *The Common Vision,* Trump exudes power. "His populist slogan on his signature red hats, 'Big Guy for You' probably harmonizes with the prosperity gospel picture of God that still holds currency in some evangelical circles."[49] This prosperity gospel is the mainstay of popular evangelical preachers such as Joel Osteen and Creflo Dollar, who argue that God's grace can be seen in the proliferation of material goods and that wealth is an indicator of spiritual health. Trump as a figure is perfectly fitted to the prosperity gospel model, using flagrant displays of wealth (and supposed business acumen) as an indicator of his presidential competency.

Second, he has a narrative of conversion. Trump's conversion story, if not one culminating in sincere profession of Christian faith, nevertheless tells the tale of an apostate turning away from liberal dogma and the same strand of progressivism that has culturally disenfranchised many evangelicals.[50] As a former registered Democrat and a New York City real estate mogul with an ambivalent attitude toward abortion, Trump transformed into a viable Republican candidate via the familiar rhetorical device of the born-again narrative. During the first candidate debate in August 2015, Trump explained his transformed position on abortion: "Friends of mine years ago were going to have a child, and it was going to be aborted. And it wasn't aborted. And that child today is a total superstar, a great, great child. And I saw that. And I saw other instances."[51] Despite the fact that his position on abortion, same-sex marriage, and transgender rights seems to fluctuate wildly, the rhetoric of personal transformation that Trump put forth throughout 2016 was legible and familiar to many evangelicals. Historian Lincoln Mullen acknowledged the currency of this conversion narrative in the *Atlantic*.[52] But for the most part, this narrative was couched within a broader frame of skepticism popular among religion reporters.

Third, Trump is immodest.[53] His boisterous and unapologetic style is culturally familiar for many evangelicals who take pride in their unselfconscious propagation of the Gospel. While the message may differ between Trump and religious conservatives, the delivery mechanism is the same. Since the 1925 Scopes Trial, when fundamentalist Christians were publicly ridiculed in both the press and popular culture for their literal interpretation of the Bible, some conservative Christians have come to take pride in the expression of fringe opinions. Evangelicals have long rallied around public disrupters such as William Jennings Bryan and, more recently, Jerry Falwell Sr., who came under intense public scrutiny when he remarked that the 9/11 terrorist attacks were punishment for America's growing culture of sexual permissiveness. Writing in the Pentecostal outlet *Charisma News* one month before the 2016 presidential election, Dominionist Lance Wallnau explained why he had supported Trump early in the GOP race: "I heard the Lord say: 'Donald Trump is a wrecking ball to the spirit of political correctness.'"[54] Trump's misogynistic "strong man" style also aligns with the cultural politics of the Religious Right.[55]

Trump also embodies the features of charismatic leadership that are culturally familiar to many evangelicals. Max Weber borrowed from religious forms of leadership in developing his notion of charisma.[56] For Weber, charisma is not about popularity or even personal charm. Rather, charismatic leadership derives authority from a promise to upend the status quo. In this sense, it is irrational, "in the sense of being foreign to all rules."[57] It makes passionate emotional appeals and, as such, inspires hatred as much as adoration. Charismatic leadership refuses to acknowledge weakness or the possibility of failure. At the same time, it succeeds by accentuating the perception of crisis and scapegoating minority groups, who are seen as the crisis's catalyst. The charismatic leader offers salvation via the embodied power of a singular, exceptional leader. Indeed, because charisma is embedded in a cult of personality, it is particularly difficult to pass it on—or in Weber's terms, to "routinise" it—into a long-lasting system of authority.[58]

Charismatic leadership is not specific to religion, according to Weber, but it is culturally familiar for many evangelicals who conceptualize Christ in a similar manner. Before the election, Trump offered salvation in the form of economic uplift and a dramatic transformation of the political status quo. After his inauguration, we witnessed the difficulty of translating his "me alone" campaign into the regular channels of public administration. Trump's protectionism centers not only on reviving American manufacturing but also on the threat of outsiders as embodied in the nebulous caricature of the "radical Islamic terrorist." White evangelicals are particularly receptive to this discourse. A study published in March 2017 by the Public Religion Research Institute (PRRI) reports that 57 percent of white evangelicals say that Christians face more discrimination than any other religious group, including Muslims.[59] And in February 2017, the Pew Center released findings that white evangelicals were the religious group most inclined to support the administration's various executive orders restricting Muslim access to the United States (76 percent of them reported being in favor of a travel ban).[60] The PRRI also found that white evangelicals were the only religious community among those surveyed whose support of the travel ban increased between May 2016 and February 2017 and the only group with a majority indicating support for the ban.[61] While many evangelical leaders have used their political influence to lobby on behalf of retaining Deferred Action for Childhood

Arrivals (DACA), white evangelicals report the lowest degree of support for the program, according to 2015 data from the PRRI.[62]

In the context of these studies, evangelical leaders' public denouncements of Trump's policies do not detract from his charisma and perhaps only serve to reinforce grassroots evangelical support for an antiestablishment president. News media foreground white evangelical leadership and the institutional structure of evangelicalism because the constraints of news reporting demands reliance on the opinion of experts or institutional authorities.[63] In doing so, however, journalists end up erasing the practices and beliefs of ordinary evangelicals. The disparity between these groups is no more evident than in the repeated denouncement of Trump by evangelical leaders such as Russell Moore and the ongoing grassroots white evangelical support of the administration. Finally, white evangelical support for Trump cannot be read as a religious issue alone; there is a racialized politics to evangelicalism in the United States that requires an intersectional approach to reporting on religion in America.

The alliance forged between white evangelical leaders and the Republican Party has been remarkably resilient, even in the face of tremendous backlash against Trump. In late 2019, the outgoing editor of *Christianity Today,* Mark Galli, published an explosive op-ed supporting the impeachment inquiry into President Trump. He wrote: "It's time to call a spade a spade, to say that no matter how many hands we win in this political poker game, we are playing with a stacked deck of gross immorality and ethical incompetence."[64] The op-ed was swiftly denounced by 177 evangelical leaders—including Jerry Falwell Jr.—who rallied behind Trump in an open letter to Timothy Dalrymple, the magazine's president.

I do not mean to suggest that there was not serious introspection about a possible Trump-evangelical alliance throughout 2016. Many evangelical news outlets debated the merits of supporting the candidate and continue to do so. However, the coalition-building work of the Moral Majority during the late 1970s and 1980s has left an indelible mark on the intersection between race, faith, and partisanship in the United States. By revisiting this history, we can begin to unpack why the election results were met with such shock in November 2016. The predominant media frame employed by journalists writing about Trump and evangelicals throughout 2016 underscored a schism that had emerged based on Trump's personal character. However, a very different kind of schism took place on Election Day: between white evangelicals, on the one hand, and Black and Hispanic evangelicals, on the other. Treating "evangelical" as an exclusively religious category ignores the huge political disparities between these groups and reifies the notion that white evangelicalism is devoid of its own racialized politics.

By advancing the myth of evangelical schism throughout 2016, journalists overlooked the long historical precedent for a unified evangelical voting bloc made up of predominantly white conservative Christians. In the academy as well as in the news media, it is often easy to forget the huge number of values voters throughout the United States and to write off the political power of the Religious Right as a long-forgotten relic of the culture wars. But such an erasure is dangerous because it compromises our ability to accurately take the religious temperature of the nation and to make thoughtful predictions about religion and politics. And perhaps most significantly, it is important to remind ourselves that the erasure of evangelicals from mainstream political reporting is not commensurate with the disappearance of evangelicals themselves. Rather than signaling the end times for a unified conservative religious movement, Trump's election has given many white evangelicals the opportunity to become politically born again.

NOTES

1. Jessica Martínez and Gregory A. Smith, *How the Faithful Voted: A Preliminary 2016 Analysis* Pew Research Center, November 9, 2016, http://www.pewresearch.org/fact-tank/2016/11/09/how-the-faithful-voted-a-preliminary-2016-analysis/. In terms of raw numbers, Bush earned about 62 million votes, while Trump earned about 62.7 million. There have been disputes in Christian media circles about the 81 percent figure. The same polling methods were used in 2004, 2008, and 2012, however, so the metric is useful for comparison over time.

2. Todd Gitlin, *The Whole World Is Watching: Mass Media in the Making and Unmaking of the New Left* (Los Angeles: University of California Press, 1980), 4–7.

3. Ibid., 6.

4. Ibid., 100.

5. Ibid., 101.

6. Michael Barbaro, "Debate Heats Up about Mosque near Ground Zero," *New York Times,* July 30, 2010, https://www.nytimes.com/2010/07/31/nyregion/31mosque.html;

Associated Press, "Fact Check: The 'Ground Zero Mosque' Debate," CBS News, August 19, 2010, https://www.cbsnews.com/news/fact-check-the-ground-zero-mosque-debate/.

7. Dan Gilgoff, "Obama Throws Support behind Controversial Islamic Center," CNN, August 14, 2010, http://www.cnn.com/2010/POLITICS/08/13/obama.islamic.center .support/index.html; Carl Hulse, "GOP Sees Mosque near Ground Zero as Campaign Issue," *New York Times,* August 16, 2010, https://www.nytimes.com/2010/08/17/us/ politics/17mosque.html.

8. Ronda Kaysen, "Condo Tower to Rise Where Muslim Community Center Was Proposed," *New York Times,* May 12, 2017, https://www.nytimes.com/2017/05/12/realestate/ muslim-museum-world-trade-center.html.

9. Jenna Johnson and Robert Costa, "Trump Makes Inroads with Evangelicals, Undermining Cruz," *Washington Post,* 26th January 26, 2016, https://www.washingtonpost .com/politics/trump-makes-inroads-with-evangelicals-undermining-cruz/2016/01/26/ e47768fe-c445-11e5-a4aa-f25866ba0dc6_story.html;

Kevin Schaul and Kevin Uhrmacher, "Ted Cruz Has an Evangelical Problem," *Washington Post,* February 21, 2016, https://www.washingtonpost.com/news/the-fix/ wp/2016/02/21/ted-cruzs-looming-evangelical-problem/.

10. Trip Gabriel, "Donald Trump, Despite Impieties, Wins Hearts of Evangelical Voters," *New York Times,* February 27, 2016, https://www.nytimes.com/2016/02/28/us/ politics/donald-trump-despite-impieties-wins-hearts-of-evangelical-voters.html.

11. Quoted ibid.

12. Penny Edgell and Eric Tranby, "Religious Influences on Understandings of Racial Inequality in the United States," *Social Problems* 54, no. 2 (2007), 263–88. See also Penny Edgell, "An Agenda for Research on American Religion in Light of the 2016 Election," *Sociology of Religion* 78, no. 1 (2017): 1–8.

13. Daniel Burke, "R.I.P. Religious Right, and Other Super Tuesday Takeaways," CNN, March 2, 2016, http://www.cnn.com/2016/03/02/politics/religion-super-tuesday/index .html.

14. Michelle Boorstein, "Why Donald Trump Is Tearing Evangelicals Apart," *Washington Post,* March 15, 2016, https://www.washingtonpost.com/news/acts-of-faith/ wp/2016/03/15/evangelical-christians-are-enormously-divided-over-donald-trumps -runaway-candidacy/.

15. Kathleen Parker, "Trump's Born-Again Campaign," *Washington Post,* June 21, 2016, https://www.washingtonpost.com/opinions/trumps-born-again-campaign/2016/06/21/ c36b94ac-37e8-11e6-8f7c-d4c723a2becb_story.html?utm_term=.11a39ad03a7b.

16. Trip Gabriel and Michael Luo, "A Born-Again Donald Trump? Believe It, Evangelical Leader Says," *New York Times,* June 25, 2016, http://www.nytimes.com/2016/06/26/ us/politics/a-born-again-donald-trump-believe-it-evangelical-leader-says.html.

17. Kurtis Lee, "James Dobson Says Trump Has Found a Relationship with Christ," *Los Angeles Times,* June 25, 2016, http://www.latimes.com/nation/politics/trailguide/la -na-trailguide-06252016-htmlstory.html.

18. Michael Gerson, "Evangelical Christians Are Selling Out Faith for Politics," *Washington Post,* June 23, 2016, https://www.washingtonpost.com/opinions/evangelical

-christians-are-selling-out-faith-for-politics/2016/06/23/f03368de-3964-11e6-8f7c
-d4c723a2becb_story.html?utm_term=.9401c02a6fd6.

19. Lincoln Mullen, "Just Another Sinner, Born Again," *Atlantic,* June 29, 2016, https://
www.theatlantic.com/politics/archive/2016/06/trump-born-again/489269/.

20. Julie Zauzmer, "By Picking Mike Pence, Trump Sends Conservative Evangelicals
a Mixed Message," *Washington Post,* July 15, 2016, https://www.washingtonpost.com/
news/acts-of-faith/wp/2016/07/14/pence-defines-himself-as-a-christian-above-all-else
-do-christians-want-him-for-vp/.

21. Alex Altman, "Why Donald Trump Picked Mike Pence as Running Mate," *Time,*
July 14, 2016, http://time.com/4406477/donald-trump-mike-pence-running-mate-vice
-president/.

22. Pew Research Center, *Evangelicals Rally to Trump, Religious "Nones" Back Clinton,* report, http://www.pewforum.org/2016/07/13/evangelicals-rally-to-trump-religious
-nones-back-clinton/.

23. Laurie Goodstein, "Nearly Four-Fifths of White Evangelicals Say They'll Vote for
Donald Trump," *New York Times,* July 13, 2016, https://www.nytimes.com/2016/07/14/
us/donald-trump-White-evangelical-voters-poll.html; Eugene Scott, "More White Evangelical Voters Back Trump than Romney," CNN.com, July 15, 2016, http://www.cnn
.com/2016/07/13/politics/White-evangelical-voters-donald-trump/index.html.

24. Sarah Posner, "How Donald Trump Divided and Conquered Evangelicals," *Rolling
Stone,* July 21, 2016, http://www.rollingstone.com/politics/features/how-donald-trump
-divided-and-conquered-evangelicals-w430119.

25. Quoted in Posner, "How Donald Trump Divided."

26. Sarah Pulliam Bailey, "'Still the Best Candidate': Some Evangelicals Still Back Trump
Despite Lewd Video," *Washington Post,* October 8, 2016, https://www.washingtonpost
.com/news/acts-of-faith/wp/2016/10/08/still-the-best-candidate-some-evangelicals-still
-back-trump-despite-lewd-video/.

27. Eugene Scott, Ashley Killough, and Daniel Burke, "Evangelicals 'Disgusted' by
Trump's Remarks, but Still Backing Him," CNN, October 21, 2016, http://www.cnn
.com/2016/10/07/politics/donald-trump-evangelical-leaders/index.html.

28. Sarah Posner, "The Religious Right's Trump Schism," *New York Times,* October
19, 2016, http://www.nytimes.com/2016/10/19/opinion/campaign-stops/the-religious
-rights-trump-schism.html.

29. Laurie Goodstein, "Donald Trump Reveals Evangelical Rifts That Could Shape Politics for Years," *New York Times,* October 17, 2016, http://www.nytimes.com/2016/10/17/
us/donald-trump-evangelicals-republican-vote.html.

30. "Evangelicals Consider Whether God Really Cares How They Vote," *All Things
Considered,* NPR, November 1, 2016, http://www.npr.org/2016/11/01/500105245/
evangelicals-consider-whether-god-really-cares-how-they-vote; Kelefa Sanneh, "The New
Evangelical Moral Minority," *New Yorker,* October 31, 2016, https://www.newyorker.com/
magazine/2016/11/07/the-new-evangelical-moral-minority.

31. Brandon Ambrosino, "How Trump Is Dividing Jerry Falwell's University," *Politico,* October 27, 2016, http://politi.co/2eHUVsy; T. Rees Shapiro, Sarah Pulliam Bailey,
Susan Svrluga, and Scott Clement, "Liberty University Students Protest Association with

Trump," *Washington Post,* October 13, 2016, https://www.washingtonpost.com/news/grade-point/wp/2016/10/12/liberty-is-not-trump-u-students-protest-donald-trump/.

32. Laurie Goodstein, "Religious Right Believes Donald Trump Will Deliver on His Promises," *New York Times,* November 11, 2016, http://www.nytimes.com/2016/11/12/us/donald-trump-evangelical-christians-religious-conservatives.html.

33. Randall Balmer, *Evangelicalism in America* (Waco, TX: Baylor University Press, 2016).

34. Balmer, *Evangelicalism in America,* 112.

35. Randall Balmer, "The Real Origins of the Religious Right," *Politico,* May 27, 2014, https://www.politico.com/magazine/story/2014/05/religious-right-real-origins-107133; Balmer, *Evangelicalism in America.*

36. Balmer, *Evangelicalism in America,* 129–31.

37. Williams, D K "Jerry Falwell's Sunbelt Politics: The Regional Origins of the Moral Majority," *Journal of Policy History 22, no.* 2 (2010): 125–47.

38. Julie J. Ingersoll, *Building God's Kingdom: Inside the World of Christian Reconstruction* (New York: Oxford University Press, 2015), 1, 5–6; Michael J. McVicar, *Christian Reconstruction: R. J. Rushdoony and American Religious Conservatism* (Chapel Hill: University of North Carolina Press, 2015), 144–46.

39. Penny Edgell, "Seeing the White in Christian America," *The Society Pages,* December 15, 2016, https://thesocietypages.org/specials/seeing-the-White-in-christian-america/.

40. Edgell, "Seeing the White"; Penny Edgell, "An Agenda for Research on American Religion in Light of the 2016 Election," *Sociology of Religion* 78, no. 1 (2017): 1–8.

41. Edgell, "Seeing the White."

42. Elizabeth A. Castelli, "Persecution Complexes: Identity Politics and the 'War on Christians,'" *differences* 18, no. 3 (2007): 152–80.

43. Ibid., 156.

44. Quoted in Frederick Clarkson, "Dominionism Rising: A Theocratic Movement Hiding in Plain Sight," *The Public Eye,* August 18, 2016, no. 87, 12–20.

45. Jonathon Van Maren, "The Painfully Obvious Reason Christians Voted for Trump (That Liberals Just Don't Understand)," *LifeSiteNews,* November 14, 2016, https://www.lifesitenews.com/blogs/the-painfully-simple-reason-christians-voted-for-donald-trump-that-liberals.

46. Alex Wilgus, "Fake News and Evangelicals," *The Common Vision,* January 19, 2017, http://thecommonvision.org/features/fake-news-evangelicals/.

47. See also Paul A. Soukup, "Church, Media, and Scandal," in *Media Scandals: Morality and Desire in the Popular Culture Marketplace,* ed. James Lull and Stephen Hinerman (New York: Columbia University Press, 1997), 222–39.

48. According to the Public Religion Research Institute's *2016 American Values Survey,* white evangelicals have the highest amount of nostalgia for a pre–civil rights 1950s era. See Robert P. Jones, Daniel Cox, Betsy Cooper, and Rachel Lienesch, *The Divide over America's Future: 1950 or 2050? Findings from the 2016 American Values Survey,* report, Public Religion Research Institute (PRRI), Washington, DC, 2016.

49. Alex Wilgus, "In Trump We Trust," *The Common Vision,* January 28, 2016, http://thecommonvision.org/features/in-trump-we-trust/.

50. Ibid.

51. First Republican Primary Debate, Fox News, August 7, 2015, https://www.youtube
.com/watch?v=mL3WKWMnytk.

52. Mullen "Just Another Sinner."

53. Wilgus "In Trump We Trust."

54. Lance Wallnau, "Why I Believe Trump Is the Prophesied President," *Charisma News,* October 5, 2016, http://www.charismanews.com/politics/opinion/60378-why-i
-believe-trump-is-the-prophesied-president. Wallnau also frequently compares Trump to Cyrus, the Persian emperor who ruled in the sixth century BCE and who, despite his non-belief, was instrumental in the emancipation of Jewish people from Babylon, as detailed in the Book of Isaiah. Wallnau argues that "the 45th president is meant to be an Isaiah 45 Cyrus."

55. Roger Friedland, "Donald's Dick: A Man against the Institutions," in *Politics of Meaning / Meaning of Politics: Cultural Sociology of the 2016 U.S. Presidential Election,* ed. Jason L. Mast and Jeffrey C. Alexander (Cham, Switzerland: Palgrave Macmillan, 2019), 115–33.

56. Max Weber, *The Theory of Social and Economic Organization* (New York: Free Press, 1964).

57. Ibid., 361.

58. Ibid., 364.

59. Daniel Cox and Robert P. Jones, *Majority of Americans Oppose Transgender Bathroom Restrictions,* report, PRRI, Washington, DC, 2017, https://www.prri.org/research/
lgbt-transgender-bathroom-discrimination-religious-liberty/.

60. Gregory A. Smith, *Most White Evangelicals Approve of Trump Travel Prohibition and Express Concerns about Extremism,* report, Pew Research Center, 2017, http://www
.pewresearch.org/fact-tank/2017/02/27/most-White-evangelicals-approve-of-trump
-travel-prohibition-and-express-concerns-about-extremism/.

61. Daniel Cox and Robert P. Jones, *47% of the Country Say Trump Has Violated the Constitution, but Few Support Impeachment,* report, Public Religion Research Institute, 2017, https://www.prri.org/research/poll-trump-impeachment-constitution-partisanship
-muslim-ban/.

62. According to the PRRI, 57 percent of white evangelicals report favorable attitudes toward DACA, as compared with 73 percent of the religiously unaffiliated, 70 percent of Catholics, 66 percent of nonwhite Protestants, and 62 percent of white mainline Protestants. White Americans generally show lower levels of support for the program (64 percent) than Hispanic (78 percent) and Black (70 percent) Americans. Harmeet Kamboj and Robert P. Jones, *Majorities of Republicans and Democrats Support the Basic Policies of DACA Program,* report, PRRI, 2017, https://www.prri.org/spotlight/trump-dream-act
-immigration/.

63. Gitlin, *Whole World Is Watching,* 28.

64. M. Galli, "Trump Should Be Removed from Office," *Christianity Today,* December 19, 2019, https://www.christianitytoday.com/ct/2019/december-web-only/trump-should
-be-removed-from-office.html.

Contributors

Randall Balmer, an Episcopal priest, is the John Phillips Professor in Religion at Dartmouth College. He is the author of more than a dozen books, including *Mine Eyes Have Seen the Glory: A Journey into the Evangelical Subculture in America,* now in its fifth edition, and *Redeemer: The Life of Jimmy Carter.*

Hannah Dick is assistant professor of communication and media studies at Carleton University (Canada). Her research focuses on the historical dominance of Christianity in liberal democratic contexts, looking at the relationship between religion, law, media, and public policy.

J. Brooks Flippen is professor of history at Southeastern Oklahoma State University and the author of four books on modern political history.

Jeff Frederick is professor of history at the University of North Carolina at Pembroke, where he also serves as dean of the College of Arts and Sciences. He is the author of *Stand Up for Alabama: Governor George Wallace.* He has published on a variety of topics, including interest groups, female support for conservative politicians, NASCAR, southern culture and identity, sport and race, southern governors during the civil rights era, the rhetoric of victimization in southern politics, and party politics in the South.

R. Ward Holder is a historical and political theologian and professor of theology at Saint Anselm College in Manchester, New Hampshire. He writes on the Reformation, biblical interpretation, and the manner in which religious convictions shape modern politics and political theory.

Among other works, he has authored *John Calvin and the Grounding of Interpretation: Calvin's First Commentaries;* coauthored *Reinhold Niebuhr in Theory and Practice: Christian Realism and Democracy in America in the Twenty-First Century;* and edited *John Calvin in Context.* His essays have appeared in *Christian Century, Church History, Politics and Religion,* and *Society.* His current work focuses on the intersection of faith and politics and history.

Andrew S. Moore is professor of history and director of summer school at Saint Anselm College in Manchester, New Hampshire. He is the author of *The South's Tolerable Alien: Roman Catholics in Alabama and Georgia, 1945–1970* and several articles and book chapters.

Randall J. Stephens is professor of American and British studies at the University of Oslo. He is the author of *The Fire Spreads: Holiness and Pentecostalism in the American South;* coauthor, with physicist Karl W. Giberson, of *The Anointed: Evangelical Truth in a Secular Age;* and editor of *Recent Themes in American Religious History.* His latest book is *The Devil's Music: How Christians Inspired, Condemned, and Embraced Rock 'n' Roll.* Stephens was a Fulbright Scholar in Norway in 2011–12 and a Wigeland Visiting Professor at the University of Chicago in 2020.

Allison Vander Broek is a historian of American religion and politics. She recently completed her doctorate in history at Boston College. Her dissertation, "Rallying the Right-to-Lifers: Grassroots Religion and Politics in the Building of a Broad-Based Right-to-Life Movement, 1960–1984," explored the origins of the right-to-life movement in the 1960s and its rise to national prominence. She currently works at Tufts University.

Dan Wells received his PhD degree from Florida State University. He researches the relationship between religion, politics, and race in the United States, with a particular focus on American conservatism in the twentieth century. He also focuses on the use of aesthetics in the study of religion, theory and method in the study of religion, and material culture. He teaches courses on religion, race, and ethnicity and religion in the Americas at Florida State University.

Daniel K. Williams is professor of history at the University of West Georgia and the author of *God's Own Party: The Making of the Christian Right; Defenders of the Unborn: The Pro-Life Movement before* Roe v. Wade; and *The Election of the Evangelical: Jimmy Carter, Gerald Ford, and the Presidential Contest of 1976.*

Index

CPSIA information can be obtained
at www.ICGtesting.com
Printed in the USA
LVHW101624010722
722550LV00003B/62